LABOR AND SOCIALISM
IN AMERICA

KENNIKAT PRESS

NATIONAL UNIVERSITY PUBLICATIONS

SERIES IN AMERICAN STUDIES

Under the General Editorial Supervision of

JAMES P. SHENTON

Professor of History, Columbia University

WILLIAM M. DICK

LABOR AND SOCIALISM IN AMERICA

IN AMERICA

The Gompers Era

1972
National University Publications
KENNIKAT PRESS
Port Washington, N.Y. / London

Library of Congress Catalog Card No.: 71-189555
ISBN: 0-8046-9005-7

Manufactured in the United States of America

Published by
Kennikat Press, Inc.
Port Washington, N.Y./London

To My Mother

Acknowledgments

I should like to thank the staffs in charge of the various archival collections mentioned in the bibliography for their assistance over the past few years. I also wish to express my gratitude to Professor Kenneth McNaught for his inspiration and encouragement in writing this book.

Finally, my thanks go to my wife Madelyn for her innumerable kindnesses and aid in the many tasks involved.

Contents

LABOR AND SOCIALISM
IN AMERICA

Introduction

In the introduction to their *History of Trade Unionism* the English Fabian Socialists Sidney and Beatrice Webb gave the classic definition of a trade union: "a continuous association of wage earners for the purpose of maintaining or improving the conditions of their employment."[1] After eighty years, this definition is still valid. The essence of the trade union is to raise wages and shorten hours; its immediate aim is to secure an agreement with employers. As George Bernard Shaw put it, trade unionism is the capitalism of the proletariat.

This definition, however, does not preclude other activities. It was the same Sidney Webb who endowed the British Labour Party with a socialist program in 1918, but this program did not rob the trade unions, on whose support it depended, of their original role. Just in case their original definition confused the issue, the Webbs changed the words "conditions of their employment" to "conditions of their working lives." Trade unions, in other words, may carry on their essential function and at the same time participate in a movement that "looks outside itself—to the good of society as well as its own betterment, and to a national following as well as its own membership."[2]

In most Western nations, this is precisely what happened. In continental Europe the development was complex. Labor organizations for the most part developed in the wake of revolutionary philosophies, but by the close of the nineteenth century they had asserted their independence and emerged as real trade unions. Most of them, however, continued to provide a mass base for socialist parties with advanced aims. In Great Britain the development was very different. Here strong independent trade unions had already developed and only gradually they resorted to independent politics, first to secure their legal basis but then acquiring far-reaching social goals in a fully fledged labor party. The British dominions of Australia and New Zealand followed a simi-

3

lar pattern. More recently Canadian trade unionists have thrown
in their lot with Canadian socialists.

The United States has provided a notable exception to this
general pattern. Today, not only do American trade unions assert
their sole function as a pressure group, but their members are
among the principal upholders of the capitalist system. In the
ferment of recent years they have been the most stalwart defenders
of the status quo. Unapologetically, they offer nothing to the
urgent needs of the society of which they are a part.

To most students of American labor it has been axiomatic that
so-called "business unionism"—working exclusively for immediate
interests within the capitalist framework—should dominate American thinking. The geographical, social, and cultural environment
provided no other choice for American labor than to take its place
as one of a number of pressure groups in the voluntary society,
and labor gladly accepted. By the same token, the socialism that
captivated the trade unions of other nations could find no roots in
America.

Some writers have given socialism credit for strengthening wage
consciousness among American workers by destroying the power
of the antimonopoly panaceas that had beguiled many earlier
labor organizations. Selig Perlman made the point in several works
published before 1930,[3] and it was an important part of David J.
Saposs' thought.[4] More recently Gerald N. Grob has brought out
the importance of socialism in destroying the reform-minded
Knights of Labor and replacing it with wage-conscious trade
unionism.[5] Grob's work contrasts sharply with the much older
study by Norman J. Ware, who regarded this development in
many ways as a step backward.[6]

Other American labor historians of the first generation besides
Ware expressed regret over the defects of the victorious craft
unions. Perlman was obviously aware of the A.F.ofL.'s failure to
cater to a large part of labor. Such reflections are undoubtedly the
genesis of his general theory that trade unions are the product of
a "scarcity consciousness" peculiar to the manual worker, which
renders him unwilling "to become completely merged with his own
class."[7] Other writers of the time were less pessimistic. Saposs and
Lewis Lorwin obviously regretted the absence of enthusiasm
associated with socialist ideals and anticipated its return. If Saposs'
book has a moral, it is that practical opportunism and evangelical

idealism can be combined. Lorwin astutely prophesied the renewal of the evangelical approach that was to come with the C.I.O.[8]

But since the New Deal and especially since the end of World War II, the majority of writers have expressed unqualified approval of the development of "pressure group" unionism, which by and large they attribute to the peculiar American environment and its culture of equality, individualism, and opportunity. In the voluntaristic "consensus" society of the 1950's, trade unions were not expected to be other than exclusivist and inward-looking.

Even J. R. Commons, whose rambling introduction to the early volumes of his monumental history had stressed the interplay of ideas and environment, changed the emphasis in his 1935 introduction to the later volumes. He now surveyed the adjustment of labor to American culture and welcomed the demise of socialism in unions where it had been a significant force.[9] Philip Taft, who with Perlman wrote the fourth volume of Commons' history, has since written several works extolling recent developments. Taft feels that environmental determinism is so widely accepted that he has to remind his readers that the American Federation of Labor in the time of Samuel Gompers "greatly contributed to the specific outlook of American labor and its unions." Its main contribution, however, seems to have been to guide labor into channels predetermined by the environment.[10]

Lloyd Ulman, another writer of the fifties, stresses geographical mobility as the key factor in labor's evolution, but in a more general sense he associates the outlook of present labor institutions with the American cultural tradition. In doing so he betrays none of Perlman's pessimism but rather expresses pride in the development.[11] Foster Rhea Dulles' widely read survey of American labor history is of the same mould.[12] Among the works of this period, only Henry Pelling's study, written from a British perspective, portrays the domination of "exclusive" over "inclusive" practices (the Webbs' terms) as a matter of regret.[13]

Works on socialism written during the fifties take a similar line to those on labor. Daniel Bell made the oft-quoted assertion that socialism failed because it was "in but not of" America. More specifically, socialism's foreignness to American soil, according to Bell, is made all the clearer by its failure to make any impression on American labor.[14] David Shannon is much more sympathetic but no less clear in his assertion of the inevitability of socialism's failure.[15]

The obvious exception to this general pattern of the inevitable development of peculiarly American institutions has been the work of the historians of the left, especially Philip S. Foner[16] and Ira Kipnis.[17] But their work is plagued by another kind of determinism, which sees the development of a class-conscious revolutionary proletariat as the only correct course. In their sympathy for the extreme left, they damn all forces that recognize the primary function of unions and really expect them to become something else. Kipnis specifically accounts for the decline of the Socialist Party by its being too right wing and thus inseparable from the Progressive movement.

If most works of the Cold War generation reveal a sense of confidence in American institutions, this is not the case with some of the most recent histories. Naturally the upheaval of the past few years has produced a change of thought. The New Left is not so convinced of the inevitability of the failure of the old. James Weinstein has evinced the Socialist Party's 'strength and relevance to the America of its day. He attributes its decline to the Communist disruption of 1919, i.e., to an internal failure, rather than to intrinsic irrelevance as Bell argues, or to the ineffectiveness described by Kipnis.[18] Melvyn Dubofsky's recent works, while less assertive than Weinstein's, clearly indicate the constructive role of socialism in the early part of the century and the omissions of the dominant labor institutions both then and today.[19] Professor John H. M. Laslett's *Labor and the Left* appeared too late to be considered in the text of this work. Laslett's study of radical influence in six unions confirms many of the conclusions reached in this book, particularly the absence of any dichotomy between unionism and democratic socialism discussed in Chapter III. Laslett nevertheless concludes that the explanation of American developments is still to be found in broad, underlying factors.[20]

Still, in spite of the writings of Marxists and the recent trends just noted, it is fair to say that environmental determinism remains the accepted key to understanding American labor's unique development toward its voluntaristic, "pressure group" stance of today, so alien to the European pattern of labor support for parties of the left. The present work is concerned with this generalization. It is an examination of that formative period in labor history between the 1880's and 1924 when socialists felt they had a good chance of reversing the American trend. It is chiefly concerned with the leadership on both sides of the issue and the clash of their personalities and aims, and how these influenced or failed to influence the developing labor institutions. The study concludes with an attempt to assess these factors against the larger background of American culture and environment.

As to arrangement, a consistent chronological narrative is possible only from the eighties up to the turn of the century, and again from World War I to the death of Gompers in 1924. In the middle period, it has been necessary to pursue three themes occurring simultaneously: the development of democratic socialism and its contribution to trade unionism; the general question of industrial unionism—a chief stumbling block to good relations; and finally, the development of the A.F.ofL.'s outlook, here termed "Gompersism."

NOTES

1. Sidney and Beatrice Webb, *The History of Trade Unionism 1666-1894* (London: Longmans & Co., 1894), 1.
2. H. A. Clegg, Alan Fox, and A. F. Thompson, *A History of British Trade Unions since 1889* (Oxford: Clarendon Press, 1964), 486.
3. Selig Perlman, *A Theory of the Labor Movement* (New York: Macmillan, 1928), 197-198, and J. R. Commons and Associates, *History of Labor in the United States* II (New York: Macmillan, 1918), 308.
4. David J. Saposs, *Left Wing Unionism* (New York: International Publishers, 1926), 9.
5. Gerald N. Grob, *Workers and Utopia: A Study of Ideological Conflict in the American Labor Movement 1865-1900* (Evanston: Northwestern University Press, 1961), 43.
6. Norman J. Ware, *The Labor Movement in the United States* (New York: D. Appleton & Co., 1929), xii.
7. Commons II, 533-537. Perlman, *Theory*, 237-251, esp. 246.
8. Lewis Lorwin, *The American Federation of Labor* (Washington, D.C.: The Brookings Institution, 1933), esp. 444-470.
9. J. R. Commons and Associates, *History of Labor in the United States,* Vols. III and IV (New York: Macmillan, 1935), III esp. xix.
10. Philip Taft, *Organized Labor in American History* (New York: Harper & Row, 1964), esp. xxi; *The A. F. of L. in the Time of Gompers* (New York: Harper, 1957), esp. xviii; *The A. F. of L. from the Death of Gompers to the Merger* (New York: Harper, 1959).
11. Lloyd Ulman, *The Rise of the National Trade Union* (Cambridge, Mass.: Harvard University Press, 1955), 594-604.
12. Foster Rhea Dulles, *Labor in America* (New York: Thomas Y. Crowell Co., 1949, 2nd rev. ed., 1960), esp. 409.
13. Henry Pelling, *American Labor* (Chicago: University of Chicago Press, 1960), 210-227.

14. Daniel Bell, "The Background and Development of Marxian Socialism in the United States," in D. D. Egbert and Stow Persons, *Socialism and American Life* (Princeton: Princeton University Press, 1952) I, 215-405, esp. 254. Daniel Bell, *The End of Ideology* (New York: Collier Books 1961), 279.
15. David A. Shannon, *The Socialist Party of America* (New York: Macmillan, 1955), 262.
16. Philip S. Foner, *History of the Labor Movement in the United States* 4 vols. to date (New York: International Publishers, 1947, 1955, 1964, 1965), esp. III *The Policies and Practices of the American Federation of Labor 1900-1909.*
17. Ira Kipnis, *The American Socialist Movement 1897-1912* (New York: Columbia University Press, 1952), 421-429.
18. James Weinstein, *The Decline of Socialism in America, 1912-1925.* (New York: Vintage Books, 1967), viii.
19. Melvyn Dubofsky, *We Shall Be All: A History of the I.W.W.* (Chicago: Quadrangle Books, 1969). Melvyn Dubofsky, *When Workers Organize: New York City in the Progressive Era* (Amherst: University of Massachusetts Press, 1968), 32-36, 151.
20. John H. M. Laslett, *Labor and the Left:* a study of socialist and radical influences in the American labor movement 1881-1924. (Basic Books, Inc.: New York, 1970).

1

Origins

In the generation following the Civil War, the United States became an industrial nation. New technologies, both developed at home and copied from abroad, transformed extractive and manufacturing industries. The railroads joined the nation into an integrated whole, bringing raw materials, manufacturing centers, and markets close together. The natural growth in population, assisted by a vastly increased immigration, provided both the labor and the necessary consumer demand. By the end of that post-Civil War generation, the United States had outpaced Great Britain and Germany in industrial output.

It is true that vast areas of the country retained their agricultural character, but in no other country were the lives of farmers so much affected by industrialization as in the U.S. Besides highly complicated agricultural machinery, the existence of large urban areas in their midst and a dependence on the giant railroad companies also had their effect. The American farming system, moreover, was based on an elaborate structure of credit centered on the industrial east. Industrialization affected all America. Even before 1890—the traditional date for the closing of the frontier—more Americans had been leaving the land for the cities than were moving on to it. America had become an urban civilization.

The immediate social response to industrialization was a bewildering variety of economic and political organizations, but mostly a hybrid of the two. Bewildering is the key word, for their rapid rise and fall, their simultaneous appearance, and their overlapping membership makes it almost impossible to trace their separate histories. To put the matter in British terms, it is almost as if the agitation resulting in the "Six Acts"—Chartism, Owenism, conservative trade unionism, the "New Unionism," and the Labour Party movement—all of which had American equiva-

9

lents in the period after the Civil War, had been crammed into one generation instead of stretching over a whole century.

While comparison between events in two countries scarcely constitutes an explanation, the exercise can be enlightening. Of course the fragmented nature of society and politics all help to explain the American cataclysm, but the compression of events due to the greater speed of industrial change compared with the British example obviously made the assimilation of experiences much more difficult and clouded the issues for contemporaries.[1]

Trade unionism, in the general sense of combinations of workers for the purpose of preserving or improving their conditions of labor, began among men in the same trade in particular localities in the early nineteenth century. The combination of local bodies took two forms: the local trades assembly combining the different trades and the locality, and the national trade union linking together all the local unions of one particular trade. Both these forms of organization first appeared in the Jacksonian period, and the 1840's witnessed sporadic attempts to form a national body representing all labor organizations. Before the Civil War, however, trade unionism followed an erratic course. The boom that began during the war and lasted into the seventies lent impetus to trade unionism generally, and in 1866 the National Labor Union, formed by representatives from both local trades assemblies and national trade unions, gave America its first comprehensive nationwide labor organization.

Two phases of the National Labor Union, from 1866 to 1870, and from 1870 until 1872, are distinguished by the form the organization took. In 1870 it decided to enter politics and the unitary structure gave place to a dual form; an economic organization on one side, and a political party on the other. At this point some of the national trade unions withdrew—an early indication of mistrust of political action.

With hindsight it is easy to credit the national trade unions with remarkable astuteness in seeing the political move as bound to lead to disaster. But from the start the National Labor Union was politically minded. Originally called in 1866 to support an eight-hour bill it drifted into greenbackism, a monetary reform scheme aimed at securing cheap government credit. From the very first, independent political action was in the air and the move of 1870 was a logical step, no matter how disastrous it proved in 1872, when the presidential candidate withdrew and left the party high and dry. With the Republican Party little more than a decade old, the political scene appeared much more flexible to contemporaries than it does to us looking back over a century.

The endorsement of greenbackism as a means of securing capital for producers' cooperatives is perhaps evidence of American labor's continuing desire to escape capitalism and revert to some kind of Jeffersonian dream. But the peculiarly American nature of the National Labor Union can be overstated. Labor's support of greenbackism bears similarities to British working-class support of Thomas Attwood's banking ideas in England in the 1830's. The notion of government credit for producers' cooperatives was the aim of Lassallean socialism, which may account for German workers' support for it in America. Moreover, the National Labor Union in some measure saw itself as the American counterpart of the International Workingmen's Association. An unofficial representative attended the Basle Conference of the First International in 1869, and the following year there was talk of affiliation. The National Labor Union was a mixed response to industrialization, typical of different countries at a similar stage of development.

With the National Labor Union at an end, the national trade unions renewed attempts at federation. However, the depression that came after 1873—the worst in the century—not only destroyed the federations but some of the national trade unions themselves. As always, some local unions survived and many began to align themselves with a new organization now making its first, somewhat shadowy appearance on the American scene: the Noble Order of the Knights of Labor.

Modern socialism was originally a German import into the United States, and not surprisingly its adherents among German immigrants suffered the same divisions as their compatriots in the home country. The chief of these concerned the relative importance of trade unionism and politics. Briefly, the followers of Ferdinand Lassalle believed in the conquest of the state through universal suffrage. The state alone could then provide credit for cooperative production, which alone could provide the economic basis for effective trade unionism. Trade unionism was therefore only possible after the conquest of the state by the working class. Marx reversed the process. True to his theory of dialectic materialism, he believed effective working-class political activity to be possible only after organization in accordance with

objective economic realities. Trade unionism, a natural outgrowth
of the capitalist mode of production, was to provide the working
class with such organization, its day-to-day struggles gradually
increasing the workers' class consciousness until the time became
ripe for political conquest of the state.

These differences were real enough, but in America theories
seem to have been more readily sacrificed to expediency, since
the decision to give more weight to politics or to unionism seems
to have depended more upon the state of business at any given
time than on theory. In other words, the Marxists or Internationalists flourished in good times, when economic action paid off;
while the Lassalleans found support during depression, when
politics seemed the only way out. Personal or theoretical disagreements were overcome in the interests of taking the most
suitable action.

Marxist groups antedating the Civil War, for instance, joined
with Lassalleans in 1866—the beginning of a postwar slump—
to form the Social Party of New York. It put forward candidates
in the election of 1868, with disastrous results. Amid the prosperity of the late sixties and early seventies, the remnant of the
Social Party affiliated with the National Labor Union and constituted itself as Section I of Marx's International Workingmen's
Association. The Internationalists then gained added prestige
when Marx transferred the headquarters of his organization from
Geneva to New York in 1872.

Though the depression in 1873 renewed dissension by reviving
political activity, emerging leaders like P. J. McGuire and Adolph
Strasser were certainly not unfriendly toward trade unions. Part
of their motive was to use the political forum to propagate socialist and trade unionist ideas more widely. And not only individual
leaders but also the political parties formed in this new upsurge
did not discount trade unionism. The Labor Party of Illinois and
the Social Democratic Party of New York, both formed at this
time, gave considerable space to the advocacy of unionism in
spite of the objection of some purist Lassalleans. For the most
part, those who broke from the International in 1873 did not
stray far from the path of trade unionism.

Besides, the split did not last long. Lassalleans and Marxists
reunited at a conference in Pittsburgh in 1876 when negotiations
were opened with the Greenback Party; then the following year,
when great strikes erupted throughout the country, all socialist

groups—the remnant of the International, the Labor Party of
Illinois, and the Social Democratic Party—as well as some others
joined to form the Workingmen's Party of the United States.
Renamed the Socialist Labor Party soon afterward, it remained
the main body of American socialism until the turn of the
century.

This was not the end of conflict over the relative merits of
trade unionism and politics, however; in fact it was the real
beginning. In the future the theoretical question as to whether
trade unions could play their most effective role before or after
the inevitable victory at the polls became irrelevant. With the
end of the depression of the seventies, trade unionism revived
not only among foreign-born socialists, but among native Americans and others who had had little contact with socialism. The
attitude the new Socialist Labor Party was to adopt toward these
bodies was bound to be a crucial question during the succeeding
decades.

Besides trade union theory, Socialists had other problems in
the generation after the Civil War. Bakunin's brand of anarchism, which split the First International in 1872, had its American counterpart in New York's Section 12, dominated by the
notorious Victoria Woodhull and Tennessee Claflin. Preaching
the supremacy of the individual in the form of women's suffrage
and free love as much as socialism, Section 12 eventually seceded
from the International and expired.

More serious than the "faddists" of Section 12 were the anarchists who gathered strength in the course of the seventies.
A fresh influx of foreign radicals after the passing of Bismarck's
antisocialist law in 1879 reinforced their ranks. Further recruits
arrived from Russia when the assassination of Alexander II led
to widespread persecution.

The new arrivals formed two groups. One consisted of "pure"
anarchists with rather vague ideas. They were centered mainly
in New York and recognized Johann Most as their leader. The
others were more "anarcho-syndicalist" in outlook, giving a place
to the trade union as the source of revolution and the future basis
of social organization. This group was centered in Chicago and
drew its recruits not only from new immigrants but also from
those Marxist Internationalists in the region who resented the
sweep into politics of the Illinois Labor Party. The anarchist
movement was shattered by the Haymarket affair of 1886, when

several of its leaders were executed. "Syndicalism" of one kind or another, however, was to remain one of the problems facing the socialist movement in America.

One segment of "working class" activity after the Civil War remains to be considered, namely the radical political parties other than socialist. Probably the most important was greenbackism in its two phases. During the first phase, when the National Labor Union took it up, the aim was to use "greenbacks" as a means of lessening the interest on credit. The second phase, starting about 1874, was concerned solely with the inflationary possibilities of the banknotes. Primarily a western movement, especially in the later period, greenbackism was of limited importance among urban workers. Nevertheless, the organizations to which workmen belonged answered the call to various congresses and often gave their support. The National Labor Union became hopelessly involved in the movement. The Pittsburgh Conference of 1876 was organized by greenbackers, but attended by Knights of Labor, socialists, and just about everyone else interested in the labor question. The socialists, it seems, were strong enough to "capture" the meeting, but this was of little importance since no future plans were formulated. In 1878 the success of the Greenback party and its labor affiliates—Terence V. Powderly, future leader of the Knights of Labor, won election as mayor of Scranton—attracted the attention of the newly formed Socialist Labor Party. Consequently it endorsed James B. Weaver, the greenback candidate for President in 1880, though separate candidates ran for other offices. The disappointing returns together with returning prosperity brought a decline in greenback activity and ended the temporary alliance of radical movements. The spirit of cooperation had only a brief revival in 1886.

Such then was the immediate impact of industrialization upon America: a flood of short-lived organizations, quickly rising and even more quickly falling; a vast quadrille comprising political and economic groups, often moving in opposite directions, constantly changing partners, occasionally all joining together for one brief turn only to separate again immediately to form some new pattern. As the nation recovered from the depression of the seventies, the process of industrialization intensified. The giant corporation came to predominate in most sections of production and in the last quarter of the century took its place as the most significant feature of American economic, social, and political life. Meanwhile, what was the nature of working-class resistance to corporate domination?

In working class politics, the Socialist Labor Party, still largely in the hands of German groups, had made its appearance, but bedeviled by the anarchist question it had little to offer as yet. Even by the end of the eighties it could scarcely be compared with the European and particularly the German movement, but it was certainly more influential than any socialist organization in England at the time.

The late seventies also witnessed the reappearance of nation-wide labor organizations. The world, however, was now different from that immediately after the Civil War. With the corporation came large-scale machinery, and as a result the division of labor intensified. The distinction between skilled and unskilled began to break down, creating between them an amorphous class of semiskilled labor. From about 1880 this development rapidly became the fundamental fact of the American working class, and yet over the next fifty years the main body of American labor came to ignore it. As a result, not only was working class solidarity in the face of corporations impossible, but the immediate interests of trade unionism were jeopardized as well. This was not an irrevocable development. What happened in the next half-century depended on particular circumstances and individual personalities. As events unfold, however, precedents set at an early stage can have a decisive effect.

In 1879 the aged Uriah H. Stevens handed over the leadership of the Knights of Labor to Terence V. Powderly, former blacksmith and labor mayor of Scranton. Powderly finally threw off the veil of secrecy that had surrounded the organization during the seventies, and the stage was set for one of the most dramatic scenes in the labor history of any country. After a steady growth up to 1884 during relative prosperity, a series of wage-cut strikes championed by the Knights suddenly brought the membership up to half a million, at a conservative estimate. Newspapers, labor and capitalist alike, created wide publicity. America had seen nothing like it before.

The following year the eight-hour movement, under the general impetus of industrial unrest, swept the country, and though Powderly was lukewarm the rank and file Knights eagerly took up the issue. So did almost every other labor organization, including the "anarcho-syndicalists" in Chicago. When the bomb exploded in the Haymarket in 1886, mass hysteria swept the country. The Knights of Labor, having enjoyed years of great publicity, now had to face a hostile public opinion. It was the start of a decline, which, along with a series of disputes with the national trade unions, rendered the Knights utterly impotent. The movement lingered on for another two decades but by then it was little more than a memory.

The very rapid rise and fall of the Knights of Labor is partly explicable in terms of its organization. The motto of the Knights —"an injury to one is the concern of all"—stood for the solidarity of all labor. In America during the eighties, when industrial machinery minimized the difference between skilled and unskilled workers, and the power of the rising corporations was evident everywhere, nothing was better fitted to capture the imagination of a vast segment of the working population. In taking over the leadership of the new organization, Powderly pointed out the inadequacy of the older institutions to meet the new industrial situation.[2] In calling together all labor into a monolithic organization, however, there was an obvious danger of unwieldiness. On paper the plan was simple. The basic unit was the local assembly of men, of the same or of different trades. These were grouped into district assemblies, which in turn were represented in a national general assembly. At each level in the hierarchy an executive committee was elected by the assembly. The constitution of the Knights was thus conducive to speedy growth, but it was a time of strikes and there was no great reserve of funds. Once disillusionment crept in, the Knights of Labor were bound to feel the lack of solidarity associated with a smaller-scale trade union.

Norman Ware, writing in the 1920's, argued that the Knights were potentially capable of accommodating the trade unions. Of course, when "the solidarity of all" was the Knights' plea, the national trade union based on a particular skill was bound to create suspicion. Hence the amendment to the constitution in 1879 permitting trade unions to enter the organizations as district assemblies was repealed after a few months. Nevertheless, Ware believed that in practice the Knights continued to accommodate the unions and only certain circumstances and personalities ruined the chances for the Knights' development.[3]

More recent scholarship, on the other hand, rejects this inter-

pretation. Lloyd Ulman, for instance, argues that the very nature
of national trade unions demanded exclusive jurisdiction over all
members of a trade for purpose of collective bargaining. It could
therefore brook no rivals to its authority, from any source. If
British unionism seemed to be able to accommodate different
kinds of organizations with overlapping jurisdictions, it was
because British industry was more localized so that the union
controlling the trade in the main center could afford to be more
tolerant toward other organizations outside. American industry,
on the other hand, was widespread throughout the country, and
more important, its employees more mobile. Hence, to bargain
collectively the national union would have to have exclusive control of all the workers in the trade.[4]

The difference between Ware and Ulman is the difference
between the historian and the social scientist. Ulman's purpose
is to trace the basic cause of the present-day national trade union,
and not surprisingly the note of determinism comes into his find-
ings. Ware, on the other hand, is struck by the fluidity of the
situation and how much depends on unforeseen circumstances
and personalities. Ulman's argument, of course, appeals to the
school of American labor historians who stress geographical and
cultural determinism behind the rise of present-day business
unionism. But it smacks of *a priori* reasoning. In the early
eighties, even when some trade unionists had organized the Federation of Organized Trades and Labor Unions as their spokesman, relations with the Knights were reasonably cordial. For a
number of years there was overlapping jurisdiction and accommodation between trade unions and Knights in the interests of
securing immediate aims and encouraging solidarity. But this
was before the sudden increase in the Knights' numbers. Then
a series of conflicts arose, and both sides expelled members refusing to give up affiliation with the enemy. All attempts to end
the quarrel in the interests of the solidarity of labor proved futile.

The failure probably lay in the fact that all labor attempted
to organize before craft unions had had time to establish themselves. It proved difficult enough in Great Britain to make the
old, solidly founded craft unions lend assistance to the unskilled
in organizing general and industrial unions.[5] How much less
feasible it must have seemed to American trade unionists when
faced not just with new unions with overlapping jurisdictions,
but with a monolithic whole that threatened to swamp them.

One of the reasons for a development in America very different from Great Britain must be the suddenness with which the United States became industrialized. Perhaps the American response was to attempt too much at one time.

However, even if the failure of the Knights meant that unskilled labor in America had no spokesman for another fifty years, at least in organized labor, it was not necessarily foreseen by the leaders of the attack on the Knights. Men like Samuel Gompers and P. J. McGuire were neither indifferent to the problems of the unskilled nor uninterested in working-class solidarity. They were, however, convinced that the Knights of Labor was not the instrument to achieve effective solidarity, and Gompers had personal animosities against the Knights as well. To appreciate their position it is necessary to examine further the general philosophy of the Knights and the national trade unionists' response to them.

In brief, it was the tragedy of the Knights of Labor to combine the most advanced ideas of the day with the most retrogressive. In consciously seeking the organization of the unskilled, the Knights were ahead of their times. Perhaps even the idea of cooperation, which obsessed the early leadership, was as much forward looking as backward looking; connections could be made with the guild socialism of a later day.[6] Powderly himself consistently advocated public ownership of mines and railways.[7] George E. McNeill, the labor writer of the day, believed that the Knights' aims were not unlike those of the Socialist Labor Party,[8] and statements made in the general assembly bear this out. In 1884, for instance, it was stated that the essential difference between the Knights and the trade unions was between the desire for a radical change in the existing system and merely its adaptation, and that the attitude of the Knights toward the existing industrial system was necessarily one of war.[9]

On the other hand, in so many ways the Knights of Labor was the culmination of that earlier American tradition that never really accepted the realities of industrial society. One proposed aim of the constitution of 1881, "to persuade employees to agree to arbitrate all differences which may arise between them and their employees in order that the bonds of sympathy between them may be strengthened and that strikes may be rendered unnecessary,"[10] suggests the appeal of an earlier, simpler society.

Cooperation of course had links with the National Labor Union back to the Jacksonian period. The dislike of strikes and the stress on education all befit a man who wished to "ban the word class" from the English language.[11]

Powderly, however, is his own best spokesman and defense against critics:

> I am aware that some young men fresh from college have tried to write the history of the organization but they failed. They applied logic and scientific research; they divided the emotions, the passions and feelings of the members into groups; they dissected the groups; they used logarithms, algebraic formulas and everything known to the young ambitious graduate of a university . . . they attributed to me certain motives, ambitions and intentions that I never dreamed of. From where they sat, while writing, they endowed me with a firmness I never possessed or a weakness almost unparalleled. Others claimed I was very inconsistent; I changed my mind and my tactics frequently. These came nearest to being right . . . .[12]

The Knights of Labor was a wide movement with many sides to it. Perhaps it was too wide, for the diffusion of energy contrasted sharply with the more concentrated purpose of the leaders of the national trade unions.

All but destroyed by the depressions of the mid-seventies, the trade unions slowly began to revive, and by the time of the heyday of the Knights of Labor in the mid-eighties, they were only just beginning to find their feet. Some of these reviving unions—the shoe workers, glass workers, miners, and brewers—grew along with the Knights. The miners and brewers have retained the industrial or intercraft basis they acquired at that time.

Other unions came to set as their model the British unions of the mid-century, which entailed a craft basis and high dues. The Cigar Makers International Union under Adolph Strasser and Samuel Gompers led the way, though it must be noted that while imposing high dues they also brought unskilled workers using new machinery into the union fold. P. J. McGuire played a similar part in organizing the Brotherhood of Carpenters and Joiners in 1881. John Jarret, an immigrant Welshman already experienced in trade unionism, helped establish the Amalgamated Association of Iron and Steel Workers in 1876. Meanwhile the National Typographical Association, the oldest union in America, was growing as a strong craft-based union.

Most of the leaders were comparatively recent immigrants into America, and they had not shared the earlier reform tradition which to them was the most obvious part of the outlook of Powderly and the Knights. Above all, they were practical men with precise aims for their own organizations and the oldfashioned reformism of the Knights had little appeal for them. However, most of them seem to have been aware of the need for a solidifying force, and though "wage consciousness" was undoubtedly the most obvious aspect of their philosophy, they were not all exclusively "business unionists" in the sense of accepting the capitalist structure of society as permanent. This was true even among those who spoke a great deal about "pure and simple" trade unionism as opposed to trade unionism with political aims. The point becomes clearer by examining the experience of some of these leaders.

P. J. McGuire, after activity in the Socialist Labor Party during the upheavals of the seventies, apparently tired of the socialists' factionalism and abandoned politics altogether.[13] The Cigar Makers' International Union had been a stronghold of socialism in New York. Adolph Strasser had played an important part in the old International Workingmen's Association, and Gompers, the most promising of its younger members, became imbued with Marxist ideas, though he did not take an active part in any political movement. Like McGuire, however, they grew tired of the factionalism and, turning to Marxism and away from Lassalleanism, grew steadily more suspicious of political activity. After the debacle with Weaver in 1880, they were thoroughly disillusioned; hence the "pure and simple" trade unionism.[14]

For several years after 1881, moreover, Gompers as president of Local 144 of the Cigar Makers' International Union in New York fought a group of socialist secessionists from the union. It started when Gompers supported certain state politicians prepared to pass a law forbidding the manufacture of cigars in New York tenements, a practice obviously detrimental to union activity. Some socialist members of the union, resentful of support given to a party other than the Socialist Labor Party, ousted Gompers from the presidency of the local in an election in 1882. Strasser as president of the whole union intervened and decreed the election invalid on the grounds that the socialist candidate was an employer of labor at the time of his election. The socialists seceded and formed the Progressive Cigar Makers' Union.

The action of Strasser was high-handed, though the rights and wrongs of the situation are not exactly clear. But right or wrong, the socialists had committed the cardinal sin of dual unionism and were never forgiven. Even worse, Gompers' ego was involved and he was never one to forget a personal slight.[15]

There was thus no shortage of quarrels between the unions and the Socialist Labor Party, but this does not mean that men like McGuire and Gompers had abandoned their own socialist ideas completely. On the contrary, the evidence suggests that it was a long time before they gave up the Marxism they had been raised on as union men. McGuire, an American representative at the International Labor and Socialist Conference in Geneva in 1881, always referred to the trade union as the germ of the future society.[16] Similarly, Gompers believed the "final emancipation of the working-class"—a phrase he loved—lay in the trade unions.[17] It is not enough to say that such concepts of a future society are too vague to give any indication of how these men felt; they are no more vague than the statements of Marx himself. Marx of course had advocated a political party as well as trade unionism, but Gompers saw that in the American context such political parties were inevitably diverted by reform panaceas, so a political party as such had to be relegated to the future while the labor movement concentrated solely on unions. Undoubtedly it would have been difficult in the 1880's not to have doubts about the future of socialist politics, but it is much too early to divorce Marxist ideas from these labor leaders.

Even the "new unionism" with its high dues and benefits was not in conflict with socialism, for the International Workingmen's Association, as opposed to Lassallean organizations, had considered a strong trade union movement necessary. Gompers, Strasser, and McGuire knew by experience that without high dues unionism was not able to survive. Benefits made men more loyal to unionism because they provided something tangible. McGuire and Gompers did not necessarily see any conflict between trade unionism and a socialist view of society.

Meanwhile, the general acceptance by most unionists of the principle of solidarity as expressed by the Knights of Labor is shown by their indifference toward a rival organization created in 1881, the Federation of Organized Trades and Labor Unions. A year earlier the Typographical, in the interests of securing support for its boycotts, took the initiative in attempting to form a new organization but met with little response. The next year a group of disaffected members of the Knights of Labor called a conference at Terre Haute, Indiana, and the Typographical seized this chance. Its representative Lyman A. Brant must have been disappointed by the turnout, for most representatives were from central bodies in cities, or local unions (about half from Terre Haute itself), but arrangements were made for a conference at Pittsburgh the following November. One hundred and seven delegates, including representatives from eight national (or international) unions, then met and launched the Federation of Organized Trades and Labor Unions of the United States and Canada.[18]

From start to finish the new organization was a failure. Most unions, like the miners, preferred to work within the existing Knights of Labor and regarded the Federation as a dual movement, which it was. At the 1882 convention of the Federation the Iron and Steel Workers left in a row over the tariff and resumed friendship with the Knights.[19] Most other unions had not even bothered to send representatives. In fact the Federation would have had no importance in the history of American labor but for one thing: certain outstanding men in it, including Samuel Gompers and P. J. McGuire, transformed it into the American Federation of Labor.

If the original movement was a failure, what had its leaders hoped to gain from it? The idea of the disaffected members of the Knights of Labor was apparently to form a rival organization based on the same lines; the Typographical wanted support; there was also some talk of a political pressure group, for Gompers in 1881 was yet to be chastened by his experiences with the New York legislature. None of these things was accomplished. Another aim of the Federation was the general encouragement of trade unionism in the broadest sense. The preamble to the constitution makes this clear: "Whereas, a struggle is going on in the nations of the civilized world between the oppressors and oppressed of all countries, a struggle between capital and labor, which must grow in intensity from year to year and work disastrous results to the toiling millions of all nations if not combined for mutual protection and benefit. . ." Historian Philip Taft's assertion that the preamble was merely "couched in the standard language of the time" scarcely proves they did not believe it.[20] For Gompers it was probably part of his broad aim of working-class solidarity, for one of his goals was a central strike fund by which one union could assist another.[21] Then why not work within the Knights of Labor, as many other members of the federation felt they ought? McGuire, for instance, showed signs of wanting to make some kind of arrangement with the Knights.[22] But Gompers was resolutely opposed. His reasons were far from straightforward, and since he played a large part in wrecking the Knights, they must be examined.

In the first place Gompers resented the Knights' tendency to attract members away from the national unions outside their jurisdiction.[23] Rival jurisdiction is bound to exist in any union movement, and the problem was not solved by the disappearance of the Knights. But with Gompers it was more than a question of general principles. The Progressive Cigar Makers, whose secession from the Cigar Makers' International had been caused by Gompers, appealed for and received the aid of District Assembly No. 49 of the Knights. One of the most important in the organization, this Assembly was controlled by a clique of Lassallean socialists collectively known as the Home Club. What their intentions for the Knights were is not entirely clear, but true to the views of Lassalle they did not disguise their hostility toward trade unionism. Although the Home Club was not typical of the Knights, when "scabbing" arose between the rival factions of the Cigar Makers and they opposed each other with different union labels, Gompers laid the responsibility on the Knights as a whole.[24]

There was also personal animosity between Gompers and Powderly that went deeper than the practical issue of the Progressive Cigar Makers' Union. Their whole personalities clashed. Gompers liked a barroom atmosphere; Powderly was rather prim, middle-class in some ways, and temperate. He once claimed he had never seen Gompers sober. Obviously, personal ill-feeling did not improve an already existing conflict.[25]

Finally, Gompers' Marxism also made him dislike the Knights. For someone who readily thought in Marxist terms the Knights appeared Utopian, born out of some odd character's mind rather than out of the experience of the workers. The progressive side of the organization Gompers chose to ignore, concentrating instead on the grandiose schemes it seemed to have inherited from the past. "The trade unions are the natural growth of natural laws," Gompers explained in an open letter to the *Cleveland*

Citizen,[26] and he went on to explain the difference between a natural growth and an ideological one. Around the same time he got an excellent opportunity for Marxist slogan making when Powderly innocently entitled one of his articles "An Ideal Union." "What a chance for a rejoinder," Gompers wrote to McGuire. "How would this caption be for a reply: 'A Real versus an Ideal Organization.' "[27] However impossible it seems today, when his name is immediately associated with exclusive craft unionism, Gompers at this point sincerely believed that the entire working class could be organized. A craft union was more "real" to him in that a common craft gave men a natural bond. Throughout his life, even at the pinnacle of fame, Gompers took great pride in his own trade. But he appreciated the new conditions and as soon as he attained a position of real authority he pressed for a partial reorganization along industrial lines. In his aims he antedated some of the developments that were to transform British trade unionism in the 1890's.[28]

The quarrel over the Cigar Makers was not the first time that relations between the Knights and the unions had soured, but two factors made accommodation much less likely than before. In the first place, the enthusiasm associated with the Knights' spectacular growth was such that some national trade unions feared serious loss of membership or even of entire locals. Second, at this critical juncture the spokesmen of the Knights were not the conciliatory figures of previous years but the members of the same Home Club that had been a thorn to Gompers. By capturing control of the executive council in New York, they effectively controlled the Knights as a whole, and they made no attempt to disguise their intentions of open war against the trade unionists both within and without the Knights.[29]

For a variety of reasons, therefore, Gompers aimed to destroy the Knights of Labor. Of course he alone did not do so, but the great changes in American labor in the late eighties are inconceivable without him. He saw the opportunity and seized it. The opportunity came with the phenomenal growth of the Knights in 1885–1886. Though trade unions outside the Knights also benefited, the rapid growth brought about a new series of jurisdictional disputes in addition to the one between the Knights and the Cigar Makers. In this atmosphere P. J. McGuire issued a circular calling for a meeting of trade unionists for May 1886, which was answered by almost all of them, including many

within the Knights. The conference drew up a document that
was to form the basis of a treaty between trade unions and
Knights, defining their respective spheres of influence. Considering the prestige enjoyed by the Knights at this point, the con-
tents of the document are decidedly impertinent. Even McGuire
felt they should not be taken too seriously but only provide
something on which to start discussion. But the attitude of the
Knights was no more conducive to compromise, and Powderly
was tactless in choosing a committee to treat with the unionists.

The treaty having failed, the trade unions' committee called a
convention for December 1886 in Columbus, Ohio, which
launched the American Federation of Labor. Gompers meanwhile had postponed the planned October meeting of the Federation of Organized Trades and Labor Unions to the day before
the Columbus meeting. It then merged with the new organization with Gompers as president. Though there were several attempts in the following years to unify the labor movement, they
all met with failure. Meanwhile the Knights were dying a natural death, for besides the war with the unions, the loose structure
of the organization made it difficult to withstand the disappointment of futile strikes and the bad publicity of Haymarket. By
1892 it was becoming obvious that the future lay with the
American Federation of Labor.

The most curious aspect of the conflict between Knights and
unionists was that it was the most radical elements of both—the
Home Club in the case of the Knights, Gompers in the case of
the trade unions—that took the initiative in attempting to destroy
the other organization, each claiming that it possessed the key to
the "emancipation" of the entire working class. In a sense it was
a latter day battle between Lassalleans and Marxists.

Gompers won the battle, but at a price. The American Federation of Labor owed its existence to the fears of trade union leaders of an amorphous, weakly structured but popular organization
that threatened to swamp them. Some of them hoped to establish
a new federal body in place of the Knights, less attracted by the
older reform tradition and more realistically based on modern
industrial conditions. But the A.F.ofL. was born in the defense
of organization by craft, and precedents once set have a habit of
restricting future developments.

Meanwhile, just as the new federation formed, a new political
movement combining all radical forces was again under way.

Gompers had scorned independent political activity; but just as Marxists had earlier joined Lassalleans when the situation demanded it, Gompers, for all his "pure and simple" trade unionism, could not resist.

NOTES

1. See Charles H. Kerr, "The Backwardness of America," *International Socialist Review*. IX, 4 (October, 1908), 294.
2. *Journal of United Labor* 1 (June, 1880), 21.
3. Norman J. Ware, *The Labor Movement in the United States 1860-1895* (New York: D. Appleton & Co., 1929), esp. xii, 163, 171-174.
4. Lloyd Ulman, *The Rise of the National Trade Union*. (Cambridge, Mass.: Harvard University Press, 1955), 45,8. 362-363.
5. H. A. Clegg, Alan Fox and A. C. Thompson, *A History of British Trade Unionism since 1889*. (Oxford: 1964 Clarendon Press), 486-488.
6. See Terence V. Powderly, *The Path I Trod* (New York: Columbia University Press, 1950), 274-275.
7. E.g., *Journal of United Labor* VIII (March 10, 1888), 2; VIII (June 8, 1888), 1; *Journal of Knights of Labor* XIII (April 14, 1892), 1.
8. George E. McNeill, ed., *The Labor Movement: The Problem of Today* (Boston: M. W. Hazen Co., 1887), 602.
9. Knights of Labor, *Proceedings* 1884, 716-717.
10. *Journal of United Labor* VIII (March 10, 1888), 2.
11. *Journal of United Labor* I (June, 1880), 21.
12. Powderly, *The Path I Trod*, 102.
13. Robert A. Christie, *Empire in Wood* (Ithaca, N.Y.: Cornell University Press, 1956), 34-35.
14. Samuel Gompers, *Seventy Years of Life and Labor* (New York: E. P. Dutton, 1925) I, 384 suggests he was never attracted by socialism. But see Bernard Mandel, *Samuel Gompers: A Biography* (Yellow Springs: Antioch Press, 1963), 17-19.
15. Ware, *Labor Movement*, 262 ff.
16. Christie, *Empire in Wood*, 41, 92.
17. Mandel, *Gompers: Biography*, 65.
18. George A. Tracy, *A History of the Typographical* (Indianapolis: The International Typographical Union, 1913), 315.
19. Ware, *Labor Movement*, 229.
20. Philip Taft, *A. F. of L. in the Time of Gompers* (New York: Harper, 1957), 11-12.
21. A. F. of L., *Proceedings* 1883, 16.
22. "The New Federation of Trades Unions," *John Swinton's Paper*, December 19, 1886, 1.
23. A. F. of L., *Proceedings* 1883, 9-10.
24. Ware, *Labor Movement*, 265.
25. Mandel, *Gompers: Biography*, 67.
26. Cleveland *Citizen*, June 30, 1891.
27. S. G. to J. P. McGuire, August 1, 1891 (Samuel Gompers Copy Books).
28. A. F. of L., *Proceedings* 1888, 14.
29. Ware, *Labor Movement*, 267, 286.

2

Henry George and After: Unionism and Politics 1886-1900

The Henry George New York mayoralty campaign of 1886 was more than an episode in local politics. Depression again encouraged political activity and the nation watched as the entire left—unionists, socialists, and progressives, in addition to Single Taxers—threw down the gauntlet before the old parties. Similar movements sprang up in several major cities of the United States, and had it been successful in New York a nationwide party might have materialized.

A special committee of the New York Central Labor Union in which members of the Socialist Labor Party were prominent first nominated Henry George. His chief journalist critics dubbed him the "socialist candidate," and when a larger convention of labor organizers of New York nominated him a second time, one paper called it an endorsement of the socialist candidate.[1] George accepted after the fulfilment of his one condition, the pledging of thirty thousand votes.

Henry George's single tax theory is not socialism. Raised in California just as the state was being settled on a large scale, he noticed a relationship between monopolization of land—including its products such as minerals—and the fall in real wages. His solution was for the government to tax to the extent of the monopolists' advantage. In single tax theory there was nothing about abolishing the wage system or the cooperative commonwealth. Karl Marx considered the movement an oldfashioned "bourgeoisie versus land owner" struggle and compared it to a similar scheme of the elder Mill's.[2]

On the other hand, once expressed on the hustings, there was a great deal in single taxism that would appeal to both socialists and labor. George's analysis of deplorable conditions and low wages as the result of monopolistic growth is not unlike Marx's.

27

The platform put forward by the delegates to the convention of trade and labor organizations responsible for his nomination aimed at "the abolition of the system which compels men to pay their fellow creatures for the use of God's gifts to all and permits monopolizers to deprive labor of natural opportunities for employment"—an astute compromise between single tax and Marxian theory.[3] Land monopoly, according to George, also brought government under the control of corrupt monopolizers—a concept very close to Marx's view of the state. One of the great campaign issues was the corruption of the two old parties. When the Democratic candidate Abraham S. Hewitt charged George with pursuing the interests of one class against all others—contrary to all that was best in American institutions—George replied that "the working class is in reality not a class but the mass, and that any political movement in which they engage is not that of any class against other classes, but as an English statesman has happily phrased it, a movement of 'the masses against the classes.' "[4]

Similarities between socialism and Single Tax theory do not obviate the differences, and it is doubtful whether the two movements could have remained permanently united. Yet Henry George probably had a greater initial impact on British Fabians than Karl Marx did, and the British left managed to unite permanently.[5] As late as 1918 one prominent Single Taxer pointed out the progress of the British and Australian labor parties in carrying out Single Tax proposals.[6] Even more recently Norman Thomas has expressed American socialism's debt to the movement.[7] An interest on the part of socialists is therefore understandable, though the rush into politics indicates the persistence of Lassallean ideas within the S.L.P. Meanwhile, what was the attitude of the national labor organizations—the Knights of Labor and the Federation—toward Henry George?

Though Powderly was suspicious of politics and withheld his support until the very end, the rank and file Knights—many attended the nominating convention—were for him. As the *Sun* put it, "Politics is tabooed in every Knights of Labor assembly, but where George is concerned it is all right."[8] With this kind of pressure Powderly changed his mind. Just before the election the *New York Times* noted his strong plea for a vote for George.[9]

The position of Gompers and the Federation of Organized Trades and Labor Unions is interesting. The 1885 convention rejected a resolution calling for support for a party "free from the

capitalist parties."[10] Yet the following year the executive committee of the American Federation of Labor announced at its open-
ing convention that it was in full accord with George's movement
and recommended to all organized labor that it use its political
power.[11] Though its situation of flux prevented the Federation
from playing any part in the election, some of the leading lights,
including Gompers, were involved—"pure and simple" trade
unionism notwithstanding.

Henry George's opponents were formidable. The press for the
most part was firmly against him and made a great deal of his
Anglophilia and alleged un-Americanism. The Catholic hierarchy,
particularly influential among Irish and Italian voters, was sav-
agely anti-George, though a strong body of the Irish led by a
Father McGlynn, who was finally excommunicated for his efforts,
supported him. George also won the recommendation of the
Irish World in spite of attempts to label him the foe of Parnell
and the Land League.[12] Some tried to drive a wedge between
Henry George and labor support by emphasizing the nonlabor
elements in Single Tax theory. At least one paper maintained that
had Powderly lent support earlier, the results might have been
different.[13] Once Powderly changed his mind, however, he stuck
by his decision and was still advocating political action in 1890.[14]
Finally, corruption probably played a large part in George's
defeat.[15]

Yet, un-Americanism, irreligion, Anglophilia, and irrelevance
notwithstanding, George managed to poll more than 67,000 votes
against 90,000 for Hewitt and 60,000 for Theodore Roosevelt,
the Republican candidate. The *Irish World* went so far as to call
it a triumph. "The deep voiced protest conveyed in the 67,000
votes for Henry George against the power of both political parties, of Wall Street and the business interest and of the publishers,"
it remarked, "should prove a strong warning to the community to
heed the demands of labor so long as they are just and honor-
able."[16]

Meanwhile, the movement had appeared in other parts of the
country. The Illinois State Labor Association (later the Illinois
State Federation of Labor) had earlier rejected independent political action, but the Haymarket affair seems to have galvanized
the left into action. When the Illinois United Labor Party emerged,
the *New York Times* indignantly reported that socialists had
"captured" the labor party—evidence of the presence of an expe-

rienced manager of primaries. It was a warning to politicians who put their trust in labor.[17] The United Labor Party achieved remarkable success both in Chicago and other areas. In Chicago 25,000 votes were cast for the party ticket, and one state senator and seven members of the lower house were elected. One United Labor nominee for congressman missed election by only 64 votes. In other industrial cities outside Illinois, like Cincinatti, the new parties made a reasonable showing.[18]

But the loss of the New York mayoralty campaign shattered hopes for a national third party. Dissension, the luxury of the defeated, soon crept in, reflecting the diverse elements in the United Labor Party. After the defeat Henry George sought to broaden his party's base by appealing to more middle class elements in the community and aroused the suspicion of the socialists. To hasten the party's conversion to socialism they had "captured" the *Leader,* the newspaper of the United Labor Party. George simultaneously brought out a new weekly, the *Standard.* Soon afterward, the Socialist Labor Party members, accused of divided loyalties, were expelled from the United Labor Party in spite of their leaders' protests that the Socialist Labor Party was not a separate political party in the usual sense. They then formed the Progressive Labor Party and chose John Swinton, the owner of an influential labor paper, as their candidate in the following state elections.[19] The United Labor Party and the Progressive Labor Party entered the 1887 campaign as rivals, with disastrous results for both.

In Chicago relative success meant there was more unity for the moment, but once the United Labor Party failed in the mayoralty campaign when the two old parties combined, a split similar to New York's appeared. One section, the "Free Lunch" party, even combined with the Democrats. The remainder of the United Labor Party under the wing of the socialist trade unionist Thomas J. Morgan changed its name to the Radical Labor Party. A fresh attempt in 1888 to reunite the left, including old greenbackers, ended dismally. The Chicago split was also reflected in the rest of the state.

The part played by organized labor in these postelection conflicts is revealing. In Illinois the State Labor Association was too weak to do anything, but the Chicago Trades and Labor Association, in which socialist influence remained strong, endorsed the Radical Labor Party. In New York, on the other hand, the Central

Labor Union, formerly dominated by socialists, condemned the Progressive Labor Party. Considering how radical city organizations usually were at this time, this seems anomalous, but it can be accounted for by the preponderance of the building trades, in which business agents often dependent on politicians for contracts predominated. Whether these supervisors represented rank and file opinion is more doubtful.

But if the Central Labor Union of New York appeared anti-socialist, the leaders of the newly formed American Federation of Labor proved different. When asked to umpire a debate between Henry George, speaking for his broad-based party, and the social-ists, now applying for re-entry into the United Labor Party at the state convention, Gompers took a neutral position.[20] But writing in the *Leader,* now under the socialists, he explained how trade unionists, though desirous of "present and tangible results," shared with socialists "certain ultimate ends, including the abolition of the wage system." "As many of us understand it," he noted, "Mr. George's theory of land taxation does not promise present reform nor an ultimate solution."[21] With such views it is not surprising that Gompers quickly granted an A.F.ofL. charter to a Central Federated Union, formed by socialist secessionists from the Central Labor Union.

But though sympathetic toward socialists, Gompers was dis-illusioned with politics. He apparently tried to keep an open mind at first, when the situation was still fluid, but the barren results of all this political activity made a permanent impression on Gom-pers. He had always suspected labor politics along Lassallean lines, preferring what he considered a more Marxian line of con-centration on trade unions, relegating political action to the future. This temporary lapse ultimately hardened his earlier position. It was a lesson he never forgot.

How did the Henry George experience permanently affect Gompers? First, it could scarcely escape his notice that whatever labor leaders said, the majority of workingmen did not vote for the labor parties. Where the two party system has flourished long enough to become a habit, no matter how corrupt or irrelevant to the workingman's needs, these parties had a strange hold. The attraction was even stronger if these parties were sufficiently flexi-ble to adapt to new demands, as the flood of labor legislation around 1886 would suggest they were, or to combine against the newcomer, as they did in Chicago during the mayoralty campaign of 1887. Political habits were hard to break. As George Schilling, an advocate of united political action in Illinois, put it: "There is an instinctive feeling among trade unionists that when they form a union they do not surrender their individual politics or religion. They will go so far in a political movement, but if repressed too far they jump the track."[22] In his report to the A.F.ofL. convention in 1888 Gompers maintained that third party activity would be unwise for the moment.[23] This implies that he still felt it might be possible later, but in 1891 he abruptly dismissed a circular from Powderly to the executive council of the Federation[24] on the grounds that it was unwise for a labor organization to meddle with politics at all. Gompers' attitude had hardened.

Undoubtedly, the "no politics" argument made a good deal of sense. The A.F.ofL. had just been lauched and even its constituent unions were far from secure. But whether Gompers was justified in making the experience of 1886–87 a permanent basis of policy is more open to question. The Henry George campaign, in a sense, corresponds with the movement in the nineties in Great Britain that culminated in the formation of the Labour Representation Committee in 1900, when trade unionists and both Marxian and Fabian socialists decided to go into independent politics. In neither country were initial results impressive, for a well-established two party system, demanding loyalties and providing excitement, existed in each. But in Britain the new movement went on to greater victories, while in America it was both a beginning and an end.

There are, of course, differences between the two countries. The American presidential system, for instance, is often quoted as a chief obstacle to third party growth, since it prevents new parties from getting in "the thin end of the wedge." But it is conceivable that the effect of such factors has been exaggerated. As with so much in American history, hindsight tends to create a general law out of very few examples. The political machine that the socialists built up in Milwaukee, and the general impact of Victor Berger as a Socialist congressman show what was possible.[25] The Republican Party at one time also had to break into the system. Leadership was probably a more important factor than the Constitution in determining the success or failure of new parties: the tireless energy with which British labor leaders attacked the political question, in spite of defeat, contrasts sharply with the way that the propaganda of North American labor was directed against third party politics. It is doubtful whether the experience of Great Britain would have proved so different if British labor had been so easily put off.

Moreover, there is something confused about the American logic. British labor went into politics almost unwillingly, after years of propaganda about the need for solidarity of the working class. The Americans, on the other hand, still in rival labor organizations, went lightheartedly into politics in 1886. Just as the Knights of Labor tried to weld one organization before strong foundations had been laid in craft unions, so labor charged into politics without any preparation. While results at the polls had little effect on British trade unions, many Americans feared the economic organization could not withstand political defeat. Immediately after Henry George's campaign Gompers wrote that the trade unions could remain a unit only if both sides of the political movement—Henry George and the socialists—could be kept outside.[26] In 1900, just when British labor was entering independent politics, Gompers wrote to Ben Tillet, a leading British socialist trade unionist, "You must bear in mind that we have not reached that stage of stability, yet, by reason of the fact that, comparatively speaking, the trade union movement in America is in its swaddling clothes, and though we are making progress, yet we cannot shut our eyes to the fact that the element of stability has not yet been reached."[27]

Perhaps Gompers was right and political action premature, but there is something odd about the logic that says independent politics are desirable yet produces constant propaganda against third parties. More than thirty years later Gompers was still preaching the lessons of the Henry George campaign. Whether A.F.ofL. leadership avoided independent political action because the rank and file opposed it, or whether the rank and file opposed it because of the propaganda of the leadership, must remain unanswered. But the British experience certainly shows how trade union support for the labor party depended upon who seized the initiative among the leadership.[28]

If one lesson learned from the Henry George campaign was a suspicion of third parties, Gompers did not turn to the two existing ones, at least at the time. Instead, he appears to have learned to dislike politics altogether. It was not immediately obvious, for on occasions Gompers practiced the nonpartisan policy he was to make official after 1906, i.e., encouraging the election of men favorable to labor, whatever their party. Martin A. Foran, for instance, a former trade unionist and later congressional representative of the 67th district of Ohio, repeatedly advised the Federation's conventions throughout the eighties to elect laboring men—presumably through the old parties.[29] At the convention of 1887, E. R. Cremer, a visiting British liberal member of Parliament with a labor background, expressed surprise that American labor did not get more men in Congress.[30] American delegates to the British T.U.C. were rather impressed by British "non-partisan methods" in the nineties and noted a desire among Americans to pursue similar tactics.[31] Perhaps acting on this kind of advice, Gompers had allowed himself to be nominated by Republicans for the New York Senate in 1889, and he dropped out only because of socialist opposition.[32] The Cleveland *Citizen* in 1897 also noted with some disgust his nomination to the New York State Republican convention and resented this fall from "pure and simple" trade unionism.[33]

But it would be wrong to assume, as Gompers would have us do later in order to emphasize the continuity of his nonpartisan approach, that he took it very seriously in the nineties. Much more frequently he took the line that American politics should be completely avoided by labor, because success was impossible. When Martin A. Foran's own state, Ohio, suffered from strikes in 1892, Gompers complained that workers were .more loyal to parties than to their class.[34] The previous year in Kansas City he gave a venomous speech against all parties. "As for your political parties," he announced, "I say a plague on all of them. I have seen men march through mud and rain wearing glazed hats and carrying candles stuck on sticks and go to the polls and vote the Democratic or Republican ticket and the next morning go to the factory and Democrats and Republicans alike found wages reduced twenty-five per cent."[35]

Dislike of politics turned into a kind of syndicalism. "With every day of my life," he wrote to George Perkins of the Cigar Makers, "I am becoming more fully satisfied that the trade unions are not only the organizations for the defense of labor today, but will be the machines by which emancipation will be secured and is today the germ of the future state."[36] By 1894, he considered it hopeless to try to reform the political system "without a previous recasting of the current opinions concerning the rights of property and duties of man."[37]

The socialists in the Cigar Makers had argued the futility of piece-meal reform in 1881, when Gompers attempted legislation against tenement manufacturing. Gompers learned the lesson even if he never forgave the socialists for pointing it out. The recommendations of the 1883 senate committee on education and labor, he mentions in his autobiography, were never even published. Even when laws were enacted, the capitalists influenced the courts, or the laws were conveniently forgotten. Eight-hour laws passed in various localities were ineffective or could even be used against labor's interests.[38] "One need but read the history of the toilers," he warned the miners much later, "to learn how potent has been the power vested in the constituted authorities of the time to twist laws intended to be of interest to the workers to their very undoing even to the verge of tyranny and enslavement."[39] The antilabor injunctions stemming from the Sherman antitrust law was another case that constantly embittered Gompers. He even asserted there was a deliberate conspiracy among judges against labor.[40]

Such attitudes are very Marxist, but at the same time there was a large element of Social Darwinism in the minds of the unionists at this period. Henry White, the editor of the *United Garment Workers' Journal*, wrote that "the supremacy of right is largely due to the element of might, and the maxim 'thrice armed is he whose cause is just' should have its application in economic warfare."[41] William D. O'Brien, an ex-socialist who in fact argued with the socialists in the pages of the mineworkers' journal, wrote: "Organized capital is responsible for some of the wrongs, organized labor for others, but the great mass of them are done from an inherent savagery of man's nature."[42] Gompers has testified to the influence of Spencerism upon his own thought. In his view corporate capitalism had to be answered by labor organization on the same scale.[43]

"Pure and simple" trade unionism stems from a Marxist-cum-Social Darwinist position, rather than from simple antisocialism. In the nineties Gompers felt his position was quite consistent with Marxism. But there is another reason why unionists wished to keep labor out of politics, and one peculiarly American: a deep fear of exploitation by politicians. The United Garment Workers, usually noted for its conservative attitudes, took a relatively strong line on this. Henry White, the general secretary, considered politics to be the "sport of knaves," and a "very doubtful weapon."[44] Bernard Rose, a frequent writer in the garment workers' journal, believed that union interest in politics merely assisted "the ambitious designs of one or more individuals who are seeking to enter the hall of fame through the door of the White House." Politicians stood on a "low moral plane," according to Rose, and went into politics merely to fill their pockets.[45] The English anarchist John Turner warned Americans against politics in Gompers' own *Federationist*.[46] In answering demands for independent political action at the A.F.ofL. convention of 1898, one "pure and simple" trade unionist declared, "Show me how to keep out the bad men and I am with you."[47]

The lessons of 1886—the impossibility of launching a third party and the disgust with politics altogether—make an interesting comparison with Great Britain. British trade unionists, for the most part, agreed that in a two party system it was well nigh impossible to attract the majority of the workers. Even when it was deemed necessary for the survival of trade unionism there were strong voices opposing it. Labor would probably have remained a wing of the Liberal Party but for the Liberals' stupidity and inflexibility. It was thus only with reluctance that the British trade unions went into independent politics.

But unlike the Americans, British unionists did not mistrust the political system itself. On the contrary, former trade unionists like John Burns were a respectable wing of the Liberal Party. Even after the growth of radicalism in the later part of the century, most maintained great respect for politics and political leaders. Factory acts, universal suffrage, favorable trade union legislation, all bore witness to the efficacy of politics. From 1875 until the Taff Vale decision, in no other country were the unions so legally secure and free from court injunctions. English immigrant trade union leaders in America attempted to secure favorable legislation on the English model.[48] American trade union experience with politics, therefore, differed radically from the British. "Pure and simple" trade unionism before 1900 was not so much an expression of belief in a pluralistic society, or faith in existing institutions, or that political action was unnecessary. Politics were taboo in America because corruption made them impossible.

Gompers' revived aversion toward premature third party politics was similar to that of the Marxists all along. Usually regarding third parties as products of bourgeois idealism, they had supported the labor party movement since it was specifically backed by trade union bodies. Now chastened by the debacle following the Henry

George campaign, the Marxist hostility to participation in politics reasserted itself. W. L. Rosenberg and J. F. Busche, the leaders of the Lassalleans who wished the Socialist Labor Party to continue the political struggle independently, were expelled. As a party that now abstained from politics, the Socialist Labor Party was something of an anomaly, but its strong trade union stand ought to have made for cooperation with the American Federation of Labor. Instead, the remainder of the nineteenth century witnessed a steady deterioration in relations.[49]

The first serious conflict occurred at the Detroit convention of the A.F.ofL. in 1890, when the committee on delegations refused to accept the credentials of Lucien Sanial as representative of the Central Labor Federation of New York, on the grounds that the Central Labor Federation was not purely a trade union organization but had representatives of the Socialist Labor Party as well.[50] Logical though this decision may have been, socialists had grounds for disappointment. Gompers had willingly granted a separate A.F.ofL. charter to the Central Labor Federation, though it was formed by socialist dissidents from the Central Labor Union dissatisfied with Henry George's United Labor Party. The Central Labor Federation returned the separate charter only after the quarrel had been patched up. When the quarrel and the division resumed, Lucien Sanial went to the Detroit convention of the A.F.ofL. believing the charter would be reissued without difficulty.

Though Sanial's argument that the Socialist Labor Party was not a political party in the usual sense was not altogether convincing—Sanial was himself not even a worker—it was not without support among trade unionists. Delegates from unions with large numbers of socialists were afraid of the effect of an adverse decision. Thomas J. Morgan, representing the Chicago Trades' Assembly, argued that refusal to seat Sanial would hurt the shoemakers' union; W. J. Dillon of the glassworkers, McBride of the mineworkers, and representatives of bakers, brewery workers, and furniture workers, made similar arguments. Other support came from the usually radical central organizations. Richard Braunschweig of the furniture workers actually thought all should join the Socialist Labor Party. The mineworkers' journal expressed surprise that figures like McGuire, William Martin of the steelworkers, and Chris Evans of the mineworkers should assist Gompers in introducing a precedent they would not dare advocate in their own organizations—an argument hotly denied by Chris

Evans.[51] A vote taken among the carriage workers on the issue of withdrawal from the A.F.ofL. over the issue supported Gompers, but the secretary resigned.[52]

Gompers' position was a relatively simple one. The A.F.ofL. was concerned exclusively with the economic organization of the working class: socialists were welcome so long as they were trade unionists, but for socialists, per se, to demand representation in the A.F.ofL. was preposterous. When Sanial claimed that socialists wished no more than was standard practice in Europe, Gompers made his stand on the English model: whatever the contributions of English socialists to the trade union movement, socialist representation on the trade union council or on city trades councils was unthinkable. "Pure and simple" trade unionism again became the slogan of the day.[53]

While it is undeniable that the 1890 convention marked an important stage in the A.F.ofL.'s relations with the Socialist Labor Party, it is untrue that Gompers' position was now that of the "business unionist," in the procapitalist sense. Admittedly, he did draw up a memorandum for his own use before the convention stressing the immediate aims of the trade union movement.[54] But his speeches suggest he thought of immediate betterment not as an end in itself, but only a means to an end. "Present practical improvements" were a means of dealing with problems it was their "mission" and "solemn duty" to solve; they were "the way out of the wage system." In other words, Gompers remained as Messianic as ever, and the trade unions "pure and simple" were the "natural organization of the wage workers to secure their present material and practical improvement *and* to achieve their emancipation."[55] As the special committee examining the matter pointed out in the course of the argument, the S.L.P. was part of the labor movement in the broadest sense.[56] The final aims of the A.F.ofL. and the Socialist Labor Party were apparently the same, but their methods were different.

Some will maintain that Gompers' "philosophy" is construed from isolated phrases he did not really mean. Yet it is odd that Gompers should urge his policy upon the members of the Second International meeting in Brussels in 1891. He added, moreover: "There can scarcely be a division of opinion that when the economic movement has sufficiently developed so as to produce a unity of thought on all essentials, that a political labor movement will be the result. In fact there is not and cannot be any economic action taken by organized labor unless it has its political and social influence."[57]

Gompers obviously believed his views were in keeping with orthodox Marxist theory. When the conflict over the Central Labor Federation was at its height, Gompers, to show he was "logically and scientifically correct," wrote to Friedrich Engels, completely confident that he would agree with him. Later, Gompers told the old Internationalist F. A. Sorge that he was absolutely willing to abide by Engels' judgment. Engels, expecting to see Gompers in Brussels, did not reply, but later told Schluter he could not understand the quarrel and that Gompers had the right to exclude anyone he pleased.[58]

Many American socialists agreed with Gompers. The Cleveland *Citizen* noted that the question before the convention had nothing to do with the merits of socialism, and that even socialists voted against receiving the credentials of Sanial.[59] The Chicago socialist, T. J. Morgan, reluctant at first, eventually agreed with Gompers.[60] Even the Socialist Labor Party was divided, for most New York socialist trade unionists disliked direct party representation in the Central Labor Federation anyway.[61] Socialist Labor Party leaders, however, thought otherwise and were beginning to think of drastic action against the A.F.ofL.

The strong line of the Socialist Labor Party was largely the result of the rise of Daniel DeLeon to leadership. A former professor at Columbia University, DeLeon joined the S.L.P. as late as 1890, after a period in the Bellamyist movement. Through his editorship of the *People*, he soon rose to a position of leadership under which the party undoubtedly became more American and increased its influence in American life generally. Nevertheless, his role in the history of American socialism was essentially destructive.

Whereas the party had previously oscillated between trade unionism and politics, DeLeon envisioned a two-armed labor movement relying on both. It might seem that he was merely bringing the American movement into European practice, but this was not the case. The trade union movements of European countries enjoyed an independent existence within the broadly conceived "labor movements." Even in Germany, where trade unionism was largely the creation of socialists, they were not in any sense subject to party control. But a broadly conceived labor movement encompassing both kinds of working class activity was not enough for DeLeon. For him it was necessary to have central direction—naturally under his leadership.

Earlier biographers were inclined to lend DeLeon a certain brilliance as a theorist who antedated Lenin in his ideas of revolutionary unionism and a highly centralized party structure. More recent scholarship, however, paints him as something of an opportunist who relied on other Americans for his ideas and who in the 1890's was little more than a power-crazy bigot.[62] His determination to control the trade unions or destroy them probably did more to alienate trade unionists from socialism than any other force. For his stubbornness and the reaction it produced on his opponents, he enjoys the dubious distinction of being one of the chief moulders of American social and labor institutions.

In spite of DeLeon's domination of the party, however, the second dispute involving socialism within the A.F.ofL. emanated not from the leader of the Socialist Labor Party, but from the more moderate Chicago-based socialist, Thomas J. Morgan, a prominent trade unionist in Illinois and frequent representative of the International Association of Machinists at A.F.ofL. conventions. DeLeon, however, watched intently from the sidelines.

At the Chicago convention of 1893 Morgan introduced a political program that included as plank 10 a resolution calling for the "collective ownership by the people of all means of production." Samuel Gompers, in his memoirs written thirty years later, called this political program a socialist trick to convert the A.F.ofL. into a socialist organization.[63] Many have reiterated this since. Yet it is difficult to discover the deceit.

Morgan, in fact, as he stated in the preamble to his resolution, used the British Independent Labour Party as his model, which he wrongly thought had just been endorsed by the Trade Union Council. Perhaps Morgan was confused by a resolution of the Trade Union Council that year to provide a voluntary fund for political purposes, but certainly the Independent Labour Party was not the child of the British Trade Union Council as Morgan seemed to think. At any rate, the program was not drawn up by the Socialist Labor Party as such, but by socialist trade unionists aiming at an alliance with the People's Party. Morgan did not ask the convention to adopt it immediately but merely submitted it "for the favorable consideration of labor organizations of America," to take place over the following year. His resolution was adopted after the word "favorable" was dropped, by a vote of 2,244 to 67.[64]

Though Gompers later claimed he merely humored the social-ists and political advocates,[65] he does not seem to have been entirely unaffected. With depression everywhere, government interference in the great Pullman strike, and for the first time talk of a general strike, 1894 was a difficult year for labor. The time was ripe for political action, as the success of the Populists in 1894 suggested. Gompers seems to have been in two minds about the whole thing. He founded the *American Federationist* in March, 1894, presumably to counteract the influence of out-right political papers among trade unionists, particularly the Cleveland *Citizen*.[66] The first *Federationist* editorial claimed the purpose of the publication was to protect trade unions from both avowed enemies and those who would unwittingly destroy them by leading them into politics. Frank K. Foster, a leading Gom-persite, interpreted this editorial as meaning that successful poli-tical action had to follow traditional American lines and acknowl-edge "that higher Americanism, catholic in its tolerance and grandly liberal in its conception of citizenship." Gompers, on the other hand, wrote that trade unionism still aimed at the over-throw of "the yoke of industrial serfdom." Nevertheless, the *Citizen* complained that since the Federation apparently paid Foster to propagate "No Politics," it should send out Morgan to explain the other side of the case.[67]

By the second issue of the *Federationist* Gompers' words strongly suggest that he was less opposed to a third party than earlier, and he regarded the political program as a step in the right direction, with or without plank 10. His general attitude seems to have been "wait and see what develops"—with the reservation that personal divisions should not divide labor's ranks. "Does it not seem that the dictates of wisdom . . . should promote all the well wishers of the wage workers to aid in inaugu-rating a thorough, a clean and an aggressive working class move-ment, economically and politically," he wrote, adding that "the best aid and impetus that (could) be given to such a movement would be a hearty cooperation to eliminate the divisions in labor's ranks and to tone down the bitterness of personal differences."[68]

By the time of the Denver convention, however, when the political program was to be voted upon, Gompers came out reso-lutely against it. Feeble attempts at "non-partisan politics" by listing favorable candidates at the 1894 elections in the *Federa-tionist* apparently renewed Gompers' disgust with the political system altogether. In addition, there was a growing feeling that adoption meant handing the labor movement over to DeLeon, whose attitude made it difficult to have any dealings with the socialists at all.[69]

With the opposition of the A.F.ofL. leaders it is not surprising that the political program was defeated at Denver by 1,173 votes to 735; but these figures do not adequately guage the strength or weakness of socialism in American unions. It was not at all clear what the delegates were voting for: a statement of final aims, a Labor Party there and then, or affiliation with the Socialist Labor Party. Procedure also confused the issue. The preamble and each clause was voted on separately, and all were accepted except for a correction in the preamble and a Single Tax substitute for plank 10. When the amended program was voted upon as a whole, however, it was defeated, when some socialists opposing the amendment to plank 10 joined forces with opponents of the whole program. A final reason for questioning the significance of the defeat of the program is that some delegates ignored the instructions of their unions by voting for the substitute to plank 10, even when the entire program had previously won acceptance by referendum.[70]

Though defeated over the political program, socialists were strong enough to overthrow the chief culprit, Samuel Gompers, who for the following year had to cede the presidency to John McBride of the mineworkers. The results were almost disastrous; because of ill health and incompetence, McBride took very little part in the A.F.ofL. If ever a socialist, his speeches suggest he was less radical than Gompers. Though he argued that since the political platform had been voted upon clause by clause, the whole must be accepted, he did not believe this committed the A.F.ofL. to independent political action, but to independent voting—what Gompers would later call "rewarding friends and punishing enemies."[71]

The McBride interlude is virtually of no significance in the history of the A.F.ofL. except that it made Gompers more wary of socialists. The personal affront was probably more responsible for setting Gompers on an antisocialist course than any theoretical differences. When he returned to office, Gompers denied it was a victory for those who would "count it as squelching or annihilating a certain school of thought in the ranks of the A.F.ofL." On the contrary, he explained the need for lively discussion and paid tribute to the intelligence and energy that "active forces" brought to the trade union movement. All he insisted was that a man should be true to his union whatever happened.[72]

Besides the A.F.ofL. debates and DeLeonite pronouncements usually stressed in the history of socialist-labor relations in the nineties, internal events in unions and local organizations are equally revealing. The innumerable conferences leave a confusing picture, but in general it is possible to detect considerable sympathy among trade unionists for endorsing the political program coupled with support for the Populist Party. Of course, many have maintained that socialism and populism are incompatible, but such arguments often depend on a very strict definition of socialism, like DeLeon's.[73] There was already present, in the left wing of the populist movement, that more moderate variety that was eventually to overthrow DeLeon and form the mainstream of the American movement.

Most populist newspapers were favorable to socialism, except those in Washington, D.C., while some socialist papers, like the Cleveland *Citizen,* abandoned the populists only after they joined the democrats in 1896. A meeting of workingmen in St. Louis in 1894 resolved to support the Populist Party and wished that party to support the A.F.ofL. program, including plank 10.[74] But precisely what confronted advocates of this course in one of the more important labor centers is best seen in Chicago, where T. J. Morgan returned to encourage the adoption of his political program after the 1893 convention.[75]

His chief opponents in the Illinois State Federation of Labor were "Skinny" Madden and William C. Pomeroy, two anti-socialists who made fortunes in exploiting trade unions in the early nineties. In opposing the political program, they were very much fortified by the result of an earlier conference of "all labor unions, labor organizations, industrial associations and political reform societies of the State of Illinois," which had thrown out plank 10, though it adopted all the others. The influence of Pomeroy was such that the convention of the State Federation of Labor not only rejected plank 10, but decided not to break with the old parties. Morgan's plea for independent political action *and* plank 10, however, lost by only 10 votes. The socialists might have bolted had not Henry Demarest Lloyd arranged a compromise, whereby on a modified plank 10 labor was to engage

in independent political action, but pending the formation of a
labor party, the State Federation of Labor was to vote the Populist ticket. With this amendment, Morgan's side won.

The battle between Pomeroy and Morgan then entered the
political arena proper. Both entered a convention called by the
Cook County Central Committee of the People's Party, in August,
1894, and the row ended only when the lights went out. Next
day, two conventions met, one led by Morgan advocating the
Lloyd compromise, the other under Pomeroy consisting mostly
of Democrats. The next convention of the State Federation of
Labor had to decide which to endorse. Morgan's seemed to be
gaining until Pomeroy called in reinforcements. Pomeroy then
brought out yet a new plank 10 advocating Single Tax—for
which he cared nothing except that it attracted downstate representatives—and so Morgan's wing of the People's Party in Cook
County failed to receive the endorsement of labor. Morgan's
faction gained the official Populist ticket in 1894, however, and
despite all the opposition the Pomeroy contingent could muster,
the ticket polled a good 3,500 votes though it elected no one. It
was a respectable showing under the circumstances, but without
much promise.

In these maneuvers at state level, the populist-labor forces felt
the lack of leadership from the A.F.ofL. a great hindrance, so
that Henry D. Lloyd and Lawrence Gronland, the socialist
author, implored Gompers to make a stand.[76] Gompers' negative
attitude may have been justified. The past provided too many
examples of labor organizations sacrificed at the altar of politics,
and he feared that the A.F.ofL., only now finding its feet, might
follow them. The Populist-Democratic fusion of 1896 eventually
revealed once again the vagaries of American politics and the
dangers inherent in placing trust in parties of the left. Still, the
continuing industrial and social changes constantly made the
relevance of earlier experiences more questionable and it certainly
makes sense to argue that labor's negativism encouraged the drift
toward the Democrats.

At any rate, a moderate socialist like Morgan found himself
defenseless against the narrow theorists like DeLeon in his own
party, making building a permanent organization at a state level
impossible. As in the aftermath of the Henry George campaign,
the left disintegrated. DeLeon was even more delighted when the
Populist Party went down in the free silver debacle in 1896.

Believing it would soon reveal its true character as a middle class movement, DeLeon looked forward to a growth of Socialist Labor Party strength in the West.[77] But he was mistaken. In the nineties socialism could have made its influence felt only by participation in a broad-based party, but DeLeon never appreciated this.

The row over plank 10 was an internal affair of the trade unions, but it could scarcely fail to attract the attention of the Socialist Labor Party. DeLeon's vision depended upon party control of the trade union movement, but the plank 10 affair revealed that Gompers was determined to keep the trade unions separate from any political party, however radical his own views. For this reason, Gompers had to be portrayed as a "labor faker," accepting capitalism and its inherent evils, and the A.F.ofL. "a mere benevolent organization dolling out charities for sick and death benefits . . . instead of being a militant class organization ever watchful of the interests of the workers and ever ready to battle against conditions that tend to degrade them."[78] This DeLeonite, antisocialist image of Gompers in the nineties has stuck and is constantly reiterated—partly, of course, because it corresponds with the later Gompers—and yet at this period, he constantly demonstrated that he was the real inheritor of the Marxist tradition, and DeLeon its abuser.

DeLeon first attacked Gompers in 1893, though at that time Gompers was conciliatory. An enemy of Morgan, DeLeon nevertheless considered the proponents of plank 10 "the progressive forces" and argued they were defeated only by trickery. Besides, the decentralization of the A.F.ofL., in DeLeon's opinion, made the leadership unwilling to embark on adventurous schemes and therefore "inefficient for all practical purposes."[79] A brief flirtation with the failing Knights of Labor, now under James R. Sovereign, who had been elected with socialist support, convinced DeLeon of that organization's "overcentralization" under corrupt leadership.[80] He was refused a seat in the 1895 General Assembly. The McBride interlude momentarily brought a possibility of change in the A.F.ofL., but Gompers' reelection signaled the launching of a new economic organization deliberately intended to destroy the A.F.ofL.—the Socialist Trades and Labor Alliance.

The Socialist Trades and Labor Alliance was never more than DeLeon's instrument. There was one attempt to show that "DeLeon was not the whole thing," but DeLeon soon forced the

executive board, elected by convention, to resign.[81] The organization made inroads into the textile workers, cigar workers, coal
miners, and glass bottle workers, but it never achieved great
success. It had petered out as anything more than a paper organization by the close of the century.

In retrospect the Alliance seems very unimportant, but the
rival organization occupied Gompers' energies to a very large
extent, and provided the occasion for some of his most vitriolic
writing. DeLeon, Sanial, and Hugo Vogt, whom he held responsible, were "a professor without a professorship, a shyster lawyer
without a brief, and a statistician who furnishes figures to the
republican, democratic, and socialist parties."[82] True, even in the
late nineties the A.F.ofL. was still not secure and Gompers' fall
from power for a year indicated considerable socialist influence,
so perhaps he had cause for alarm. But the Socialist Trades and
Labor Alliance perhaps also satisfied Gompers' psychological
need for opposition. Even after there ceased to be any danger
from the rival organization, there could be no "honest difference"
with the party, and he refused every challenge to public debate
on the issue, "until reason shall take the place of bigotry."[83]

But in spite of the venom that Gompers poured forth on the
dual unionists and spilled over at times on to all socialists, the
astonishing thing about this episode is how Gompers and his
supporters stressed that DeLeon's activities were contrary to real
socialist theory.

Philip Taft has argued that Gompers, though deploring socialism, remained on good terms with a few socialists.[84] In fact, the
reverse seems truer. He deplored a few socialists—those who pursued dual unionism—but still considered that he and the socialists really had the same ends. At the height of the controversy,
for instance, Gompers wrote:

> There was a time when trade unionists could fraternize with
> socialist partisans and both could co-operate for agitation,
> organization and educational purposes on practical lines, but
> since the advent of this adventurer DeLeon, this protegé of
> capitalism . . . men in sympathy with each other's aspirations
> to advance the great cause of the wage earners the world over,
> have been forced apart in *apparent if not real* hostile camps and
> bitterness and strife have taken the place of real co-opera-
> tion."[85]

There was nothing to compare with it in England, Gompers
told Ben Tillet, for even socialist trade unionists were not safe

from DeLeon's attacks.[86] Gompers, therefore, seems to have agreed with W. S. Carter, who replaced Eugene Debs as editor of the Locomotive Firemen's magazine after the disastrous Pullman strike, that trade unionisms and socialism "are by their very nature allies."[87] Sam Leffingwell, another friend of Gompers, believed it was necessary to distinguish between different degrees of socialism and that every member of a trade union was a socialist, "if only he knew it."[88]

On the other hand, DeLeon, according to Gompers, led a movement absolutely unique, for there was "not an authority on the labor movement from the time of Marx to the present day, in England, Germany, in fact in any part of Europe or the United States—but who this fellow does not practically declare is 'out of step' mentally, and that he, and he alone, has the patent process to emancipate labor."[89] "The *so-called* socialists of New York," Gompers remarked elsewhere, "are all at variance and in conflict with the best writers, thinkers, and actors in the socialist movement in every other part of the world." Thus Gompers could claim, with justice, that his differences were "not so much with the socialists of America as such, but rather a few of them in New York City."[90] He believed that people who had spent their lives building up the trade unions, so that they were feared and respected by the money class, were unsafe from the attacks of a few who had never worked for wages in their lives.[91]

This issue was taken up in a series of articles in the *American Federationist*. G. A. Hoehn, the socialist editor of the St. Louis *Labor* and prominent in the typographical union, argued that the A.F.ofL. participated in the class struggle and had not placed itself in opposition to the teachings of Marx, who had supported British "pure and simple" unions and advocated immediate benefits. Objectives like the limitation of the working day, according to Hoehn, were "the voice of true Marxism." And not only was the historic Marx portrayed as a Gompersite: a declaration on labor and politics by the Socialist and Trade Union Congress held in London in 1896 insisted, like Gompers, that "differences of political views ought not to be considered a reason for separate action in the economic struggle." Hoehn then pointed out that Gompers had shown wage earners the meaning of class interest—"a sound Marxian principle"—and only added that it should not be lost sight of in the political field.[92]

In the nineties, most of Gompers' ideas and his general outlook reflected "sound Marxian principles." His declaration that the culmination of the class struggle would bring the "abolition of classes based on possession of wealth and power," and that "with its disenthralment [would come] the abolition of all profit and interest . . ." caused the Cleveland *Citizen* to say he should join the socialists.[93] Even Gompers' specific denial, in which he claimed his conception of the emancipation of the working class was for the benefit of all, sounds more like Jaures or Bernstein than the "business unionist" usually portrayed.[94]

This discussion of Gompers' relations with socialists in the nineties does not deny the traditional picture of Gompers as a "pure and simple" trade unionist, nor does it intend to make him a revolutionary socialist. What it does show is that "pure and simple" trade unionism did not mean simply higher wages and better conditions as the sole aim of the unions. It meant that the trade unions were apolitical. It was a trade unionist's duty "to study and discuss questions that have any bearing upon their industrial or political liberty," Gompers editorialized, but he declared it was "not within the province of the A.F.ofL. to designate to which political party a member [should] belong or which political party he [should] vote."[95] But "pure and simple" trade unions were not "business unions." They were a morally regenerating force, "the only power whose mission it is to evolve order out of social chaos, to save us from reaction, brutality and perhaps barbarism." Though the trade unions might make "no pretensions of what their highest aim or ultimate ideal may be," they were "the germ of a future state which all will hail with glad acclaim."[96]

Was Gompers' position in demanding both immediate improvements and some rather vaguely expressed final aim logically untenable? DeLeonites at the time claimed it was, and so have most labor historians since. A majority of socialists at the turn of the century, however, agreed with Gompers.

NOTES

1. New York *Star,* October 21, 1886. Henry George's Scrap Book in New York Public Library contains newspaper clippings from the campaign.
2. Note in Socialist Party Papers, Duke University, dated Feb. 8, 1913.
3. New York *Star,* September 24, 1886.
4. Open letter to Hewitt, New York *Irish World,* Oct. 19, 1886.
5. Anne Fremantle, *This Little Band of Prophets,* (New York: Mentor Books, 1960), 25.
6. Cleveland *Citizen,* March 30, 1918.
7. Columbia University Oral History Project, *Norman Thomas Memoir,* 48.

8. New York *Sun,* October 22, 1886.
9. New York *Times,* November 2, 1886.
10. A. F. of L., *Proceedings* 1885, 17-18.
11. A. F. of L., *Proceedings* 1886, 8.
12. New York *Irish World,* October 23, 1886.
13. *Labor News,* November 3, 1886.
14. New York *Times,* November 2, 1886 and *Journal of the Knights of Labor* X, 44 (May 1, 1890) 1.
15. Commons II, 453.
16. New York *Irish World,* November 3, 1886.
17. New York *Times,* September 30, 1886.
18. Eugene Staley, *History of Illinois State Federation of Labor* (Chicago: University of Chicago Press, 1930), 29, 71-83.
19. Socialist Labor Party, *Proceedings* 1887, 18.
20. Samuel Gompers to Friedrich Engels, January 9, 1891, (Samuel Gompers Copy Books, Library of Congress).
21. New York *Leader,* July 25, 1887.
22. Staley, 81-82.
23. A. F. of L. *Proceedings* 1888, 13.
24. Cleveland *Citizen,* January 30, 1891.
25. See for instance, Sally M. Miller, "Victor L. Berger and the Promise of Constructive Socialism 1910-1920" (Unpublished Ph. D. Dissertation, University of Toronto, 1966), and Frederick L. Olson, "Victor Berger: Socialist Congressman," *Wisconsin Academy of Sciences Arts and Letters,* Volume 58, 1970), 27-38.
26. S. G. to P. H. Donnelly, Secretary of the Illinois Miners' Protective Association, August 20, 1887.
27. S. G. to Ben Tillett, June 28, 1900.
28. See H. A. Clegg, Alan Fox and A. F. Thompson, *A History of British Trade Unions since 1889* (Oxford: Clarendon Press, 1964), 303-304.
29. A. F. of L., *Proceedings* 1882, 18; 1884, 17; 1885, 7; 1887, 21.
30. A. F. of L., *Proceedings* 1887, 18.
31. *American Federationist,* January, 1896, 210.
32. Nathan Fine, *Labor and Farmer Parties in the United States 1828-1928.* (New York: Rand School of Social Science, 1928), 140.
33. Cleveland *Citizen,* December 4, 1897.
34. A. F. of L., *Proceedings* 1892, 9.
35. Cleveland *Citizen,* March 6, 1891.
36. S. G. to George Perkins, March 22, 1894.
37. *Federationist,* October, 1894, 172-173.
38. Samuel Gompers, *Seventy Years of Life and Labor* (New York: G. P. Dutton, 1925), I, 413, 444, Chapter 9; II, Chapter 33.
39. *United Mine Workers' Journal* XXVI (November 11, 1915), 8.
40. Cleveland *Citizen,* April 1, 1893.
41. Henry White, "Concerning Industrial Harmony," *The Garment Worker* V (May, 1901), 4-6.
42. O'Brien letter in *United Mine Workers Journal,* December 17, 1903, 4.
43. Gompers, *Seventy Years* I, 362. A. F. of L. *Proceedings* 1898, 14-15.
44. Henry White, "Politics and Salvation," *Garment Worker* V (February, 1900), 1.
45. Bernard Rose, "Politics in the Union," *The Weekly Bulletin,* III (March 18, 1904), 10.
46. J. Turner, "A Peculiar Policy," *Federationist,* July, 1896, 81.
47. A. F. of L. *Proceedings* 1898, 107.

48. R. T. Berthoff, *British Immigrants in Industrial America* (New York: Russell & Russell, 1953), 102-103.
49. Howard J. Quint, *The Forging of American Socialism* (New York: Bobbs-Merrill Co., 1953), 52-59.
50. A. F. of L., *Proceedings* 1890, 22-27.
51. *United Mine Workers' Journal,* July 23, 1891. Chris Evans to Editor of *Mine Workers' Journal,* July 25, 1891 (S. G. Copy Books).
52. S. G. to Executive Council of International Union of Carriage and Wagon Workers, October 4, November 22, 1890 (S. G. Copy Books).
53. A. F. of L., *Proceedings* 1890, 23-24.
54. Memorandum dated August 12, 1890 (S. G. Copy Books).
55. A. F. of L., *Proceedings* 1890, 13, 17.
56. A. F. of L., *Proceedings* 1890, 22.
57. S. G. to Delegates of International Labor Congress, Brussels, August 4, 1891 (S. G. Copy Books).
58. S. G. to George Schilling, January 6, 1891. S. G. to Friedrich Engels, January 9, 1891. S. G. to F. A. Sorge, November 21, 1891. Engels to Schluter, January 29, 1891. Engels to Sorge, January 6, 1892. Last two letters in Alexander Trachtenberg, ed., *Letters to Americans* (New York: International Publishers, 1953), 233-4, 240. (Others in S. G. Copy Books.)
59. Cleveland *Citizen,* July 25, 1891.
60. S. G. to P. J. McGuire, August 4, 1891 (S. G. Copy Books).
61. Cleveland *Citizen,* February 6, 1892.
62. Don J. McKee, "Daniel DeLeon: A Re-appraisal," *Labor History* I (Fall, 1960), 264-297.
63. Gompers, *Seventy Years,* I, 393.
64. A. F. of L., *Proceedings* 1893, 37-38.
65. Gompers, *Seventy Years,* I, 391-392.
66. A resolution in A. F. of L. convention sought to make the *Citizen* the official A. F. of L. organ. A. F. of L. *Proceedings* 1893, 29, 68. See also Columbia University Oral History Project, *Eva Valesh Memoir,* 85.
67. *Federationist,* March 1894, 5-6, 10. Cleveland *Citizen,* May 5, 1894, 2.
68. *Federationist,* April, 1894, 31.
69. S. G. to H. D. Lloyd, July 2, 1894 (S. G. Copy Books).
70. A. F. of L. *Proceedings* 1894, 36-40. See also Cleveland *Citizen,* April 28, 1894, and December 1, 1894.
71. A. F. of L. *Proceedings,* 1895, 15-16.
72. Federationist, February, 1896, 224.
73. For instance George Harmon Knoles, "Populism and Socialism," *Pacific Historical Review* XII, 3 (September, 1943), 295, 304.
74. Cleveland *Citizen,* September 22, 1894, 1.
75. Staley, 113-137.
76. H. D. Lloyd to S. G., July 30, 1894 and Lawrence Gronland to S. G., August 9, 1894 (A. F. of L. Papers, Wisconsin State Historical Society, Madison, Wisconsin).
77. S. L. P., *Proceedings* 1896, 10.
78. S. L. P., *Proceedings* 1896, 10, 13.
79. S. L. P., *Proceedings* 1896, 25.
80. S. L. P., *Proceedings* 1896, 28.
81. *Federationist,* August, 1898, 115.
82. *Federationist,* April, 1896, 33.
83. *Federationist,* September 1898, 146.

84. Philip Taft, *A. F. of L. in the Time of Gompers* (New York: Harper, 1957), 74.
85. *Federationist,* August, 1898, 116.
· 86. S. G. to Ben Tillett, May 25, 1896 (S. G. Copy Books).
87. W. S. Carter, "Trade Unionism and Socialism," *Federationist,* September, 1897, 132.
88. Cleveland *Citizen,* November 18, 1899.
89. *Federationist,* August, 1898, 116.
90. *Federationist,* April 1898, 37-38.
91. S. G. to Ben Tillett, May 2, 1896 (S. G. Copy Books).
92. G. A. Hoehn, "Marxism and Trade Unionism," *Federationist* September, 1898, 130-131; October, 1898, 153-154; November, 1898, 175-177.
93. Cleveland *Citizen,* July 10, 1897.
94. Cleveland *Citizen* September 11, 1897.
95. *Federationist,* January, 1899, 222.
96. A. F. of L., *Proceedings,* 1898, 15.

3

American Revisionist Socialism

Marxist socialism contains an inherent contradiction: it prophesies increasing misery to end only with the final cataclysm; yet in beckoning workers to unite economically and politically, it automatically improves conditions and renders revolution less likely. "Revisionism"—the attempt to alter Marxism in the light of this paradox—became a chief source of dissension in most of the parties constituting the Second International.

The attitude toward trade unionism was not the only issue at stake. Eduard Bernstein's questioning of Marxist theory was anathema to the orthodox in Germany. The question of participation in bourgeois governments hindered unity in France. But as the most obvious means of immediate improvement, trade unionism and its relationship to the political party was bound to be a crucial issue facing socialists in all countries. In the United States it was paramount.

A tendency toward revisionism, as in most countries, was always present among American socialists. Lassalleanism, for instance, a major influence on Bernstein in Germany, had repercussions in the United States. During the 1880's the Lassallean wing of the socialist movement was not necessarily any more revisionist than its Marxist rival. As we have seen, Lassalleans forced the Socialist Labor Party to abandon the Progressive Labor Party in 1888, in the interests of a clear-cut socialist political stand. But once expelled from the Socialist Labor Party in 1889 just as DeLeon's star was rising, the Lassalleans, or Rosenberg-Busche faction, seemed to revert to a more revisionist position. In the nineties they played a role in bringing midwestern sections of the Socialist Labor Party into the Socialist-Populist movement. They even got as far as having the much more revisionist St. Louis *Labor* temporarily endorsed over the head of DeLeon's *People* at the 1893 Socialist Labor Party convention.[1] Eventually, the Rosenberg-Busche faction became the Social Democratic Federation, based in Cleveland.

Meanwhile, in Milwaukee, Victor Berger, an Austrian immigrant whose experience in America turned him to socialism, organized a Social Democratic Union composed chiefly of ex-members of the Socialist Labor Party. Berger himself had abandoned the Socialist Labor Party at the same time as the Rosenberg-Busche faction in 1889, and later, as editor of the leading Labor paper in Milwaukee, developed a revisionist brand of socialism which really antedated Bernstein's. In 1893 the Social Democratic Union participated in a broad coalition of Socialists and Populists, until the Populist fusion with the Democratic Party in 1896.

Another approach of revisionists, namely Eugene Debs' Social Democracy, emerged independently of the Socialist Labor Party. Debs' career forms a strange counterpart to his contemporary and protagonist Samuel Gompers. While Gompers' pure and simple trade unionism gradually caused him to abandon Marxism, Debs at first denied the class struggle and was chiefly concerned with the craft-conscious Brotherhood of Locomotive Firemen, of which he was secretary. Even when he formed the American Railway Union, an industrial organization attracting men from the craft-based brotherhoods, he was motivated by common sense rather than any theory of the working class. Only when faced by the power of organized capital during the disastrous Pullman strike in 1894 and imprisoned for refusing to obey a Supreme Court injunction did socialism have any meaning for him. A visit by Victor Berger and Keir Hardie, the leader of the British Independent Labor Party, to Debs in the Woodstock jail seems to have confirmed him, and he spent the remainder of his life in the service of socialism. DeLeon considered Debs the "American Lassalle."[2]

The Social Democracy grew out of the remnant of the American Railway Union and parts of diverse socialist organizations— Fabians or Bellamyite Nationalists. These were then joined by various secessionists from the Socialist Labor Party, including Berger's Milwaukee movement and the Social Democratic Federation of Cleveland. The Social Democracy was as much interested in colonization schemes as politics, but in 1898 colonizers and political activists split, leaving the latter to form the Social Democratic Party of America.

But in spite of the growth of revisionism, the Socialist Labor Party probably remained the most important branch of American socialism and, under DeLeon, a bastion of orthodoxy. Its development in the nineties is curious. The Lassallean faction had been ousted for preferring politics and antagonizing trade unions. Yet starting in 1892 the DeLeonite Socialist Labor Party fought elections and by 1896 was actively trying to destroy the A.F.ofL. through the Socialist Trades and Labor Alliance. In its intolerance of anything suggesting revisionism, the Socialist Labor Party under DeLeon was without parallel. The result was the series of secessions throughout the nineties. Its attack on the A.F.ofL., however, all but brought about its own destruction.

Engaged in a day-to-day struggle for immediate gains, trade unions by their very nature are almost bound to be revisionist. The European experience makes this clear. The socialist founders of German trade unions, for instance, may have regarded them as class-conscious organizations, but they soon came to assert an independent spirit. Their obvious success in achieving immediate aims provided justification for Bernstein's revisionism. Similarly, the French trade unionists refused to be dominated by the "orthodox" Guesdistes. But in both France and Germany socialism and trade unionism remained allies, and it might be said that trade unionism helped to remold political socialism along revisionist lines. The same might be said of the trade unions in Great Britain, for once the Labour Party was formed it was bound to attract diverse leftist elements, and orthodox Marxism gradually lost any small influence it might have enjoyed.

But even while such developments were taking place in Europe, DeLeon insisted that trade unions act only as the economic instrument of the revolutionary socialist political party. As an independent force seeking gradual improvements, they were worse than useless, for not only did conditions deteriorate, according to DeLeon, but workers were misled. Gompers, in fact, was like the leaders of the British trade unions "all down the line, a band of the very worst kind of labor skates and crooks who are misleading our class all the time."[3] "Pure and simple" trade unionism was a corrupting influence among good socialists, for as soon as they became office holders in a trade union their faces changed. Isaac Bennet of the Cigar Makers had been deliberately wooed by the "fakers," according to DeLeon. John F. Tobin of the Boot and Shoe Workers was another that pretended to be a socialist and yet allowed "poisonous principles" of "pure and simplism" to be expounded in his presence. Other DeLeonites pointed out

how even when socialists managed to capture a union, their fear
of disruption caused them to take half measures. Even only one
socialist who prevaricated in this way could render the socialist
movement inestimable harm through his influence. The only solution was a clean break with the A.F.ofL. and a new trade union
organization wedded to socialism.[4] In this mood DeLeon had
launched the Socialist Trades and Labor Alliance in 1895.

In the face of these developments, the position of socialist
trade unionists was obviously becoming impossible. Interestingly,
some of the more outstanding of them had attended the launching
convention of the Socialist Trades and Labor Alliance under the
impression that the new movement would organize the unskilled
and so only complement the American Federation of Labor.
John F. Tobin of the Boot and Shoe Workers and J. Mahlon
Barnes of the Cigar Makers actually made speeches. But by the
1898 convention of the A.F.ofL. their embarrassment was acute.
Tobin, as was customary with socialist delegates, proposed a
resolution recommending that trade unionists should vote only
for such political parties as stand for nationalizing the means of
production. But he was at pains to point out that his trade unionism came before his socialism and that he was not necessarily
seeking the endorsement of the Socialist Party, but merely
"endorsing the principle as to whether we can endorse some
party when the occasion arises." The point was echoed by other
socialists who claimed that their political views did not bind
them to the Socialist Labor Party.[5]

The question of revisionism must have been very close to
Tobin. In his own shoemaking town of Haverhill, Massachusetts,
the trade unionist James F. Carey won election to the Common
Council in 1897 on the Socialist Labor Party ticket. Chosen as
president of the Common Council, he attracted considerable attention, particularly in the New York headquarters of the party,
where his moderate views had always been suspect. The following
year he was officially booted out of the party for alleged heresy
in connection with voting funds for a new armory, but Carey
had already left. In 1898 Carey and another socialist, Louis M.
Scates, entered the state legislature, and John C. Chase became
mayor of Haverhill, all on the Social Democratic ticket. Revisionist socialism was obviously taking hold. Needless to say, the
Socialist Labor Party took a dim view of the victories of these
socialists. Members in Massachusetts sent clippings from "bour-

geois papers" showing how Chase and Carey were "denying the class struggle, were fishing for bourgeois support, and were seeking to establish harmony between capitalists and workingmen."[6] Unfortunately, however, when Tobin asked the A.F.ofL. convention for some token of support for these socialists, some critics, including Gompers, failed to distinguish between the Social Democratic Party and DeLeon's Socialist Labor Party, which was out to destroy the A.F.ofL.[7]

At the 1899 A.F.ofL. convention, Max S. Hayes of Cleveland, one of the most important spokesmen for socialism among trade unionists, also showed embarrassment over Socialist Labor Party pronouncements. While recommending the nationalization of trusts, he was forced to state he was not enjoining delegates to join the Socialist Labor Party. According to the official report of the convention, "he wasn't quite sure that he was in that party, but served on the floor as a trades unionist."[8]

By 1899 the revisionist revolt against DeLeon was well under way. Later DeLeon blamed the Rosenberg-Busche faction and traced the trouble back to the St. Louis *Labor* dispute.[9] But the most dramatic resistance came from the German and Jewish elements around the *Volkszeitung* in New York, led by Morris Hillquit, a prominent figure among Jewish trade unionists in the needle trades and organizer of the United Hebrew Trades. In 1895 the *Volkszeitung* group had already shown revisionist tendencies at the time of the plank 10 controversy, when, according to DeLeon, they "hinted quite clearly at the advisability of a new 'labor' party."[10] But the real blow came in December, 1898, when the *Volkszeitung* editorially attacked the trade union policy of the Socialist Labor Party. DeLeon countered as best he could with individual expulsions, but in July, 1899, the *Volkzeitung* group, after an open battle, set itself up as the National Executive Committee of the Socialist Labor Party, on the constitutional grounds that the committee was elected or suspended "by a general vote of the section or sections located in the city chosen as the seat of the National Executive Committee." Arguing that the city included greater New York, DeLeon declared the actions of the rebels illegal. The result was that two Socialist Labor Parties were now in the field. The DeLeonite executive committee ordered a general vote of the party, which according to its own account, accepted its actions, except for the locals of Philadelphia, Chicago, and Cleveland.[11] These cities provided notable excep-

tions, however, and there were others. Recounting these events a
few years later, A.M. Simons, editor of the *International Socialist Review,* pointed out how widespread the revolt was.[12]

DeLeon bitterly explained the rebellious "Kangaroos" as a
group of tired Germans who were, somewhat paradoxically, both
"going into small businesses and utterly detached from American
life."[13] But in 1905 he came nearer the truth when he castigated
them for having sought "the flesh-pots of the American Federation of Labor."[14] Fleshpots they may have been to DeLeon, but
to socialist trade unionists it was a question of conscience. "In
the future," wrote the Cleveland *Citizen,* "Cleveland socialists
in cutting loose from DeLeonism will no longer be forced to
apologize for the peculiar action of those who have posed as
leaders in New York."[15]

Predictably, the Kangaroos combined with the Social Democratic Party. During the election year 1900 they merely cooper-
ated—sometimes rather unwillingly. An increase in the socialist
vote, however, brought about a real drive for unity. A convention
in Indianapolis the following year launched the Socialist Party of
America.

Throughout its existence, the Socialist Party was revisionist in
outlook. True, in opposing collaboration with other parties, it
differed from, say, French revisionist socialists who did participate
in bourgeois coalitions, or the British Independent Labour Party,
which joined the Labour Party proper. But in its broadly ethical
as opposed to dialectical outlook, and in its acceptance of piece-
meal improvements, both through trade unionism and legislation,
the Socialist Party of America closely resembled the philosophy
and tactics of European revisionists.

Revisionism, admittedly, did not go unchallenged. Factionalism
between right and left wings consistently plagued the party during the first two decades of its existence, mainly over the question of trade unionism. The left, a rather amorphous group lacking nationally known leaders, became increasingly antagonistic
towards the A.F.ofL. and the revisionist attitude of the dominant
right. The left eventually seceded in 1919. But before World
War I, the Socialist Party remained united as a broad coalition
of forces opposed to corporate capitalism, and during that time
official policy, and probably also the majority of rank and file
opinion, were decidedly revisionist. This becomes clear from a
study of some of the major policy statements of the party with

regard to the labor question generally, and to the A.F.ofL. in particular.

The Socialist Party convention of 1904, for instance, declared that the trade unions were a natural product of the class struggle and deserved the support of all socialists. Echoing the London conference of the Second International in 1896, the convention asserted that "neither politics nor other differences of opinion justify the division of forces of labor in the industrial movement"[16]—a sentiment earlier expressed by Gompers. By and large, this was meant to discourage socialist-inspired dual unionism, at the expense of the A.F.ofL. Algernon Lee, the head of the socialists' Rand School of Social Science, maintained at this time that the pro-A.F.ofL. policy had shown such good results that the proposition to abandon it could be put aside as academic.[17]

The party program in 1908, following the decisions of the international conference at Stuttgart the previous year, emphasized the analogy of the two-armed labor movement—but with the two arms completely independent.[18] On this same theme, the National Executive Committee announced in 1909: "We must get away from the notion of considering the trade union movement simply a recruiting ground for socialist propaganda and the Socialist Party." Thus, Stuttgart's statement that "the proletarian struggle will be carried on more successfully but with more important results if the relationship between the unions and the party are strengthened without impinging the necessary unity of the unions," was again interpreted so as to discourage dual unionism.[19] Unity in the labor movement, according to the Socialist Party information officer, was true Marxism.[20]

Again, in 1912, the convention declared the party duty-bound to support unions morally and materially and called upon individual socialists to join and participate in union activities. On this occasion, the convention pointed out the need for more organization of migrant workers and the unskilled, but took care to declare the party neutral in any dissension arising from this question.[21]

The revisionist attitude of the Socialist Party was not only expressed in convention resolutions. Carl D. Thompson's Information Department,[22] established in 1912, provided leaflets, briefs for debates, etc., for the guidance of advocates of the party line. The information department also kept files for every state showing all legislative activity supported by socialists. This included bills for housing, minimum wages, workmen's compensation and old age pensions. Some legislation was specifically pro-labor. In Illinois, for instance, socialists sought legislation to permit peaceful picketing and the right to boycott, and to forbid "yellow dog" contracts. Though Gompers opposed a great deal of this socialist legislation, particularly minimum wages, the Socialist Party, after full debate, concluded it was in the interest of labor as a whole.

Some have argued that the dominant revisionist right wing ultimately destroyed the Socialist Party by making it indistinguishable from any other reform group (and alienating a very active left wing). Such historical questions are, of course, not open to verification, but this theory contains several flaws. Revolutionary socialism such as was advocated by the left wing had succeeded nowhere in the democratic world. There is little reason to believe that a left-wing socialist party before World War I would have succeeded in the long run any more than the American Communist Party has since. Unlike the German Social Democratic Party, which pursued revisionist tactics under revolutionary banners, the Americans preached what they practiced. In other words, like the British, they were admittedly revisionist. It becomes a little illogical, therefore, to account for the failure of the American Socialist Party by its revisionist approach, when in this respect it was no different from socialists elsewhere in the world. Meanwhile, the party always distinguished itself from the progressive movement by a broad policy of public ownership, which was the most obvious part of its program. Thus, although revisionist, the Socialist Party of America was definitely a socialist party.

The general outlook is well summed up in an address by the Socialist Party National Committee to the annual convention of the A.F.ofL. in 1901.[23] It begins with a gesture in the direction of orthodox Marxism by stating that a political revolution would eventually be necessary. The body of the document, however, is an exposition of the necessity of both trade union and political action. Trade unions had improved the standard of living and would continue to do so within certain limits. Nevertheless, trade unions could not control problems arising from periodic depression nor from automation. Moreover, capitalist control of courts placed trade unionism itself in jeopardy. For these reasons political action was also necessary. Finally, the statement attempted to put the relationship between the A.F.ofL. and the Socialist Party into perspective. The Socialist Labor Party had erred in antagonizing trade unions, with the result that those in the trade unions with socialist aims were put off politics. The rise of the pro-A.F.ofL. Socialist Party meant that those who shared its ends of the cooperative commonwealth now had the responsibility of supporting it.

Gompers' statements in the nineties obviously placed him in the category of trade unionist this document was aimed at. Unfortunately, since the foundation of the Socialist Party, Gompers had been rapidly changing his opinion. While in the nineties he had lamented lack of cooperation among leftist elements in America, he now resolutely believed this cooperation to be impossible. "I declare it to you, I am not only at variance with your doctrines, but with your philosophy," Gompers expounded. "Economically you are unsound, socially you are wrong, industrially you are an impossibility."[24] He became positively paranoid about socialists. They were in the pay of capitalists, they schemed to defeat trade union men standing for election, and they seized every possible movement of secession among trade unionists to foment trouble. In other words Gompers, after 1900, insisted there was a dichotomy between socialism and trade unionism that could not be resolved. A true unionist could not be a socialist trade unionist.

This extreme position—almost a *volte-face* from the nineties—which had such a profound effect on American labor, probably made Gompers and his close associates unique among world labor leaders. Yet historians usually accept it as so natural as scarcely to require explanation. He is portrayed as the American leader responding to the different American situation in which socialism has no place. In fact, though his experiences with DeLeon in the nineties gave Gompers grounds for suspecting socialism as a whole, personal and selfish factors probably had at least as great an influence. These factors must be discussed later in the chapter on "Gompersism." For the moment it is necessary to dwell on how explicit Gompers made this dichotomy, and then to consider its falsity.

In 1910 Gompers engaged the revisionist Robert Hunter in a highly theoretical argument on the subject of what he called "Mr. Hunter's dilemma"—the dilemma of increasing misery as opposed to immediate improvement.[25] First, he took exception to Hunter's claim that socialism had brought improvement in Europe. Marxist theory prophesied deepening degradation, therefore improvement could never be laid at the door of socialism. Socialists could only help bring about improvements despite their socialism, not because of it. On Hunter's objection, Gompers showed himself well aware of the changes in Marxian theory under the impact of revisionism, but he now insisted that the American Socialist Party remain unrevised.

Gompers' statement of the dichotomy contrasts sharply with the view of the socialist trade unionist James H. Maurer. "After the question was thoroughly discussed" [in 1904], Maurer pointed out, "the party took a sound position of co-operation with and support of the unions, a position it never afterwards abandoned." After forty years as a socialist and sixty years as a union man, he never found that his "interest in the daily struggle over wages and hours conflicted with [his] interest in advancing towards a classless society."[26] As the Information Officer explained to debaters, not only was there no antithesis but socialists hoped to achieve their goal by immediate developments.[27] Even in the most radical locals, like that in Jerome, Arizona, where revolutionary ideas had greatest force, it was claimed that Socialist Party locals "would constitute an effective fighting organization for the improvement of intolerable present day conditions *and* a revolutionary army striving with discipline and intelligence along progressive and evolutionary lines for the unconditional abolition of the capitalist state."[28]

Many claimed that socialism and unionism aided each other. One writer in the *Bakers' Journal* saw a correlation between a decline of socialist feeling and an unwillingness to serve in the union and a tendency to "make disparaging remarks about the mob."[29] In the needle trades, according to one of their historians, the reverse happened, for when "the appeal to organize for immediate betterment failed not merely to bring any organization, but also to achieve betterment," the situation was saved by socialism.[30] Interestingly enough, Ray Stannard Baker claimed that radicalism in the clothing trade unions did not get in the way of good working relations with employers.[31]

Gompers seems to have obtained a certain intellectual satisfaction in insisting on a dichotomy between socialism and trade unionism and believing that the destruction of trade unions was the socialists' principal aim. The activity of revisionist socialists in the trade union movement readily obviates such a conclusion. Revisionists used the term "boring from within" to distinguish the new policy of cooperation from DeLeon's Socialist Trades and Labor Alliance. Perhaps the choice of phrase was unfortunate, for it almost suggests a desire to destroy from within and so confirm Gompers' dichotomy. But most socialists took care to present themselves as loyal trade unionists and their actions, both at the national A.F.ofL. level and in individual trade unions, reveal that they were.

Some socialists at A.F.ofL. conventions seemed to aim at an official political program like T. J. Morgan's of 1894. Thus, resolutions about making collective ownership of the means of production and distribution one of the final aims of the trade union movement continued to appear. For the most part, however, socialists now simply demanded working-class political action. Partly in response to this, the 1901 A.F.ofL. convention resolved that it was "the duty of all trade unions to publish in their official journals, to discuss in their meetings and all members to study in their homes, all question of public nature, having reference to industrial or political liberty, and to give special consideration to subjects directly affecting them as a class." The chairman of the Committee on Resolutions even stated that, as a trade union body, the A.F.ofL. had the same aim as the socialists. At the same time, however, he warned that it was "not within the power of this organization to dictate to members . . . to which political party they [should] belong or which party's ticket they [should] vote."[32] But it is not clear that this is what the Socialist Party sought. Victor Berger, for instance, claimed he did not want the A.F.ofL. to endorse the Socialist Party, for experience in Milwaukee had shown that the socialists did better there when not endorsed by the state federation or the trades council of the city. "We don't ask for the endorsement of the Socialist Party," he declared in 1906. "But we ask for action on class lines."[33]

The fact is that the trade union socialists seem to have been sufficiently Marxist to believe that economic realities would force the Socialist Party and the trade unions together. "A party is a political expression of economic conditions," Berger believed. Elsewhere he echoed Gompers in stating that trade unionism itself was a "living witness of the constant change of economical and political systems."[34] All socialist trade unionists asked, therefore, was that the A.F.ofL. leadership take a neutral attitude toward the party instead of criticizing it, and at the same time encourage local trade unionists to study the economic and political situation. It was with this in view that very many resolutions appeared in the A.F.ofL. conventions in the ensuing years.

There was one great danger in advocating that a labor assembly make plans for using its political power, namely, the danger of a labor party separate from the Socialist Party. This is, of course, precisely what had happened in Great Britain at the same time as the Socialist Party was forming in America. H. M. Hyndman, the leader of the Marxist Social Democratic Federation, never tired of warning American socialists of the dangers.[35] On the other hand Pete Curran, an English socialist unionist, pointed out that the Labour Representation Committee, as the British Labour Party was originally called, comprised socialist organizations and the trade unions in such a way that, instead of rivaling each other, they fought for the same end. He admitted that this line of action would not "appear quite clear to the aggressive American socialists," but insisted that even those on the "extreme side of the trade union movement" in Great Britain now accepted it.[36] Curran's advice eventually came to dominate American socialists' thinking. In the early years of the century they were suspicious of the British party, for the place of socialism within it was not yet clear. But an increasing number of socialist leaders gradually came round to the view that a labor party with which the Socialist Party could amalgamate on the British model was the only visible course open to them. It was not until the 1920's, however, that this became the official policy of the Party.

Meanwhile, the question of "fusion" raised a few storms. The first of these occurred around 1902-03, when a Union Labor Party appeared in California and Job Harriman, the leader of the Kangaroo revolt in that state, threw in his lot with it. Explaining his policy to Morris Hillquit, Harriman wrote: "The unions had determined to go into politics and we were forced to join them . . . the prejudice that our opposition would arouse if we put up an opposing ticket would throw our work back some years." The Socialist Trades and Labor Alliance had caused bad relations between socialism and labor in San Francisco, but the action of the socialists in the Union Labor Party had brought "considerable relief from the estrangement and a much better understanding." Harriman distinguished between fusion with the old parties and with a new working-class party, and took cog-

nizance of the fact that the "holier than thou" attitude of the
British Social Democratic Federation, which had just left the
Labor Representation Committee, got it nowhere. He believed
that the labor party movement was gaining strength in other
states besides California.[37]

Harriman's activities caused a storm on the National Executive Committee of the party. At the end of January 1903, it
resolved to expel any local or member, "compromising with a
labor party."[38] In the upheaval, Leon Greenbaum, the National
Secretary who sympathized with Harriman, was overthrown and
the party headquarters removed from St. Louis to Chicago.

Harriman for the moment lost his Socialist Party card, but he
remained unchastened. In 1906 he took exception to bad notices
in the Los Angeles socialist press. "If the Socialist Party desires
to act in that way because I say that the economic organization,
when it enters politics should be supported, they are at liberty to
do so," he told Hillquit. "I shall never enter a protest but shall
stay with the economic organization."[39] The party organizers in
that year were after him, and he debated publicly with Arthur
Morrow Lewis on "The Socialist Party versus the Union Labor
Party."[40] By 1908 Harriman was back in the party, but as he
explained to Hillquit, he stood by his earlier policy.[41] By 1910,
however, he placed the Socialist Party organization at the service
of the trade unions and but for the disaster of the Los Angeles
Times explosion would probably have won the mayoralty campaign in 1911.

Harriman's correspondence with Hillquit provides a fine gauge
of labor party sentiment within the Socialist Party leadership. As
early as 1907 Harriman wrote that the only difference between
them was that Hillquit wished to hold the Socialist Party solid
until the United Labor Party achieved national proportions, while
Harriman urged an amalgamation at a local level in order to
hasten the national movement.[42] That this was an accurate estimate of the opinion of other socialists besides Hillquit was
revealed in 1909, in one of the fiercest rows that ever rocked the
party.

In November 1909 Algie M. Simons, the former editor of the
International Socialist Review, wrote a confidential letter to
William English Walling suggesting that the Socialist Party had
reached a turning point. At the Toronto A.F.ofL. convention,
which he had just attended, he claimed perhaps two-thirds were

ex-members of the Socialist or Socialist Labor Parties. He also found an "intense hatred against the Socialist Party, combined with a perfect willingness to accept the philosophy of socialism." The party, according to Simons, had failed to get through: it had become too intellectualized, and was no longer really a workers' party at all. "We must have the union men," he wrote. "No one has denounced the defects of the American Federation of Labor more than I, but I am forced to recognise that it comes nearer to representing the working class than the Socialist Party, and unless we are able to so shape our policy and our organization as to meet the demands and incarnate the position of the workers, we will have failed in our mission." There were several cryptic references to the need for "reorganization," and though he did not actually mention a labor party, he wrote, "I do not like the English policy, but I say frankly it is better than the Socialist Party." Simons indicated that he had been constantly interrupted while writing and that the letter was not clearly thought out; it was not a formal statement of any kind of plan.[43] He must have been surprised by the reaction.

Had Walling been known as a firebrand against the A.F.ofL.—a member of the left wing—his reaction might have been more understandable. But as a moderate syndicalist he was extremely sympathetic toward the A.F.ofL., and in fact not even a party member at the time. In an argument with the well-known revisionist Robert Hunter, in the *International Socialist Review,* Walling disapproved of British labor's involvement in politics, so he was unlikely to sympathize with a similar course in America. To him the A.F.ofL. was a natural growth that should not be hampered in any way. "The time may come when labor and socialism will join together, but in the future," he wrote. "Meanwhile, they must develop separately."[44] His position, in fact, was exactly like Gompers' in the eighteen-nineties.

But Walling took grave exception to Simons' letter. Not only did he question Simons' facts and ideas, but concluded there was some kind of plot afoot on the part of the right wing, led by Simons, Berger, John Spargo, Hunter, and even Hillquit, to invalidate the forthcoming elections to the national executive committee and maintain themselves in power. Walling showed the letter to Gustavus Myers, who read it to the New York central committee. At this point the storm arose. The right obviously feared a victory by an "impossibilist" anti-A.F.ofL. group, yet there is little evidence of a plot. True, Spargo admonished Simons for intimating to Walling their "plans." But the "plans" referred to general talk about a labor party, and Simons claimed to have discussed this with Walling previously. A chance remark in the letter that the present committee did "not propose to surrender to those who [had] never worked save with their jaws," scarcely constituted "plans" for remaining in power. All members of the group were indignant at the suggestion. Berger believed that if any plot was afoot, it was more likely among those who wished to use Simons' letter as propaganda against the national executive committee in order to turn the party over to the "impossibilists."[45]

Before the squabble ended, Charles H. Kerr produced Simons' original letter in the *International Socialist Review* and called upon all candidates for the forthcoming national executive committee election to state their views on the subject. The answers brought no surprises.[46] Berger merely reiterated the official line about two separate movements complementing each other. "I do not propose to run the trade unions into a political machine nor the Socialist Party into a trades union," he wrote. "However, I want the trade union to be part of the same movement as the political party . . . this is the Wisconsin idea." Some, like Hillquit, Hunter, Spargo, and James H. Maurer, said the Socialist Party would have to wait until it saw what kind of labor party was produced, then it would act by referendum. It was a perfectly straightforward position, which Hillquit summed up in a private letter to J. G. Phelps Stokes:

I have at all times maintained that the prime object of the Socialist Party is to organize the working class of this country politically; that it would be very desirable to have the Socialist Party as such perform that task; that it has so far not succeeded in doing so, and that if a bona-fide workingmen's party should be organized in this country for political purposes, on a true workingmen's platform and upon the principle of independent and uncompromising working class politics, our party could not consistently oppose such an organization, but that it would have to support it and co-operate with it. This, as I understand it, has also been the position of Hunter, Berger, Simons and Spargo, and if I am not mistaken, this is today the position of the overwhelming majority of the members of our party. At any rate, I always considered and still consider it the only sane and logical attitude for Marxian socialists to take. None of us ever made a secret of these views.

On the contrary, we have been discussing them in private and public very freely, whenever an occasion presented itself.[47]

This particular storm abated as quickly as it had arisen, for the A.F.ofL. did not form a labor party and the socialists officially maintained their antifusionist stand. Noting some labor party activity in the A.F.ofL. convention the following year, Max S. Hayes remarked that socialist delegates would "not take very kindly" to the scheme.[48] But the labor party idea remained in the background and became one of the dominant issues again after 1917.

The socialists' aim was the modest one of making the unions politically conscious. Such a policy, they felt, was bound to be in the interests of the party. At the New Orleans convention of the A.F.ofL. in 1902 the voting on a proposal to "advise the working people to organize their economic and political power to secure for labor the full equivalent of its toil" indicates the socialists had grounds for hope. Hayes' proposal was defeated, by show of hands, 140 to 90, with 78 abstentions, but in terms of votes cast—4,897 to 4,171 with only 309 abstentions, the result was much closer.[49] Yet Gompers denied there was any such victory for socialism at the 1902 New Orleans convention on the somewhat spurious grounds that nonsocialists voted for it.[50] At the Boston convention, the following year, he rejoiced at the decisive defeat of a socialist resolution. It might be noted, however, that the highhanded process of lumping all socialist resolutions together was of doubtful constitutionality. When the galleries opposed it, Gompers had them cleared.[51] By the 1905 Pittsburgh convention, the *International Socialist Review* reported that "the few socialists in attendance presented almost a pitiable if not a ludicrous spectacle." It seems the proceedings on this particular occasion were so dull that some delegates asked the socialists to "start something."[52] But in spite of this sad spectacle in 1905, Max S. Hayes managed to receive fully one-third of the votes for president of the A.F.ofL. in 1912.[53]

Though socialists obviously suffered great disadvantages owing to the structure of the A.F.ofL., the fact remains that their A.F.ofL. policies failed, and in this failure probably lies the main clue to their general failure. Daniel Bell sees 1902 as the peak year in the A.F.ofL., followed by a sharp decline, just as socialist influence grew elsewhere in the country. From this he concluded that whatever the source of socialist strength in America, it had nothing to do with trade unions.[54] But by concentrating purely on performance at A.F.ofL. conventions and the general attitudes of A.F.ofL. officials, Bell gives a very wrong impression of the place of socialism in American trade union history. A closer examination of the individual organizations constituting the Federation shows that the driving force behind them often came from socialists, and that socialists enjoyed considerable rank and file support. Moreover, there are indications that socialists steadily gained in influence until World War I. Considering these factors, the similarity between the experience of American and European labor becomes much greater.

Take, for instance, three of the largest A.F.ofL. unions: the United Mine Workers, the International Machinists' Association, and the International Ladies' Garment Workers Union. The extent to which they were influenced by socialism does not make them markedly different from their equivalents in Great Britain.

The United Mine Workers as explained by one lifelong prominent trade unionist, John Brophy, bears this up. Brophy at an early age had come from England and settled in the important Belleville district of southern Illinois. Though his early recollections stress the divergence between the remote objectives of the Socialist Labor Party members and the trade unionists as a whole, he nevertheless felt that socialism and the United Mine Workers grew together: "Socialism just grew out of the special conditions of struggle and expanding labor activities, and idealism of the time." Brophy claims he first became aware of the strength of the socialists among the mine workers when a delegate to their convention in 1908—the last one presided over by John Mitchell. Here he noted socialist ideas being put forward which were "not offered as a substitute for trade unionism, but rather as a supplement, a means of strengthening the union, not an alternate to it." "The socialists of that day," he wrote—people like Frank J. Hayes, secretary of the Belleville subdistrict, and the same region's vice-president, Adolph Germer—"were miners of standing in their separate communities." These two men had interesting but different careers during this period.[55]

Adolph Germer, a German immigrant, remained, like Brophy, a firm member of the Socialist Party until the New Deal. After serving as subdistrict vice president of the Belleville District of the United Mine Workers in 1907, he was secretary treasurer of the same area from 1908 until 1912, after which he was appointed an international organizer. In 1914 he became a district vice-president of the Illinois United Mine Workers. But during the same period he was an active member of the Socialist Party and became national secretary from 1916 to 1918. Robert Hunter hoped to get Germer and other miners, like Duncan McDonald and Frank J. Hayes—"men in daily touch with labor, instead of those nationally known"—on to the National Executive Committee of the Socialist Party. Germer was willing to run, but only if McDonald and Hayes would not, since he feared having too many candidates from one organization.[56] When organizing in Colorado in 1913, Germer seems to have maintained little distinction in his mind between the two organizations, for he held meetings on behalf of the party, not the union. As he explained to the mine workers' president, John P. White, "they feared that if it was held as a meeting of the United Mine Workers of America, the company might be more drastic in the persecution of the active local men."[57] It is unfortunate that men of Germer's and Brophy's importance as organizers for both the Socialist Party and the United Mine Workers should have remained very much behind the scenes at this period, rarely attracting the attention of the labor press.

Frank J. Hayes, at one time secretary of the Belleville sub-district, became president of the mine workers between 1917 and 1919. After years of membership of the Socialist Party he abandoned it in 1917 over the war, and took a violently antisocialist line. By means of organizers on the union's payroll, he influenced the United Mine Workers' convention to his way of thinking. As Germer pointed out to him: "Had it not been for the progressive element that you now seem to scorn, you would never be International President. The Socialist Party and its press gave you popularity." He then went on to say, "You were pictured as one of the coming men who could be depended upon to cleanse the labor movement of its carrion. But what have you done since you have been president and vice-president of the organization, except to turn against those who gave you your present official standing."[58]

The history of the United Mine Workers in terms of its presidents is in this respect extraordinary. Socialists not only supported Hayes, but also the much more dynamic John Mitchell who preceded him, and John L. Lewis who followed him. Both of these men placed socialists in a quandary for, though not socialists themselves, Mitchell and Lewis often supported socialist policy and disagreed with other A.F.ofL. leaders, particularly over industrial unionism. Much of their role in the history of American labor during our period must be seen as being supported and encouraged by socialists.

The *United Mine Workers Journal,* perhaps more than any other trade union periodical, is so crammed with material about socialism that one member complained that the organization, contrary to its constitution, must now be socialist. The editor, while claiming not to be a socialist himself, defended himself by pointing out that many of the members were believers in the theories advocated by the Socialist Party. "These men pay their full dues; they are active workers in our organization," he declared. "They subscribe to the journal just the same as other members, only we believe in larger numbers." Later, in an article on trade unionism and socialism, the same editor, William Scaife, remarked, "It is useless to attempt to divide trade unionism from socialism. It cannot be done . . . the man or men in the movement today who are not more or less socialistic in their belief are few and far between and do not know what the principles of unionism are or what it stands for."[59] These are admittedly strange words for a nonsocialist. At any rate, the anomaly was rectified when the socialist Ed Wallace succeeded as editor in 1912. Frank J. Hayes took the trouble to express his approval of his appointment to Adolph Germer.[60]

Socialists also influenced the conventions of the United Mine Workers. In 1909 they successfully brought in a resolution calling for public ownership of all means of production, and the miners' delegates to the A.F.ofL. convention the same year, Frank J. Hayes and W.D. Van Horn, introduced a similar resolution there.[61] Two years later, socialists managed to pass a resolution at the miners' convention forbidding members of the National Civic Federation, an organization that denied the class struggle, from holding office in the union. John Mitchell protested, but had to abandon his membership of the Civic Federation. When the question arose at the A.F.ofL. convention in Atlanta, however, a similar resolution was defeated.[62]

In the miners' convention in 1912, an attempt was made to endorse the Socialist Party, but the committee on resolutions substituted for this resolution one simply saying that political action was necessary.[63] This merely conformed with socialist policy with regard to the A.F.ofL. As J. L. Engdahl put it in his *Trade Unions and the Present Social Crisis*: "Following the recognized tactics of the Socialist Party the socialist delegates on the resolutions committee and on the floor of the miners' convention opposed any declared endorsement of the Socialist Party. It was considered a great victory to have the largest majority declare in favor of the principles of socialism and of working class action."[64]

In 1914 Gompers, apparently alarmed at the extent of the influence of the socialist Duncan McDonald's attack on him for not supporting a miners' strike in Michigan, went down to Indianapolis especially to address the convention. On his return, he launched a ferocious attack on the socialists in the *Federationist,* linking them with union haters such as the National Association of Manufacturers.[65] While it is impossible to gauge the effect of such harangues on the labor movement as a whole, the attitude of the chief spokesman of American labor provides a marked contrast with his opposite number in any European country.

Turning to the needle trades,[66] it is true that in the women's garment industry during the DeLeonite ascendancy socialism was a disruptive influence. The United Brotherhood of Cloakmakers, incorporated in 1896 from a group of short-lived unions, opposed the Progressive Cloak Makers, formed a few months earlier and affiliated with the Socialist Trades and Labor Alliance. At this period, the United Hebrew Trades—an organization combining most locals in New York in which Jews predominated—was also part of DeLeon's organization. Soon, however, many cloakmakers were leaving the Socialist Labor Party and finding support in the United Brotherhood. One group of secessionists founded the *Forward,* which in time became a strong supporter of the Socialist Party.

Unity in the socialist movement in 1900 also brought unity to the women's garment industry in the shape of the International Ladies' Garment Workers Union. Though this union immediately affiliated with the A.F.ofL., it provides one of the best test cases for the influence of socialism on the trade union movement.

The I.L.G.W.U. adopted a socialist constitution at its foundation in 1900 and declared for socialism at its 1902 and 1903 conventions. Curiously, considerable socialist support came from western delegates, and they were chiefly behind the election, as president, of Benjamin Schlesinger, the former manager of the cloakmakers' joint board and a delegate to the A.F.ofL. convention. Easterners, who dominated the following convention of the I.L.G.W.U., however, seem at this point to have been wary of direct socialist politics. The committee responsible divided on the question, the minority wishing to exclude party politics altogether. Besides, though all seemed to be eager to declare themselves basically socialist, Schlesinger lost the presidency, while John A. Dyche, known for his antisocialist views, became secretary treasurer and editor of the journal. For the moment the I.L.G.W.U. took a much more "business unionist" course; socialism seemed at a low ebb.

The historian of the very influential Local 10 in New York gives a clear picture of what followed at local level.[67] The leaders of what was to become Local 10, from the eighties up to the early years of the new century, had apparently tended to avoid politics in the interests of "pure and simple" unionism, but gradually as younger men replaced them, socialist influence grew, reaching a peak just before World War I. Thus, by 1914, Local 10 helped to elect Meyer London as socialist congressman. Later it aided socialist candidates in winning election to the New York State Legislature.

The movement was similar in the I.L.G.W.U. as a whole, for after 1907, radicalism revived. Partly it resulted from the economic situation, partly from the influx of immigrants after the abortive revolution in Russia. Though the exiles appear to have been more interested in anarcho-syndicalism, at first, experience in the union turned them gradually to the methods of the more constructive Socialist Party. The needle trades, including the I.L.G.W.U., are probably the best refutation of the Gompersite dichotomy between trade unionism and socialism, for it was precisely those unions in which socialism came to predominate that paved the way toward industrial stability in the United States.

An important landmark in this process of stabilization was the so-called Protocol of Peace, signed between the I.L.G.W.U. and the employers group in 1910. The protocol ended a series of large-scale strikes among the women's garment workers in 1909 and 1910, yet, in spite of the fact that socialists played a part in its formation, it was not a socialist document. It basically assumed an identity of interest between capitalist and workers such that

disagreements could be easily settled. Thus, for all its importance
as the beginning of regular procedures of collective bargaining, it
almost disrupted the union. Before many years it was finally
declared obsolete.

The disruption over the protocol centered around John A.
Dyche, the conservative secretary-treasurer, and a Dr. Hourwich,
who as head of the New York Joint Board[68] had more immediate
contact with employers. While Dyche was perhaps guilty of too
much deference toward employers, Hourwich seems to have regarded the protocol as the beginning of workers control. The
hostility between these two men and the disruption it caused in
the union is of interest in assessing the impact of socialism upon
trade unionism on two counts. First, though neither was a
socialist—Hourwich had formerly been a DeLeonite but was a
Progressive in 1912—both sides seemed anxious to placate
socialist opinion, thus proving its strength in the union. Dyche,
writing in the *Ladies' Garment Worker,* for instance, was at pains
to show that trade unionists in Germany made agreements with
employers though they were Social Democrats. He insisted he had
no differences with even the extreme socialists as far as principles
were concerned, and that there was nothing in the protocol that
denied the class struggle.[69]

The other point is that, although they brought in a new preamble
to the I.L.G.W.U. constitution redefining the aims of the union in
terms of political and economic class consciousness, socialists were
a moderating influence. They were thus rewarded when the affair
came to an end in 1914. Hourwich then resigned, and at the convention that year, President Rosenberg and Secretary Treasurer
Dyche did not stand again. In their places, Benjamin Schlesinger
and Morris Sigman, both socialists, were elected. Two years later,
with protocolism at an end, and in its place a more aggressive
system of hard bargaining, Schlesinger was enthusiastically re-
elected. At this time, as its historian has shown, the I.L.G.W.U.
was "greeted by the leader of the American labor movement as
an organization by far the most advanced and progressive at the
present time," and "hailed by the socialists as the stronghold of
the American class conscious socialist proletariat."[70] It is difficult
to see, therefore, the reason for Gompers' insistence on a
dichotomy between socialism and unionism.

The equivalent union to the I.L.G.W.U. in the men's clothing
industry was originally the United Garment Workers, formed in

1891. Since its largely immigrant membership chose American born officers in the hope of gaining prestige, the union tended to be "pure and simple" at the start. As time went on it became even more conservative. It seems to have been dominated by the cutters—the aristocracy of the trade—who showed little interest in the tailors. However, just as in Local 10 of the I.L.G.W.U., radical influence grew among the rank and file. Dissatisfaction with the leadership reached a peak during strikes in Chicago and New York in 1910–11, resulting in agreements inspired by the protocol. But there were still charges of corruption on the part of the unions' officers, and selling out to the employers. The result was secession from the United Garment Workers at the convention of 1914, and the appearance of the Amalgamated Clothing Workers of America. Though the Amalgamated was not accepted by the A.F.ofL., it might be considered here.

Sidney Hillman, who played a prominent part in the Chicago strikes, and later moved to New York as head of the New York Joint Board of the I.L.G.W.U., was chosen president of the new union. As leader of a union with socialist influence among the rank and file, Hillman occupies a position similar to the leaders of the mineworkers. On the whole, he was probably more sympathetic toward socialists than Lewis. He always stressed the broad social aims of the Amalgamated, for instance, and appreciated the fervor of the socialists. Yet he probably used his influence to avoid too close association with the party. Hillman might be considered a "pure and simple" unionist, at least until the New Deal, but he was far from being a stereotype "business unionist."

Besides, concentrating on the president of a union should not hide the important part that socialism played in its daily life and growth. The humdrum life of needle workers is not by itself much on which to build a large organization. Without the socialist fervor of its organizers and rank and file, the spectacular growth of the Amalgamated would have been almost unthinkable. As one historian puts it, "they issued calls to union meetings in terms of proclamations exhorting the masses to rise against the Czar."[71] And even among the long term leaders of the union, J. Schlossberg, the secretary treasurer and editor of the journal, was a dedicated and influential socialist.

There is only one curious anomaly in this, namely that Schlossberg, throughout the period before World War I, was a strong Socialist Labor Party supporter. As editor of the Jewish

weekly, *Der Arbeiter,* he attacked the *Vorwarts* and the socialists
in the I.L.G.W.U., and encouraged secession from the A.F.ofL.
By the time he became secretary of the Amalgamated, however,
he appears to have mellowed. In an open letter of congratulation
to the revisionist socialist, Algernon Lee, after his election as
New York alderman, Schlossberg wrote: "I have taken part in
every campaign since 1890, when the socialist movement in this
country for the first time entered the political arena as a permanent and independent political movement of the working class."[72]
He thus ignored the fact that Lee was in the rival party.

The Machinists also present an interesting case in the story of
socialism and trade unionism as a skilled group that showed considerable socialist influence. The earliest union affiliated with the
A.F.ofL. was the International Machinists' Union, of which the
socialist T. J. Morgan was president, but in 1895 its charter was
revoked and it was replaced by the International Association of
Machinists, under the "pure and simplist" James O'Connell, who
remained head until 1911.

O'Connell was the business unionist par excellence, interested
in the craft union, imposing high dues, seeking agreements with
employers at all costs. Mark Perlman, the historian of the machinists, sees him as having "a vision of successful unionism"—by
which he means job-consciousness—but he has to admit that
O'Connell failed.[73] His administration was marked by a growing
socialist influence, which successfully managed to democratize the
union, chiefly by wide use of the referendum. Resolutions in favor
of industrial unionism and the endorsement of socialism won by
approximately 4 to 1, when put to the vote of the rank and file.
Socialists also submitted to referendum instructions to A.F.ofL.
delegates to the effect that they should vote against Samuel
Gompers as president and that they should support the endorsement of socialism by the A.F.ofL. Though the latter resolution
won in the referendum, no change in policy came about.

If it is argued that these results are little indication of socialist
strength since so few members bothered to vote, this scarcely
applies to the 1911 election of the socialist William H. Johnston
as president. Johnston won by an overwhelming majority, with
43 percent of those eligible voting—an exceedingly high figure
for any trade union referendum.

In describing Johnston's administration, the historian of the
machinists both stresses the dissensions which socialism brought

and is at pains to show that it was not really socialism.[74] But this is all beside the point. The history makes it clear that however differently the machinists' union developed later, the rank and file during the Gompers' era found nothing incompatible between successful trade unionism and democratic socialism. In this respect it followed the pattern of the socialist trade unions in Great Britain.

Besides the miners, garment workers, and machinists, all of whom remained a constant fighting force within the A.F.ofL., there were two unions whose attachment to the parent body was more erratic. The Western Federation of Miners and the United Brewery Workers were both socialist-led. The latter's declaration of principles made their position clear. "The emancipation of the working people will be achieved only when the economic and political movements have joined hands." Under this banner, they contributed freely to the Socialist Party.[75]

The socialist outlook of both unions obviously created dissatisfaction with the A.F.ofL.'s leadership and partly accounts for the Western Federation's secession in 1898 and for the expulsion of the Brewery Workers in 1906. Neither case, however, could fairly be described as the clash of irrelevant socialist dogma and practical common sense trade unionism. Each union had serious grounds for dissatisfaction. Moreover, the reaffiliation of the Brewery Workers in 1908 and the Western Federation in 1911 renewed the energy of socialists in the A.F.ofL. Against this background they presented a fresh challenge to Gompers' leadership in 1912.

These five are the most important unions either led by socialists, or subjected to strong socialist influences before World War I. They provide remarkable contrasts: the homogeneity of the Jewish workers in the garment industry and the concentration of Germans in brewing differs from the ethnic mixture among the miners and the preponderance of native born or English speaking in the machinists. With the exception of the machinists, however, they are distinguished by their industrial as opposed to craft base.

In addition to these industrial unions, the socialists made their presence felt in some of the purely craft unions as well. Even Gompers' own cigar makers' union regularly chose J. Mahlon Barnes, the later national secretary of the Socialist Party, as one of its A.F.ofL. delegates. The union's journal, too, shows that socialism remained very much a live issue. The International Typographical Union in 1900 declared itself to be "a distinctly

class organization embracing in its membership, all workers following the kindred crafts of the printing industry,"[76] and it constantly chose Max S. Hayes, a prominent socialist, as one of its
A.F.ofL. delegates. In 1902 he was also a fraternal delegate of
the A.F.ofL. to the British T.U.C. A few other narrowly based
craft organizations, like the Metal Polishers, Buffers, Plate Brass
Molders and Silver Workers Union, and the Paper Hangers, also
resolved in favor of collective ownership and at one time or
another passed socialist resolutions.[77]

Unfortunately, in some craft unions where socialism had been
a potent force in the nineties, the disruptive and impossibilist
tactics of DeLeon effectively smothered it. The impact of
DeLeonism in the Boot and Shoe Workers' Union and the Bakers'
Union, for instance, caused effective unionism to be seen as incompatible with support for socialism. Thus, while the revisionist
Socialist Party made strides in some of the most successful unions
after 1900, it stagnated in others where DeLeonism had had great
influence. With DeLeonism in the recent past and the propaganda
of the A.F.ofL. afterward, it is not surprising that socialism did
not recover its momentum in these craft unions.

Nevertheless, the evidence from both great and small organizations forced J. L. Engdahl to conclude in 1914 that even those
unions originally organized purely for the purpose of securing
immediate advantages were "meeting the present social crisis" and
that organized labor as a whole was becoming "more and more
imbued with the working class ideals."[78] Robert Hunter went
further. Writing to Adolph Germer in 1910, he mentioned: "I
have thought for some time that if the socialists in the United Mine
Workers' Union, in the Western Federation, in the tailors' union,
in the machinists' union, in the bakers' and brewery unions,
together with all other progressive labor organizations were to
send out a call for a national conference on political action, that
conference could be dominated at the start by socialist elements."[79]
Hunter, who at this time was contemplating a labor party, was
certainly not above wishful thinking. Nevertheless, he was
possessed of sufficient evidence to conclude that the national
federative body of American labor did not adequately represent
rank and file opinion on political and economic questions.

On the other hand, the federative bodies at both city and state
level sometimes showed greater radical influence than the national
trade unions. The central bodies of cities as far apart as New

York, Toledo, Ohio, Little Rock, Arkansas, Seattle, Washington, and Chicago, all appointed socialists or expressed sympathy with the Socialist Party on occasions. In Milwaukee the Federated Trades Council and the Social Democratic Party formed an "interlocking directorate," from 1899 up to the war. When some antisocialists tried tó form a new city central in 1902, Samuel Gompers repudiated it as a dual body.[80]

The success of Berger's party in Wisconsin was also reflected in the Wisconsin State Federation of Labor. In 1900 it declared for collective ownership, and in 1909 demanded that in accordance with the A.F.ofL.'s policy of "rewarding its friends and punishing its enemies," the State Federation should report on the activity of Social Democratic members in the state legislature, instead of just that of the old parties.[81] The Michigan State Federation of Labor in 1901 adopted resolutions in favor of socialism and also one to the effect that officials of the organization were prohibited from making speeches for either of the old parties.[82]

In such crucial industrial states as Illinois and Pennsylvania socialists were presidents of the State Federation of Labor. John H. Walker headed the Illinois Federation from 1914 to 1929 and was a member of the party until 1917. After the war he headed the labor party movement. James H. Maurer of Pennsylvania, elected president of the federation in Pennsylvania, remained a socialist all his days, active in state politics.

To sum up, the Socialist Party of America was formed in a revolt against the revolutionary and anti-trade union tactics of the Socialist Labor Party. In attempting to organize politically the forces of democratic socialism, the Socialist Party regarded the support of the trade union movement as essential. Trade unions were not only potential sources of funds for party organization, but the natural vehicles for the growth of class consciousness and political awareness on which the party would ultimately depend. Trade unions, of course, were immediately concerned with wages, hours, and conditions of labor, but socialists believed this need not reduce them to mere pressure groups within the structure of capitalism; there was nothing incompatible between immediate ends and broad social and political aims. In this belief members of the Socialist Party played a considerable part in building the trade union movement between 1900 and World War I, and though their influence on the federative body declined during this time, this was not true of all individual unions.

And yet, in their attempt to carry the trade unions, the Socialist Party ultimately failed, and in this failure probably lies the fundamental reason for the failure of socialism in the United States. Many reasons have been given: lack of class feeling, social mobility, political ties. These explanations assume an active body of trade unionists, consciously rejecting even revisionist socialism as foreign and irrelevant to their situation, and equally consciously adopting the "American way." However, it makes as much sense to argue that trade unionists were essentially passive in outlook, while being continually bombarded with antisocialist propaganda from their newspapers, and those parts of the trade union movement—particularly the A.F.ofL. central organization—which attracted the attention of the larger newspapers. Significantly, those parts of the labor movement which relied on a labor press for its daily news, were usually socialist.

British trade unionists were guided into independent politics and democratic socialism through the hard work of some leaders. Americans were told by their nationally known leaders that the aims of the Socialist Party were not only impossible of realization or un-American, but contrary to trade union principles. Max S. Hayes once said that Gompers would never discuss the principles of socialism at A.F.ofL. conventions, but instead "proceeded to knock the stuffing out of straw men."[83] Too often, the ordinary trade unionist's image of the socialists was Gompers' "straw men."

Moreover, though there were the Brophys and Germers and others among the trade unions who proselytized for both organizations, the Socialist Party itself did less than it might have done. As Morris Hillquit put it, "We have often tried to coax, cajole and browbeat the trade unions into socialism, but we have made but little systematic effort to educate their members in the socialist philosophy."[84] White of the Molders' union, while organizing for the Socialist Party, was "surprised at times at the density of the ignorance as to the meaning of socialism, but found that they were willing to come and listen." Yet when a properly organized campaign was launched in 1909, by White and Collins of the machinists, these men were "of the opinion that (the Socialist Party) had never taken any form of agitation . . . so fruitful of results." "Hundreds of men in the union movement were under entirely wrong impressions regarding the position and principles of the Socialist Party," according to the organizers, but "when they heard the position of socialism stated they were glad to buy books and pamphlets, to learn more of the movement." The results were apparently so heartening that it was resolved by the executive committee, "to select six first class socialist trade unionists to undertake this special propaganda during the next year, part of their time to be given to general propaganda for the locals, and part of their time exclusively to trade union propaganda." The results are not recorded.[85]

There was in the American labor movement, therefore, a body of untapped support, which given the proper organization and encouragement from above might have supported separate political action as readily as, say, its British counterpart. But the situation was more complex than this, for most of the potential socialist voters lay among the unskilled and unorganized outside the A.F.ofL. The Socialist Party's policy was probably affected by the British experience for, as an "aristocracy of labor," the A.F.ofL. was similar to the British T.U.C. before the advent of "new unionism" during the eighties and nineties. What socialists looked forward to was not merely the conversion of the already organized, but the organization into unions of the mass of unskilled workers, whom the socialists were sufficiently Marxist to believe could not fail to be socialist. Their hopes then lay more in the vertical expansion of the labor movement than in its conversion. Socialists were already successful in those unions already industrially based.

The difficulty arose, however, when the A.F.ofL. seemed unwilling to expand in this direction. It was inevitable, then, that some socialists should expect the initiative to come from elsewhere, causing bad relations not only between the Socialist Party and the A.F.ofL., but also within the party itself.

NOTES

1. S. L. P., *Proceedings* 1896, 10-11, 21.
2. S. L. P., *Proceedings* 1900, 32.
3. S. L. P., *Proceedings* 1900, 228.
4. S. L. P., *Proceedings* 1900, 211-217.
5. A. F. of L., *Proceedings* 1898, 106-108.
6. S. L. P., *Proceedings* 1900, 45, 286.
7. A. F. of L., *Proceedings* 1898, 108-110.
8. A. F. of L., *Proceedings* 1899, 149-150.
9. S. L. P., *Proceedings* 1900, 10-11.
10. S. L. P., *Proceedings* 1900, 271.
11. S. L. P., *Proceedings* 1900, 297 and 304.
12. *International Socialist Review*, December, 1903, 356.
13. S. L. P., *Proceedings* 1900, 300.
14. Address in Minneapolis, July 10, 1905, 34 (Tamiment Institute, N.Y.).

15. Cleveland *Citizen,* December 2, 1899, 1.
16. Socialist Party, *Proceedings* 1904, 206.
17. *I. S. R.,* August, 1904, 73-75.
18. Socialist Party, *Proceedings* 1908, 94-102.
19. S. P., *Minutes of National Executive Committee,* January 22-24, 1909. "Resolution of the Stuttgart Congress on Relations between Trade Unions and Socialist Party" (Typescript in S. P. Papers, Duke).
20. Carl D. Thompson, "Karl Marx and his Theory of Class Struggle," c. 1913 (Typescript in S. P. Papers, Duke).
21. S. P., *Proceedings* 1912, 195.
22. Carl D. Thompson's files in S. P. Collection, Duke.
23. Statement contained in Leon Greenbaum to Frank Morrison, December 3, 1901. (A. F. of L. Papers, Wisconsin State Historical Society).
24. A. F. of L., *Proceedings* 1903, 198.
25. *Federationist,* April, 1910, 332-333; June, 1910, 482, 484; May, 1915, 355.
26. James H. Maurer, *It Can Be Done* (New York: Rand School Press, 1938), 144, 321.
27. Carl D. Thompson, Information Department Statement c. 1914.
28. S. P. *Weekly Bulletin,* January 22, 1910.
29. *Bakers' Journal,* March 13, 1909.
30. J. M. Budish and George Soule, *The New Unionism in the Clothing Industry* (New York: Harcourt, Brace & Howe, 1920), 167.
31. New York *Evening Post,* February 18, 1920: quoted in Budish and Soule, *New Unionism,* 156.
32. A. F. of L., *Proceedings* 1901, 234.
33. A. F. of L., *Proceedings* 1906, 186.
34. A. F. of L., *Proceedings* 1906, 186; 1902, 180.
35. For instance see *I. S. R.,* July, 1900, 17-22.
36. *I. S. R.* September, 1901, 185-187.
37. Job Harriman to Morris Hillquit, November 6, 1902, December 24, 1902, March 31, 1903, May 2, 1903 (Hillquit Papers, Wisconsin State Historical Society).
38. S. P. *Weekly Bulletin,* June 20, 1903.
39. Harriman to Hillquit, September 28, 1906.
40. S. P. *Weekly Bulletin,* February 10, 1906.
41. Harriman to Hillquit, November 10, 1908; September 23, 1910; December 19, 1911.
42. Harriman to Hillquit, February 25, 1907.
43. The original letter and other correspondence published in *I. S. R.,* December 1909, 594-609.
44. *I. S. R.,* March 1909, 683-689; April, 1909, 753-764.
45. Victor Berger to A. M. Simons, December 6, 1909 (quoted by David A. Shannon, *The Socialist Party of America* (New York: Macmillan, 1955), 66.
46. See I. S. R., December 1909, 594-609.
47. Hillquit to J. G. Phelps-Stokes, December 3, 1909. (Hillquit Papers).
48. *I. S. R.,* October, 1910, 246.
49. A. F. of L., *Proceedings* 1902, 178-183.
50. *Federationist,* January, 1903, 19.
51. A. F. of L., *Proceedings* 1903, 188-199.
52. *I. S. R.,* December 1905, 368-369.
53. A. F. of L., *Proceedings* 1912, 374.

54. Daniel Bell, "The Background and Development of Marxian Socialism in the United States," in D. D. Egbert and Stow Persons, eds., *Socialism and American Life* (Princeton: Princeton University Press, 1952), I, 254.
55. Columbia University Oral History Project, *John Brophy Memoir,* 250-251, 365.
56. Robert Hunter to Adolph Germer, December 17, 1912; Germer to Hunter, December 23, 1912 (Germer Papers, Wisconsin State Historical Society).
57. Germer to John P. White, February 6, 1913 (Germer Papers).
58. Germer to Frank J. Hayes, January 25, 1918 (Germer Papers).
59. *United Mine Workers Journal,* October 8, 1908, 4; August 26, 1909, 4.
60. F. J. Hayes to Adolph Germer, May 11, 1912 (Germer Papers).
61. A. F. of L., *Proceedings* 1909, 328-329.
62. *Federationist,* April, 1911, 307, and A. F. of L., *Proceedings* 1911, 217, 258.
63. United Mine Workers, *Proceedings* 1912, 215-238.
64. J. L. Engdahl, *Trade Unions and the Present Social Crisis* (Chicago: Socialist Party, n.d., c. 1914).
65. *Federationist,* March 1914, 189 ff.
66. The following narrative is taken from Lewis Lorwin, *The Women's Garment Workers* (New York: B. W. Huebsch, 1924).
67. James Oneal, *History of Local 10, I.L.G.W.U.* (New York: Ashland Press, 1927), 58, 219-220.
68. The joint board was the central organization of all locals in one city. It was the chief negotiating agent.
69. *Ladies' Garment Worker,* January, 1914, 8-13.
70. Lorwin, *Women's Garment Workers,* 318-319.
71. Joel Seidman, *The Needle Trades* (New York: Farrar & Rinehart, Inc., 1942), 87.
72. *Advance* (Amalgamated Clothing Workers), November 1917, 4.
73. Mark Perlman, *The Machinists* (Cambridge, Mass.: Harvard University Press, 1961), 35-37.
74. Perlman, *Machinists,* 20, 35.
75. See S. P. *Weekly Bulletin,* September 24, 1904 and October 16, 1906.
76. *I. S. R., September,* 1900, 189.
77. *I. S. R., October,* 1905, 240.
78. J. L. Engdahl, *Trade Unions and the Present Social Crisis.*
79. Robert Hunter to Germer, March 18, 1910 (Germer Papers).
80. Thomas W. Gavett, *Development of the Labor Movement in Milwaukee* (Madison: University of Wisconsin Press, 1965), 97.
81. *I. S. R.,* August, 1900, 116. S. P. *Weekly Bulletin,* July 31, 1909.
82. *I. S. R.,* November, 1901, 386.
83. *I. S. R.,* January, 1901, 421.
84. Quoted in *Federationist* April, 1914, 302.
85. S. P., *Minutes of National Executive Committee,* December 11, 12, 1909.

4

Industrial Unionism

American socialists considered their party to be part of a general labor movement, but as we pointed out, experience taught them to adopt a policy of noninterference with the structure of the A.F.ofL. and stress instead the theory of two separate arms. But this does not mean they dropped interest in organized labor. Some members of the "right wing," either too eager to be amicable toward labor leaders or simply piqued at their inability to influence them, might talk about seeking a "political solution only" and leaving the trade unions alone, but most realized the future of socialism was somehow bound together with that of labor.

The mutual aid that political socialism and organized labor brought to each other in Europe made this quite clear. But since continental unions were the creation of socialist parties or at least had grown up with them, their example was less applicable to the United States. In Great Britain, however, where a strong labor movement existed before political socialism, socialist influence had grown as trade unionism expanded. Only in America, it seemed, did the leading organization of labor stand apart from the socialist movement. For socialists, part of the explanation of this lay in the fact that the A.F.ofL. was chiefly based on exclusive craft unions and represented only the skilled workers. It was not illogical to conclude, therefore, that the future of American socialism depended upon industrial unionism. "Industrial unionism," accordingly, became one of the socialist battle cries.

Unfortunately, the term has meant different things to different people—a fact causing considerable confusion about the subject. Of course it means organization according to industry rather than craft and including unskilled as well as skilled; but differences naturally arose as to how this organization should be implemented.

To some, the term industrial unionism meant starting afresh with an entirely new movement, which would include all workers. While its advocates imagined administrative divisions based on separate industries, they usually thought in terms of a highly centralized body—"one big union" in one form or another. Naturally this focus implied replacing the existing federation. Perhaps a second group of industrial union advocates envisioned some kind of compromise, a new body but complementing rather than replacing what already existed. But if there was such a group it never had a chance to put its ideas into practice.

To most socialists, however, industrial unionism implied development of the existing unions through amalgamation and expansion and the creation of new unions in industries where none existed. This was the British model and it is more or less what was achieved by the C.I.O. in the thirties. For the most part, it was also the policy of the Socialist Party of America, and remained so during the period covered by this work.

The Socialist Party, or at least its dominant "right wing," has nevertheless been accused of abandoning the policy of industrial unionism and accepting craft unionism in order to woo the A.F.ofL. leadership.[1] But this is a misunderstanding arising from the fact that the term industrial unionism was also applied to dual movements antagonistic to the A.F.ofL. Though the party leaders largely opposed dualism, it did not mean that they were wedded to the principle of craft unionism. In 1913 Max S. Hayes, who "took the lead in the battle for new ideas" in the A.F.ofL., explained to the Seattle *Star* that the organization was capable of accommodating industrial unionism since existing rules did not forbid it. He felt that a majority of the rank and file of organized labor wanted it.[2] Thus, in the socialist caucus at A.F.ofL. conventions, trade union socialists planned the introduction of "industrial union" resolutions and introduced them on the floor with such regularity that they were known simply as "socialistic resolutions."

Meanwhile, outside the A.F.ofL. "right wing" intellectual socialists constantly advocated the principle of industrial unionism. Robert Hunter wanted Adolph Germer to sponsor a meeting of progressive craft unions to discuss the question; his idea is reminiscent of the Committee on Industrial Organization that was to revolutionize the American labor scene a generation later.[3] John Spargo's book, *Syndicalism, Industrial Unionism and Socialism,* was an attempt to clear up the party's position.[4]

Nevertheless, the issue of industrial unionism not only led to the worst relations between the Socialist Party and the A.F.ofL. but caused serious dissension within the party. On both counts, therefore, it might be considered one of the chief contributing factors in the failure of American socialism.

In urging the organization of the unskilled, socialists wished for no more than A.F.ofL. leaders professed. In the very first issue of the *American Federationist* G. W. Perkins, the president of the Cigar Makers and "one of the soundest trade unionists" Gompers had ever known, wrote: "I feel that there is still a vast amount of work in what is known as the trade union movement, for the organization of the workers upon trade lines in industrial organization, and that the sooner and the more perfect labor becomes on these lines, the more rapidly and complete will be their emancipation upon other or political lines."[5] The Socialist Party of America could scarcely have said it better. In the following issue of the *American Federationist,* the general secretary of the National Longshoremen's Association pointed out how, in spite of the fact that "the remark is often made that a union among (the unskilled) would never enjoy a long life or a wide range of usefulness," he now offered his union as "an illustration of the benefits to be gained by the organization of so-called unskilled labor."[6]

Gompers himself put his finger on the essence of the problem, the same problem that had brought the "new unionism" into English industry in the eighties:

> There is unquestionably a wrong opinion as to what constitutes the dividing line between skilled and unskilled labor. We have in mind a number of trades in which only a decade ago a regular series of years were required to serve an apprenticeship in order to qualify a worker to become a journeyman, an effective tradesman, yet within a brief period these men have found that their entire early training, study and practice acquired at their trade become absolutely useless to them. A machine or a series of machines were invented, rendering their skill superfluous since any one with ordinary intelligence and ability could apply himself to operate the machine.

He concluded with socialistic directness:

> All history demonstrates that it is not so much the question of skill in labor as it is the part of that skill devoted to an appreciation of existing economic and social conditions, that is, the recognition of the necessity of organization, which is the real means by which wages, hours, and conditions of employment are permanently improved.[7]

Addressing the machinists convention in Toronto in 1901, Gompers expressed disapproval of any unwieldy "one big union" idea but added that it was "equally true that the trade organization which fails to deal with the new industrial conditions as they develop, puts up a stone buttress against further progress."[8] In spite of such protestations, it was precisely such a "stone buttress" that Gompers erected.

In reply to Henry George, who pointed out the need for labor to organize in a way sufficient to meet the trusts, Gompers replied that the experience of the Knights of Labor showed the A.F.ofL. to be better than "a trust form of labor organization."[9] He was probably right, but instead of re-emphasizing the need for great expansion on an industrial basis within the existing structure, just as the British had accomplished and the C.I.O. might have done later, Gompers believed that "the attempt to force the trade unions into what has been termed 'industrial organization' is perversive of the history of the labor movement . . . and is sure to lead to a confusion which precedes dissolution and disruption. It is time for the A.F.ofL. to solemnly call a halt. It is time for our fellow unionists entrusted with grave responsibilities to stem the tide of expansion madness lest either by their indifference or encouragement, their organizations will be drawn into the vortex that will engulf them to their possible dismemberment and destruction."[10]

Two years previously, the so-called Scranton Declaration of 1901 had affirmed craft autonomy as the official A.F.ofL. policy, though it was hedged with vague reservations about amalgamation sometimes being necessary. Philip Taft has called the declaration a "compromise," an attempt to avoid the chronic jurisdictional rivalries that threatened to disrupt the Federation.[11] This kind of compromise may have been the original idea, but by 1903 the principle hardened and became an argument against general' expansion.

Gompers, in wishing to preserve above all what had already been accomplished, indeed had a point. Like a majority of the socialists, he had a healthy suspicion of the "one big union" idea. But neither the experience of other countries, nor of industrial unions already existing within the A.F.ofL., such as the United Mine Workers, could have led him to believe that industrial unionism necessarily meant "one big union." Yet with stubborn perversity he insisted on regarding demands for industrial unionism as dualist and destructive.

This point is well illustrated in his reply to a letter from A. Rosebury, the assistant secretary of the I.L.G.W.U.—a self-conscious industrial union—seeking a contribution for the *Ladies' Garment Worker*. Rosebury wanted to give readers "an exhaustive view on the A.F.ofL. and Industrial Unionism, that is, so far as the principle of complete trade organization is concerned." He made it clear in his letter that he believed that the whole principle of industrial unionism was "being perverted by hot headed leaders of the I.W.W.," and therefore had in mind some statement about expansion within the A.F.ofL. To Rosebury's request for a straightforward statement on the subject, Gompers replied:

> Industrial unionism, so called, for no comprehensive definition has as yet been found to prescribe its boundary lines, or to classify the elements to be contained therein, is a theory, which, if carried to its logical, (or better still illogical) conclusion, is harking back to the primitive battlefield. The advocates of this form of organization, at least a great many of them, assume that the organizations of labor can be successfully combined into one gigantic union and the power of that union so concentrated that it would or could be moved at an instant's notice as an automaton.[12]

It is curious to note that in the same month he made this condescending statement, so obviously based on a misconception, his conscience must have been slightly stirred. Writing privately to the presidents of the unions in the A.F.ofL., he stressed that recent increases in membership, "while encouraging, should yet be an incentive of organizing the yet unorganized, of instilling a better spirit of unity and fraternity among the organized, of inaugurating a campaign for greater agitation, education and organization." He concluded by asking for articles on the subject for the *American Federationist*.[13]

If this approach signified a slight change of mood, it did not last. At the following 1912 A.F.ofL. convention, a United Mine Workers' resolution calling for A.F.ofL. initiative in industrial unionism met with a reaffirmation of the Scranton Declaration.[14] Similarly, three years later, when a delegate from the Oregon State Federation of Labor demanded an investigation into the feasibility of a gradual transformation from craft into industrial unionism, the committee on resolutions denied the need for this on the grounds that industrial organizations already existed in the A.F.ofL., and that the trade union movement was sufficiently flexible to change spontaneously when the need arose. The committee denied the need for A.F.ofL. initiative in this matter by again asserting that the autonomous nature of the affiliates placed the matter outside A.F.ofL. authority.[15]

If the A.F.ofL. leadership acknowledged no responsibility, some international unions and state organizations did. This was particularly the case where socialism was strong or where an industrial form already existed, which often amounted to the same thing. But it also arose where it was felt that organization industrially was the only solution to the constant jurisdictional battles that plagued the craft unions where skills overlapped.

It was the Wisconsin State Federation of Labor that called for a committee to study industrial unionism at the A.F.ofL. convention in 1903.[16] Two years later, the Illinois State Federation of Labor took up the question of the unskilled. It recommended to the A.F.ofL. that some provision be made for organizing "a class of workmen who are operating machines in various factories and shops" but who were not machinists. In 1911 the same state federation offered to cooperate with the A.F.ofL. in the attempt to organize migratory workers, and in 1913 a vigorous debate took place on the subject at state level.[17]

The United Mine Workers was probably the greatest advocate of the industrial principle, and the question constantly arose in its journal and at conventions. Edgar Wallace, the socialist editor, and James Lord, a United Mine Workers' official and head of the A.F.ofL. mining department, even extolled the old principle of the Knights of Labor. "An injury to one is an injury to all," they argued, "is still the ideal of every conscientious advocate of better conditions for the workers." They acknowledged, however, that the change had to come from within the A.F.ofL., but that advocates should remain within the craft organization, "pointing out the necessity of amalgamation with the nearest craft union, and then further affiliations."[18] Lord was optimistic that change could come, for he believed the A.F.ofL. to be flexible enough to remold itself industrially.[19] Like President White, also of the United Mine Workers, he felt the sentiment for industrial unionism to be growing in the A.F.ofL., though, rather significantly, he had to add, "at least among the rank and file."[20]

Others were less optimistic. When the United Mine Workers' convention declared for the organization by industry instead of by craft, whenever and wherever possible, and instructed its

A.F.ofL. delegates to use every endeavor to bring this about, the socialist Duncan McDonald declared:

> We have just about as much chance of getting a resolution of that character through the A.F.ofL. as it is at present constituted, as you have of flying across the Atlantic ocean without an airship. Your delegates to the A.F.ofL. brought this matter to the attention of the convention as instructed and tried to have it adopted, but they almost threw us out of the convention. If anybody can get a progressive idea through the A.F.ofL., he deserves a monument bigger than that built to George Washington . . . reactionary, fossilized, mossgrown, worm-eaten bunch as there is in the A.F.ofL. . . . When we suggest that we have crafts organized industrially we are charged—even by their vice-president John Mitchell—with working to make propaganda for the Socialist Party.[21]

McDonald spoke with some authority for he had seen a similar resolution also sponsored by the United Mine Workers squashed in 1912.

The question was also crucial in another of the great industrial unions of the A.F.ofL.—the United Brewery Workers. But here passions arose much higher, for not only was the union very socialist in sympathy but also constantly involved in jurisdictional conflicts with other unions, particularly the engineers and firemen. The result was the expulsion of the United Brewery Workers from the A.F.ofL. in 1907. The dispute had raged from 1902 and became particularly bitter in 1904, when the Boston convention of the A.F.ofL. ordered the brewery workers' union to turn part of its membership over to the Brotherhood of Stationery Firemen, which, as Louis Kemper, the secretary of the United Brewery Workers, was not slow to point out, was suspended for nonpayment of dues.[22] Socialists were naturally outraged by this kind of decision and were prone to explain it in terms of the A.F.ofL.'s fear of the potential radicalism of large industrial unions.[23] Perhaps fearing this accusation, Gompers emphatically stated that opposition to him in the United Brewery Workers' journal had no political overtones.[24]

It would be untrue to say, however, that Gompers took no practical steps to attempt to deal with the problems seeking solution in industrial unionism. The A.F.ofL. was too much racked by internal disputes, and the plight of the unorganized was too obvious, to be ignored entirely. Two steps were taken by the

A.F.ofL.: first, the organization of "industrial departments"—subdivisions within the A.F.ofL. bringing together the national trade unions within one industry; and second, the chartering of local "federal unions," for the benefit of workers with no national union. Neither of these attempts dealt with the problem directly, and neither was pursued with much vigor.

Gompers thought of the idea of industrial departments very early in his career. Surveying the question in 1888, he had felt that perhaps the future lay in a reorganization of the A.F.ofL. along industrial lines.[25] He thought of a plan whereby conventions of all trade unions in a given industry would meet in the same city as the A.F.ofL. convention, the A.F.ofL. meeting as soon as the others had adjourned. But he admitted that the idea was perhaps premature, and nothing was done.

With no initiative from the A.F.ofL., therefore, the trade unions in the building industry formed a Building Trades Council, which one socialist hailed as evidence that the American labor movement was being forced together by natural events. "In spite of this conscious avowal [of the undesirability of industrial unionism]," he wrote, "the conditions of our economic and industrial growth have forced many of these warring individual interests into harmonious co-operation."[26] Gompers, however, smelled a dualistic rat, and feared an organization usurping the powers of the A.F.ofL. The Structural Building Trade Alliance, which replaced the Building Trades Council in 1903, was no more welcome. Finally in 1907 the A.F.ofL. was forced to charter a Building Trades Department as an adjunct to the A.F.ofL., though the Department's relations with the federative body remained far from smooth. Its attempts to settle jurisdictional disputes naturally involved disciplinary action, which the A.F.ofL. claimed as its prerogative. But the new organization at least gave Gompers ammunition with which to reply to socialist blasts about the A.F.ofL.'s failures to deal with industrialism. Perhaps with this in mind, he encouraged others—the Metal Trades, Mining and Railway Employees departments—but with indifferent success. The fact is that the departments did not meet the challenge of industrialism. They might be said to have presented a cover for inaction. Jurisdictional disputes continued and, of course, they did nothing about the unorganized unskilled.

These were to be the province of the so-called local trade and federal labor unions, of which Gompers in 1902 boasted 274, organized and chartered within the previous year. Their members, on the other hand, together with the proponents of industrial unionism, constantly declared they were given little real encouragement, and they failed to attract more than a small percentage of the unskilled. Their more vociferous leaders demanded greater representation on the A.F.ofL., in order to promote organization, and when it was refused, some seceded and tried to form an International Laborers' Union. Gompers disliked this. He explained that the federal unions were not to be regarded as fixed, but simply as the pathway to the gradual formation of a laborers' union that each federal union would join "as soon as there was a sufficient number of workers in a federal union engaged in one given employment." To attempt to organize a general laborers' union, however, he felt would be like trying to reorganize the defunct Knights of Labor. "It would be an aggregation of conglomerate elements where the interests of none could receive attention, and would end in chaos and confusion."[27] Gompers thus would not abandon the craft principle even among the unskilled.

Seeing the threat of secession by the federal unions in 1902, Gompers did try to organize a strike fund for their benefit, but little more was done.[28] It was not strike benefits that the unskilled needed so much as initiative in organization. Under A.F.ofL. auspices an International Laborers' Union might have been formed that would have anticipated the British Transport and General Workers' Union. Perhaps suspicion of a similar hotbed of radicalism was why it was discouraged.

President Wright of the Illinois State Federation of Labor attempted to provide something on a state level, in the form of a smaller replica of the Knights of Labor. He envisioned a "school for trade unionism" in an organization binding the unskilled in a statewide federation with local chairmen, secretaries, and treasurers, under the control of the State Federation of Labor. After being trained in the principles of trade unionism they were to be divided out among craft unions. Though Wright's scheme was similar to Gompers' in that the ultimate aim was organization in craft unions, he felt that organization on a state level rather than the remote A.F.ofL. would give them greater initiative. The plan was approved unanimously by the Illinois State Federation of Labor, but the executive council of the A.F.ofL., seeing no constitutional provision for a state body of directly affiliated local unions, discouraged the whole idea.[29]

There was only one other place from which stimulus could

come for the organization of the unskilled, namely, the local city central bodies. Under the A.F.ofL. constitution, however, the role of city centrals was very much circumscribed, and efforts to change this in the interests of permitting them to play a more active part in the labor movement were discouraged—possibly because of a fear of the city centrals' traditional radicalism.[30]

The A.F.ofL. therefore more or less abdicated responsibility for the unskilled or semiskilled. The mass of workers in such huge concerns as the steel industry had to wait until the 1930's before they were properly organized, and even then the A.F.ofL. held back. In his memoirs the socialist John Brophy, whose active work covered the years from the Gompers' era to the thirties, rather magnanimously believed that had Gompers been alive in the thirties he could have avoided the C.I.O. split. Brophy argued that Gompers occupied an independent position on the A.F.ofL., whereas William Green, his successor, though a sympathizer with industrial unionism, was afraid of the conservatives in the A.F.ofL.[31] This is an interesting point for, as the next chapter explains, Gompers never completely lost something of his old idealism. Yet unlike his friend, P. J. McGuire, who clung to his socialist idealism and vainly tried to reconcile labor unity and complete unionization with craft exclusiveness, even in spite of the opposition of the conservatives, Gompers refused to permit ideals to influence policy. Gompers' secretary, Eva Valesh, knew him better than Brophy. On several occasions she prompted Gompers about both the unskilled and the constant jurisdictional disputes, and she maintained that he simply evaded the issue. On one occasion he said that since the unskilled could be replaced during a strike there was no point in organizing them, though as Miss Valesh pointed out, the C.I.O. managed to do it later. The fact is that Gompers was aware of the need for industrial unionism, but he put his head in the sand. "Mass production naturally made great changes in the form and procedure of the union," Miss Valesh wrote. "Mr. Gompers sensed this, but he preferred the older trade union as being more practical for organization."[32]

Since industrial unionism was crucial to socialist success, and since the A.F.ofL. refused to budge on the question, something of a crisis was bound to arise when industrial movements appeared outside the A.F.ofL. The first test came in 1902, when a convention in Denver, Colorado, launched the American Labor Union and threatened "to unfurl its flag in every state in the union."[33]

The name was new but not the organization. The American Labor Union was the child of the Western Federation of Miners, which Ed Boyce had organized in the western nonferrous metals industry. Having affiliated with the A.F.ofL. in 1897, the Western Federation returned its charter the following year over disappointment at the A.F.ofL. response to requests for strike aid. On more general grounds, however, Boyce, who had attended the Cincinatti A.F.ofL. convention in 1896, felt the main body of American labor was moribund and not particularly interested in the problems of the West. Accordingly, at a conference in Salt Lake City in 1898, he helped form a new organization for the West, the Western Labor Union, into which the Western Federation of Miners was integrated. Though Gompers' attempts at Salt Lake to have the Western Federation reaffiliate with the A.F.ofL. were thwarted, the organizing committee pointed out that the new organization was not dualistic but aimed primarily at "unattached bodies of workmen."[34] When the Western Labor Union reconstituted itself as the American Labor Union in 1902, however, the "no dualism" policy changed.

Gompers was not the kind to do nothing. Denying that the Western Labor Union or the American Labor Union really promoted "industrial unionism," he pointed out that they created jurisdictional disputes where none had existed before by issuing charters to local organizations for which there were already national unions.[35] For example, he claimed that certain parts of the shoe trade, which he wished to amalgamate with the Boot and Shoe Workers International Union, were taken over by the American Labor Union. Groups like the American district of the British-based Amalgamated Engineers, claimed by the International Association of Machinists, and the Brotherhood of Railway Employees, which the A.F.ofL. had failed to charter for a variety of reasons, looked to the American Labor Union, thus encouraging division rather than unity.[36] Gompers, however, did not mention the American Labor Union's work among the unskilled.

For the A.F.ofL., the most likely explanation was a socialist plot. In November, 1903, Gompers published in the *American Federationist* a letter signed by F. G. R. Gordon. "It is said that a certain animal will not change its spots," it announced. "And certain socialists do not change in tactics simply because they migrate from DeLeon's Socialist Labor Party into the Socialist Party." The letter claimed that the leaders of the Socialist Party had once supported the Socialist Trades and Labor Alliance, and only belatedly discovered it to be "a crime against organized labor." The party, it is true, had ignored the Western Labor Union, but as soon as it changed into what Gordon called a "socialist" American Labor Union, the party had rendered it aid and encouragement. Gordon pointedly added that the party's occasional sympathy with the American Federation of Labor was due solely to the A.F.ofL.'s numbers and owed nothing to a similarity in outlook.[37] Gordon, a former member of both the Socialist Labor Party and the Social Democratic Party, had opposed the union of Social Democrats and "Kangaroo" bolters only a few months before; he eventually became an employee of the National Association of Manufacturers. His views at this time, however, admirably sum up Gompers' own, and they are a gross distortion of the facts.

In insisting that the American Labor Union was "a second edition of DeLeon's Socialist Trades and Labor Alliance without the candor to acknowledge its desire to destroy the trade union movement," Gompers took the same line he took during the quarrels with the Socialist Labor Party in the nineties—a line he then believed to be orthodox Marxist:

> The trade unions are the naturally, historically developed organization of the wage earners. They were not born in the brain of any particular man. They are the growth of our industrial conditions and they will continue to grow and gain in strength, fight the battles for labor's rights and secure labor's final emancipation, and this too, in spite of the antagonism of the capitalist class or the false and the foolish in the ranks of labor.[38]

Gompers would have found that all socialists agreed in principle that trade unionism was a natural growth. The trouble was that the A.F.ofL. was no longer growing. This was attributed to the Scranton Declaration, which was undoubtedly "born in the brains" of some particular men. A. M. Simons, the editor of the *International Socialist Review,* though wary of the new movement and eager that the split in the ranks of labor be healed, foresaw that Gompers would explain the American Labor Union as a new version of the Socialist Trades and Labor Alliance. In denial, he termed the American Labor Union "a response to conditions," and drew attention to the fact that the west attracted more enterprising men, who presumably would not tolerate the existing conditions.[39] As far as the dualism in the east was concerned,

Max S. Hayes admitted that the refusal of the A.F.ofL. to acknowledge socialism as a working class principle had something to do with it, but it was also the natural result of Gompers' stress on autonomy of crafts.[40] Recent research has confirmed the socialists' analysis at the time, namely, that the events leading up to the formation of the American Labor Union were a natural and spontaneous expression of working-class radicalism produced by what can only be termed "capitalist exploitation."[41]

Moreover, it was not only sins of omission on the A.F.ofL.'s part that produced the challenge to its authority. The actions of the A.F.ofL. were not as conciliatory as Gompers asserted. For instance, recounting the events after 1898, Gompers maintained that "when the Western Federation of Miners . . . became separated from the A.F.ofL., we found no fault and were simply willing to await the time when better judgement would follow . . ."[42] What stung the miners, however, was that A.F.ofL. unions sent organizers into the region only after the Western Labor Union posed a threat to their respective jurisdictions. Moreover, though the Western Labor Union in these years supported the A.F.ofL. boycotts, the A.F.ofL. bluntly refused to do the same for the Western Labor Union.

Again, Gompers undoubtedly sent Secretary Frank Morrison and Thomas Kidd of the A.F.ofL. Executive Council to the 1902 Denver convention in order to plead that it was the duty of the men to return to the A.F.ofL. They should try to change it if they were dissatisfied, according to the envoys, but it was treachery to create a rival organization. The argument is thus reasonable enough through A.F.ofL. eyes, but this is not how it appeared in Denver. One delegate at the convention gave a very different story.

"I venture to say that a majority of the members of the Western Labor Union convention came to Denver with the determination to bring about reconciliation between the A.F.ofL. and the Western Labor Union," this delegate from Wyoming wrote. But he went on to explain that "during the days of the convention a strike was in progress in Denver between the building trades and their employers, which was utilized by the A.F.ofL. for the most aggressive and extraordinary means to injure the organization of the Western Labor Union ever invented by men." He also referred to Morrison's mission as a "show at an attempt to reconciliate the two organizations." "It made the poorest attempt anyone could ever have seen," he maintained, "showing plainly that it was not their intention to have us with them, at the same time throwing sand into the eyes of the rest of the labor world . . ."[43]

A. M. Simons believed there was much provocation. "While Gompers was writing articles in the *American Federationist,* breathing the spirit of brotherly love and was sending delegates ostensibly to secure harmony between the Western Labor Union and the A.F.ofL.," Simons reported, "he was also sending out private letters in large quantities most bitterly attacking that organization with its leaders. There may even be reason to believe that he was playing this apparently two faced game with the expectation and intention of being found out, and hoped thereby to keep the two organizations apart."[44]

Finally, there seem to have been strong rumors of A.F.ofL. threats to send in thousands of organizers unless the westerners capitulated. Some maintained such threats were even posed by the so-called conciliators at Denver. Whatever its truth, it was not the kind of challenge miners were likely to bow to. Debs claimed the creation of the American Labor Union was thus an act of defense, and even suggested it was the A.F.ofL. that was dualistic.[45]

But not only was the American Labor Union a natural response to industrial conditions and the product of A.F.ofL. neglect and provocation; it was also avowedly socialist. The union adopted a political program markedly similar to the party's, and Max S. Hayes reported that the miners were about to call a convention and nominate candidates on the socialist ticket.[46] Later, five socialists won election to the Montana Legislature and the party swept the Anaconda municipal elections with the aid of the union.[47]

The organization was obviously too tempting for some members of the party. Job Harriman feared that middle class socialists in the west might "embrace" the American Labor Union and thus alienate A.F.ofL. unionists whom he felt were turning to independent political action at a state level.[48] But there is no evidence to have justified his fears. On the other hand, Eugene Debs, the party's standard bearer, attended the Denver convention and unequivocally supported the new organization as "a radical departure from the effete and reactionary non-political policy of the A.F.ofL."[49]

But with the disasters of DeLeon's dualism so recently in the past, it is not surprising that the Socialist Party as a whole could not endorse the American Labor Union. Influential writers like A. M. Simons and Max S. Hayes, though fully aware of the justification for the new organization, regarded its dualism as dangerous for the future of socialism. Leon Greenbaum, the national secretary of the Party, and the local quorum at St. Louis rejected the American Labor Union outright. Gompers, of course, claimed that Greenbaum and his supporters were overthrown for their defense of the A.F.ofL., but this was untrue.[50] Greenbaum was dismissed for endorsing Job Harriman's Union Labor Party in California and the new national secretary, William Mailly, did not change the Party policy.[51] The 1904 Party convention declared against division in the labor movement.

The American Labor Union had placed the newly formed Socialist Party in an embarrassing position. Confronted by the refusal of the A.F.ofL. to adopt the industrial union policies necessary for the success of socialism, the party nevertheless did not support the new industrially based organization. It was inevitable that some of its members would dissent. Fortunately, the party splits in 1902–03 were not serious, partly because the American Labor Union proved a failure, especially in areas where it might have posed a threat to the A.F.ofL. But the trouble fore-shadowed what was to follow.

In January 1905 a "secret" meeting in Chicago of various left-wing elements produced an "Industrial Unionism Manifesto," which emphasized the sociological changes brought about by industrial advance and the inapplicability of craft unions to the new situation. It therefore called for an "Industrial Conference" to meet in June the same year.

On hearing of the projected conference Gompers immediately went into action and announced that the socialists had called yet another convention to smash the American trade union movement, "the sixth concentrated effort" in a decade. "The socialist trade union smashers and rammers from without, and the borers from within," he announced, "are again joining hands."[52] This view was confirmed by the attendance at the June meeting. "The gathering at Chicago on June 27th," he wrote, "brought together the old elements of the Socialist Trades and Labor Alliance—Daniel De Loeb alias DeLeon, Eugene V. Debs, the Socialist Party candidate for President of the United States, and a few pretending to represent the defunct American Labor Union."[53] Thus, in this and subsequent attacks on the movement which resulted in the

Industrial Workers of the World, Gompers made two points: first, that there was no real dissatisfaction with the existing state of things and no cause for any; and second, that the whole thing was another socialist plot—he lumped all factions together— aimed at the destruction of the trade union movement. Again, Gompers distorted the facts.

The journal of the Western Federation of Miners, one of the most important organizations represented in Chicago, had pro- duced evidence of demands for industrial unionism among A.F.ofL. affiliates. These Gompers dismissed. To the accusation that the Pennsylvania State Federation of Labor had voted for the new plan of organization, he produced a letter from its presi- dent, E. E. Greenwalt, saying that the resolution indeed had been introduced, but, in order to dispose of it, it had been referred to the organizations for their consideration. Gompers also asserted that a resolution supposed to have been adopted by a local of the Baker and Confectionary Workers' International Union demanding affiliation with the American Labor Union—also behind the June convention—was in fact voted down, and put forward only later with forged signatures. He finished with a rather racist statement hinting that opposition only came from Japanese on the west coast.[54]

Gompers was partly right. Few A.F.ofL. unions were at all interested in anything like a repetition of the American Labor Union. Of forty-three organizations represented at the June con- vention, only sixteen were A.F.ofL. affiliated, and of these, eleven were represented by only one local. But this does not mean there was little dissatisfaction. William E. Trautmann was removed from the editorship of the brewers' journal for his unauthorized activity at the Chicago convention, but none could say that indus- trial unionism was not supported in this strongly socialist union.[55] Even a member of the boot and shoe workers union, which had had trouble with the American Labor Union, had to admit that the idea of the conference might have had some merits, and that "all fair union men" would have to admit that the A.F.ofL. could still be enlarged and perfected, though he felt this was no excuse for attacking A.F.ofL. leaders.[56]

Possibly a considerable number of those attending the con- ference—out of 203 delegates, 61 were purely individuals and 72 with no authority to commit their organizations—went with a vague idea of finding a means of obtaining industrial unionism, but were unsure as to how to proceed. This seems to have been the view much later of Joseph Schlossberg, in 1905 a member of the Socialist Labor Party, but at the time he wrote, in 1917, supporting the Socialist Party.

Schlossberg asserted that there had been a demand for an organization to meet the power of combined capital, and went on: "It did not mean the promiscuous organization of all workers in the land in one body. It meant the organization of the working-men with the consciousness of being members of the working class instead of 'tradesmen' workers in a given trade, thus establishing the interdependence and full cooperation of all labor organizations for class interests against the common enemy of the working class. By 1905 that movement gained sufficient form and solidarity to make possible the holding of a great convention in Chicago. There, the new form of organization was given the name industrial unionism." He continued that this industrial unionism, which many sought, was not opposed to agreement with the employer "provided the agreement is made with the organization of all workers involved and is of benefit to them and it is done with the authority and consent of the organized workers." In spite of this, however, Schlossberg concluded that "the organization formed at the convention proved a bitter disappointment to those who had pinned their hopes for the American labor movement to it."[57]

Seeing such genuine demands within the labor movement for industrial unionism—deemed essential for the future of socialism —the party again seemed to fall between two stools. But the response to the 1905 conferences on the part of socialists was far from monolithic.

"What signs are there," asked A. M. Simons, "that the A.F.ofL. is moving towards industrial unionism?" He could find very few. Consequently, he went on to declare that the A.F.ofL. was "something almost wholly distinct from the rank and file of the membership." "Indeed it is practically outside their control," he argued, "and the general effect of educating a man to socialism has been to educate him out of the A.F.ofL., that is out of the official Gompers' machine."[58] Thus, in contrast with his more cautious stand in 1902, Simons took an active part in the industrial movement and even participated in drawing up the original industrial manifesto in January. Like many others involved, he probably hoped for some dramatic mass defection of entire unions from the A.F.ofL. Simons had reservations when he saw DeLeon's interest rising, but nevertheless considered this was no excuse for socialists, especially those in the A.F.ofL., to attack the movement as anarchistic and "impossibilist."[59] After the Chicago meeting he bitterly attacked "the editors of socialist papers and officials of the Socialist Party, who [had] organized unions for the purpose of getting themselves elected to national conventions and posing as trade union leaders," and promised that if they attempted to blacklist anyone who did "not subscribe to the A.F.ofL. catechism," there would be trouble ahead.[60] It is a good indication of how things turned out very differently from what some of the promoters were after, that Simons ended by attacking the I.W.W. and losing the editorship of the *International Socialist Review* as a result.

Though Simons was personally involved in the movement, he also pointed out that while nearly every offiicial of the new organization was a member of the Socialist Party, not one of them, so far as he had been able to discover, wished to involve the party in any way.[61] In being sensitive about this, Simons resembled Max S. Hayes, the labor writer for the *International Socialist Review*. Hayes, unlike Simons, was personally involved in A.F.ofL. affairs. Though not above pointing out I.W.W. successes as justification of the need for change, he was adamant that change had to come from within. Consequently, he joined Victor Berger in refusing an invitation to the January conference. Nevertheless, he thought that Gompers, in lumping all socialist groups together in his attack, was "maliciously attempting to throw discredit on the Socialist Party, otherwise he would have been honest enough to state that some thirty odd persons [at the January meeting] were trying to form a rival organization, and then he could have decently explained the error of taking such a course."[62] Hayes offered to debate with Gompers on the subject but the latter refused, perhaps with good reason. Gompers was perfectly well aware that the new organization was not the child of the Socialist Party. One of his informers at the June convention reported that socialists were ridiculing the whole scheme and predicting that no more conventions would be held.[63]

Of course, the feather in Gompers' cap was Debs, who again unequivocally supported the new movement. He did not attend the January meeting on grounds of ill health, but he took a very active part in the proceedings in June. Afterward, when many original supporters had been repelled by the presence of DeLeon, Debs specifically stated that he was not disgusted by the outcome. He took the trouble to deny that the movement had been captured by DeLeon, but some of his remarks at the conference could have been interpreted as subscribing to the current talk about socialist unity.

Debs' relationship with the Socialist Party is a fascinating subject. His lack of dogmatism and broadly humane views placed him squarely in the revisionist camp, yet his outspoken dislike of the A.F.ofL. made him almost the sole nationally known figure on the left wing of the party. His immense popularity and personal magnetism bore him a large following both within and outside the party, so that he was chosen four times as presidential candidate, yet he remained aloof and detached from its day to day business. Debs was like a flag unfurled every four years, but the rest of the time he seemed to cause constant embarrassment to many of the national office holders.

About the newly founded I.W.W., Victor Berger, for one, wrote: "If Debs stays with that crowd he will land them some prestige for a little while, but I am also sure that would be the end of E. V. Debs." Berger was probably the most vehement in opposing the new organization, and he even had some part in having Trautmann thrown out of the brewery workers' union. Rather extravagantly, he claimed: "There can be no doubt that it is the intention of Trautmann and his coterie to split the trades union movement and lead as big a part of it as they can into the Socialist Trades and Labor Alliance, and then split the socialist movement and lead as many as they can into the Socialist Labor Party."[64] The quarrel between the two became intensified when Trautmann retaliated by unsuccessfully trying to have Berger thrown out of the party for supporting a Democrat in a Milwaukee election.[65]

The intraparty quarrels in 1905–06 seemed so destructive that some attempt was made to declare out of order any correspondence in the party publications dealing with the I.W.W.–A.F.ofL. conflict. But this resolution savored too much of a gag rule and failed to pass. For the moment, most socialists probably approved the resolution of the members of the party in Michigan, who declared themselves to be "thoroughly convinced that the form of organization advocated by the I.W.W., namely industrial unionism, [was] superior to the old form of craft unionism as advocated by the A.F.ofL.," but nevertheless deemed it unwise for the party to endorse the new organization.[66] Neutrality became the order of the day. Fortunately, the immediate course of events in the I.W.W. helped clear the air for the moment.

There was a period of labor and socialist cooperation early in 1906, when three Western Federation of Miners leaders, the union president, Charles A. Moyer, George Pettibone, and William D. Haywood were arrested in Colorado, kidnapped across the state line into Idaho, and charged with the murder of a former governor of Idaho, Frank Steuenberg. Even Gompers participated in fund raising for their defense. But the mood did not last long; even original supporters of the I.W.W. soon became bitterly disappointed.

If Debs was right in asserting that the 1905 conference had not been taken over by DeLeon, he could scarcely say the same of the following one in 1906. Then the administration, most of whom had been Socialist Party members, was overthrown and a new group in which DeLeon was prominent assumed control. The new leaders altered the preamble to the constitution in order to prevent the endorsement of any political party, though they were still committed to some kind of political action.

This position represented a new phase of DeLeonism, brought into being through the master's contact with the anarcho-syndicalism of leaders like William Trautmann. Unlike the old Socialist Trades and Labor Alliance which was really only a trade union appendage to the Socialist Labor Party, the I.W.W. now represented a revolutionary industrial unionism, ultimately aiming at the political conquest of the state. It is this theorization for which DeLeon is best remembered and which was supposed to have influenced Lenin, but, as has recently been shown, the theory was developed by others and only belatedly accepted by DeLeon in order to capture the I.W.W.[67]

DeLeon's victory almost ended the new organization, for immediately afterward a majority of the Western Federation of Miners withdrew. This almost caused a disruption in the Western Federation, but by 1907 the entire body severed all connection. Meanwhile, sensing the rise of socialist strength within the A.F.ofL. unions, and encouraged by the United Mine Workers, the Western Federation reaffiliated with the A.F.ofL. in 1911, though negotiations had started much earlier. The A.F.ofL. socialists naturally regarded this as a considerable accretion in strength.

From 1906 to 1908 the I.W.W. under DeLeon's influence accomplished little. There was some attempt at general organizing of the unskilled, particularly at Goldfield, Nevada, but there was also an attack made upon A.F.ofL. positions in the east. Stagnation was not necessarily due to DeLeon, but opposition to him mounted. DeLeon professed to believe that the political should be a reflection of the economic. His earlier attempt at economic organization, however, the Socialist Trades and Labor Alliance, had been but a shadow of his Socialist Labor Party, and many rightly feared the I.W.W. was heading in the same direction. As a result, DeLeon was overthrown in 1908, and the I.W.W. entered into a most spectacular and most successful phase. It also resulted in the most serious disruption within the Socialist Party thus far.

Generally speaking, critics of the I.W.W. have emphasized two factors about the organization and its unskilled, largely immigrant membership. In the first place, it is argued, the tactics of the I.W.W. were unsound; and second, its temporary recruits were unorganizable on a permanent basis. Thus, John Dyche of the I.L.G.W.U. pointed out: "The I.W.W. wins strikes in Lawrence and then goes on to Patterson, leaving Lawrence workers leaderless."[68] Frank Doyle, a General Board member of the conservative United Garment Workers, claimed he met an I.W.W. organizer in the socialist headquarters and told him to go ahead and organize the shirt makers in Philadelphia with the United Garment Workers' blessing. The reply was that the I.W.W. "didn't have time to bother with small propositions like that." Doyle concluded that the I.W.W. was not willing to organize any kind of union.[69]

Likewise, the socialist A. Rosebury wrote in the *Ladies' Garment Worker:* "These methods have temporarily succeeded among unorganized and untrained and undisciplined workers, among workers who can easily be got to participate in a strike, but whose ideas of the value of maintaining a permanent organization are very hazy and confused."[70] A socialist organizer in Louisiana claimed that socialists attracted by the idea of industrial unions rushed to join the I.W.W., but soon left disappointed.

These statements may be partly true, but nevertheless disguise the real significance of the I.W.W. in labor history. The most recent historian of the organization has shown that its ultimate failure depended neither on wrong tactics nor on the decline of the workers' interest; the real trouble lay in the divisions among the working class that employers could exploit to their own advantage.[71] The striking thing about the I.W.W. is not its failure but its relative success in the face of what proved to be insurmountable difficulties. The general impression left by its experience is that had organization of the unskilled in the East been undertaken by a secure body like the A.F.ofL. the results might have been vastly different.

Some of the more radical unions were prepared to lend support. Gompers complained that when the I.W.W. flooded the country with appeals for funds, they received from various bodies—even A.F.ofL. unions—seven times as much money as was received from the appeals made by A.F.ofL. affiliates.[72] But this was atypical. More often A.F.ofL. unions were willing either to assist employers in breaking I.W.W. strikes, or at least take the opportunity to present themselves as a moderate alternative.

Under these circumstances it was inevitable that many socialists felt the I.W.W. to be worthy of support. While DeLeon's domination lasted, most members of the party were cool. Though the secretary of Local Globe, Arizona, argued that a "pure and simple" socialist was as bad as a pure and simple trade unionist, and that the Socialist Labor Party would sweep the entire west and southwest, William E. Trautmann was unceremoniously dropped from the Socialist Party for speaking under the auspices of the Socialist Labor Party.[73] But with DeLeon's secession and the dramatic impact of the I.W.W. on the country, attitudes were again changing.

The relationship between the I.W.W. and socialism was a curious one. In 1908 the so-called "political clause" of the constitution's preamble was removed, making the aims of the organization entirely economic. In one sense this did not make the I.W.W. antipolitical, but merely nonpolitical in the same way as the A.F.ofL. in the nineties. It certainly did not prevent individual members of the I.W.W. being members of the Socialist Party. William D. Haywood, for instance, even was named to the national executive commitee of the party in 1911. Nevertheless, the anarcho-syndicalism of other leaders gave the movement an antipolitical complexion. It ridiculed the Socialist Party as conservative and placed great stress on "direct action." which apparently could mean anything from strikes in the A.F.ofL. style to sabotage.

It is difficult to determine what groups of socialists were

attracted by the I.W.W. Perhaps rank and file in the west, where the I.W.W. fulfilled greatest needs, were sympathetic. Complaints reached the central office of the Party from Montana that the "unofficial secretary" of the local I.W.W. propaganda league was trying to impose conditions upon applicants for membership of the party that were "contrary to socialist principles," and "at variance with the broad working class character of the party."[74] James D. Graham, an active socialist and later prominent in the Montana State Federation of Labor, however, led in opposing the new movement.

In addition, a number of socialist "intellectuals" who occupied no important office in the party seem to have gone over. Thus Charles H. Kerr, the owner of the *International Socialist Review,* deposed A. M. Simons in 1908 from the editorship. "Long enough we have cringed before the autocracy of labor begging for votes that we did not get," argued the new editor. "Let us put immediate demands out of our platform and leave reformers to wrangle over reform. Let us make it our chief task to spread the propaganda of revolution and of the new industrial unionism."[75] Previously, he wrote: "The events of the past few months have convinced us that the I.W.W., as now reorganized, offers the best available rallying point for socialists on the economic field, and it is on that field that the main battle must be fought and won before capitalism will end."[76]

The young "bohemian" intellectuals in New York, centered around the *Masses* magazine—Max Eastman, John Reed, and Floyd Dell, for instance—naturally found its stress on action appealing. The *Masses* had first been unequivocally anti-I.W.W., and Max Eastman, on assuming the editorship in 1912, claimed it was time to unite the warring factions within the party, but constant articles and reports showed sympathy with the I.W.W. Robert Hunter considered Eastman's review of his book, *Violence and the Labor Movement,* an "infamous libel," and asked Adolph Germer to reply to it.[77]

The official leaders of the party led the socialist opposition to the I.W.W. and for their efforts again faced accusations of conspiring to remain in office illegally. The charge has since been repeated.[78] The argument runs that the impact of the I.W.W. turned men like Haywood into nationally known figures who could secure sufficient votes in party elections to challenge the "old guard" for the first time. The danger of this was signaled by the election of Haywood to the National Executive Committee in 1911.

But to say the motives of the party officials were purely selfish is unrealistic. The A.F.ofL. socialists among them, like Max S. Hayes, Morris Hillquit, and Victor Berger, were aware of rising socialist influence with A.F.ofL. unions and realized how damaging association with the I.W.W. might be. "Come what will," Hayes had argued, "the present trade union movement is bound to go forward, changing its character where necessary to fit conditions as they are met, replacing old leaders with new ones naturally enough, and the very struggles in which it engages will serve to enlighten and discipline the membership until they are in readiness to play their part in changing from one system to another."[79] Hayes' relative success in challenging Gompers as A.F.ofL. president in 1912 must have convinced him.

But in addition to A.F.ofL. ambitions, it was a little much to expect the leaders who spent their lives trying to increase votes to accept an organization that denied the efficacy of political action. "It is foolhardy to declare in one breath that organized co-operative effort is a matter of evolution on the political field," Hayes argued, "while in the industrial shambles all that is required is to prepare a nice little chart, and Presto! the millenium is ushered in." It was illogical to support an organization "with its semi-anarchist, take or hold pronunciamento, and grandiloquent endeavour to shove political action into a secondary position."[80] This was also the argument of John Spargo's book, *Syndicalism, Industrial Unionism and Socialism.*[81]

Besides being illogical, moreover, it was politically inexpedient as the I.W.W. became more and more associated in the public mind with "sabotage." The move of the "old guard," therefore, to expel from the party anyone who advocated violence, was not simply a piece of treachery against left-wing rivals. But this is how it appeared to many in 1913, when Haywood was driven not only from the national executive committee but from the party itself. Considerable numbers of left-wing socialists went with him.

It is impossible to calculate the effect of the "expulsion." A.F.ofL. socialists felt it was the prelude to great victories. "The party is being cleansed of that turbulent element that has marred its growth in the past," Adolph Germer had written to Keir Hardie. "It might result in a split and if so, you will find that the constructive wing of our movement will build up an organization that will challenge the admiration of the world."[82] This was wishful thinking of course; parties rarely grow as a result of expulsions. In fact, some writers have designated 1912 as the turning point in the history of the Socialist Party, after which it steadily declined.[83] These writers partly, if not wholly, attribute this decline to the expulsion of the left. But such reasoning is questionable to say the least. The war question that confronted Americans soon afterward distorted all trends in domestic politics. Moreover, the evidence collected by the most recent writer on the decline of American socialism suggests that the party's momentum continued long after 1912.[84] Still, the dissension over industrial unionism certainly tarnished the Party image, and, as a cause of the failure of socialism, is worth pondering.

It has been argued that Party dissension in itself was a manifestation of socialism's nonviability; that socialism was "in but not of" America. This chapter, on the other hand, has shown that almost all the crises facing the party between its foundation and World War I had their roots in the vital issue of industrial unionism. The experience of other industrial countries, the temporary but significant achievements of the Knights of Labor and the I.W.W.—not to mention the events of the thirties that can be appreciated with hindsight—all point to the fact that the A.F.ofL. during the Gompers' era did much less for American labor as a whole than it set out to do, or could have been expected from it. While it is impossible to determine whether A.F.ofL. initiative in industrial unionism would have assisted the growth of the Socialist Party, as socialists thought, it is nevertheless logical to say that the dissension within the party can be attributed to the A.F.ofL.'s inertia.

But what is the explanation of the A.F.ofL.'s inertia? Most historians, intent on tracing the origins of "business unionism" have scarcely bothered to raise the question. Yet as Chapter II has shown, the class-conscious idealism of people like Gompers and McGuire in the nineties was as strong as most in Europe, and might have been expected to lead to the wider, more militant, even if nonrevolutionary, unionism that socialists anticipated when they abandoned DeLeon and gave their support to the A.F.ofL. Besides, in many respects Gompers' own attitude even after 1900 was more idealistic and less that of the "business unionist" than is often portrayed. Instead of promoting a comprehensive working-class movement, however, the A.F.ofL. seemed to stagnate. This early twentieth-century outlook of the A.F.ofL. must now be examined.

NOTES

1. E.g., Ira Kipnis, *The American Socialist Movement 1897-1912* (New York: Columbia University Press 1952), 236-237.
2. Seattle *Star,* November 8, 1913 (clipping in Max S. Hayes Papers, Ohio State Historical Society, Columbus).
3. Hunter to Adolph Germer, March 18, 1910 (Germer Papers, Wisconsin State Historical Society).
4. John Spargo, *Syndicalism, Industrial Unionism and Socialism* (New York: B. W. Huebsch, 1913), 11.
5. *Federationist,* March, 1894, 16.
6. *Federationist,* April, 1894, 35.
7. *Federationist,* February, 1897, 256.
8. *Federationist,* July, 1901, 251.
9. *Federationist,* July, 1901, 245-247.
10. *Federationist,* December, 1903, 128.
11. Philip Taft, *A. F. of L. in the Time of Gompers,* (New York: Harper, 1957), 196-198.
12. *Federationist,* May, 1912, 371-375.
13. S. G. to Presidents of International Unions, May 24, 1912. (S. G. Copy Books, Library of Congress).
14. A. F. of L., *Proceedings* 1912, 243, 309-312.
15. *Federationist,* 1915, 199, 296-299.
16. A. F. of L., *Proceedings* 1903, 160-161.
17. See Eugene Staley, *A History of the Illinois State Federation of Labor* (Chicago: University of Chicago Press, 1930), 227 and A. F. of L. *Proceedings* 1911, 192-3, 305.
18. Ed Wallace, "Industrial Unionism and How to Attain It," *United Mine Workers Journal,* June 6, 1913, 4 and September 4, 1913, 2. James Lord was coauthor of the second article.
19. *U. M. W. J.,* June 13, 1912, 1, 3.
20. United Mine Workers, *Proceedings* 1914, 353-361.
21. United Mine Workers, *Proceedings* 1914, 353-361.
22. *Federationist,* March, 1904, 241-242.
23. E.g., Max S. Hayes, "World of Labor," *I. S. R.,* September, 1902, 185.
24. *Federationist* July, 1902, 374-375.
25. A. F. of L., *Proceedings* 1888, 14.
26. S. V. Lindholm, "The Chicago Lockout," *I. S. R.,* August, 1900, 65.
27. *Federationist,* December, 1902, 925.
28. A. H. Dickerson, a federal labor union organizer, sent several dismal reports to Gompers, August 9, 1905; April 20, 1907. (A. F. of L. Papers, Wisconsin State Historical Society, Madison).
29. Staley, *History of Illinois State Federation of Labor,* 227 ff.
30. See Lewis Lorwin, *The American Federation of Labor* (Washington D.C.: The Brookings Institution, 1933), 348-349.
31. Columbia University Oral History Project, *Brophy Memoir,* 721, 756.
32. Columbia University Oral History Project, *Eva Valesh Memoir,* 107-109, 139-140.
33. Vernon H. Jensen, *Heritage of Conflict: Labor Relations in the Non-ferrous Metals Industry up to 1930* (Ithaca: Cornell University Press, 1950), 69.

34. Jensen, *Heritage of Conflict,* 66.
35. *Federationist,* May, 1902, 237-239.
36. *Federationist,* April, 1905, 214-217.
37. *Federationist,* November, 1903, 1189.
38. *Federationist,* July, 1902, 376.
39. *I. S. R.,* July, 1902, 46-49.
40. *I. S. R.,* September, 1902, 187.
41. Melvyn Dubofsky, "The Origins of Western Working Class Radicalism, 1880-1905," *Labor History* VII, 2 (Spring, 1966), 131-155.
42. *Federationist,* May, 1902, 238.
43. *I. S. R.,* August, 1902, 107-109.
44. *I. S. R.,* July, 1902, 47.
45. *I. S. R.,* November, 1902, 257 ff.
46. *I. S. R.,* July, 1902, 56.
47. Kipnis, *American Socialist Movement,* 150.
48. Harriman to Hillquit, March 10, 1903 (Hillquit Papers, Wisconsin State Historical Society).
49. *I. S. R.,* November, 1902, 257.
50. A. F. of L., *Proceedings* 1903, 197.
51. See argument contained in *Cigar Makers Official Journal* November 15, 1903, 4; December 15, 1903, 6-7; January 15, 1904, 5-6.
52. *Federationist,* March, 1905, 139-141.
53. *Federationist,* August, 1905, 514.
54. *Federationist,* May, 1905, 282-284.
55. *Weekly Bulletin* (United Garment Workers), May 12, 1905, 5.
56. *Shoe Workers Journal,* June, 1905, 23-24.
57. *Advance* (Amalgamated Clothing Workers), July 6, 1917, 4.
58. *I. S. R.,* August, 1905, 69.
59. *I. S. R.,* April, 1905, 623-627.
60. *I. S. R.,* August, 1905, 76-77.
61. *I. S. R.,* August, 1905, 76.
62. *I. S. R.,* May, 1905, 692-695.
63. Part of a letter dated June 1905 (A. F. of L. Papers, Wisconsin State Historical Society).
64. Berger to Hillquit, March 27, 1905 (Hillquit Papers).
65. Berger to Hillquit, April 8, 28, 1905 (Hillquit Papers).
66. S. P. *Weekly Bulletin,* October 2, 1906.
67. Don K. McKee, "Daniel DeLeon: A Reappraisal." *Labor History I,* 3 (Fall, 1960), esp. 276.
68. John A. Dyche, "The I. W. W. and the Unskilled," *Ladies Garment Worker,* April, 1914, 12-14.
69. Frank Doyle, "The Way They Organize," *Weekly Bulletin* (U. G. W.), November 22, 1912, 1.
70. A. Rosebury, "Industrialism, The Bugbear of Society," *Ladies Garment Worker,* July, 1912, 15-18.
71. Melvyn Dubofsky, *We Shall Be All: a History of the I. W. W.* (Chicago: Quadrangle Books, 1969), 256-258.
72. S. G. to Executive Council, A. F. of L., July 20, 1912. (A. F. of L. Papers).
73. S. P. *Weekly Bulletin,* May 24, 1906. S. P. Special Circular, July 26, 1906.
74. Statement dated May 1913, Montana File, S. P. Papers, Duke.
75. *I.S.R.,* November 1909, 451.
76. *I.S.R.,* October 1909, 360.
77. Hunter to Germer, June 30, 1914 (Germer Papers).

78. Kipnis, *The American Socialist Movement*, 376, 390.
79. *I.S.R.*, September 1905, 182.
80. S. P. *Weekly Bulletin*, April 13, 1907.
81. John Spargo, *Syndicalism, Industrial Unionism and Socialism* (New York: B. W. Huebsch, 1913).
82. Germer to Kier Hardie, February 18, 1913 (Germer Papers).
83. E.g., Kipnis, *The American Socialist Movement*, 418, 424.
84. James K. Weinstein, *The Decline of Socialism in America 1912-1925* (New York: Vintage Books, 1967).

5

"Gompersism"

In view of the dominant position of Samuel Gompers, the term "Gompersism" might best sum up the outlook of the A.F.ofL. in the early twentieth century. Usually it is portrayed as a simple philosophy: a rejection of socialism combined with an attempt to integrate labor into the mainstream of American capitalism. In the official accounts "Gompersism" is the beginning of "pressure group" trade unionism, the path that leads inevitably to today's voluntaristic, consensus society.

While this aspect was clearly one side of what Gompers stood for, it is only part of the whole picture and taken in isolation gives a distorted impression. This chapter attempts to describe the rather complex whole of "Gompersism," at once violently anti-socialist and in curious ways more radical than the Socialist Party. Supposedly apolitical, "Gompersism" led to involvement in politics in a way that alternately encouraged and dismayed socialists. Explained on appropriate occasions to be without final aims, it anticipated nevertheless the evolution of a better social order.

It is certainly not difficult to see how a very simplistic conception of "Gompersism" should have evolved. Clearly, by the turn of the century, Gompers was given to periodic diatribes against socialism. Previously he had forcefully rejected political action, and he had violent quarrels with the Socialist Labor Party leaders, but during the nineties his "pure and simple" trade unionism was antipolitical, not necessarily antisocialist, and he retained much of the socialist outlook. After 1900, however, his dislike of particular socialists became transferred to the Socialist Party as a whole. He justified his position by associating the Socialist Party with "dual unionism." But it went further than this; the vilification of the Socialist Party, revisionist or not, came to be one of Gompers' chief objects in life. "I declare it to you," he said in 1903, "I am not only at variance with your doctrines, but with your philosophy. Economically you are unsound, socially you are

111

wrong, industrially you are impossible."[1] This was at the Boston convention—the "climax" according to Gompers, when socialists were resoundingly defeated. "They live in a sphere all by themselves," he said the following year. "A sphere ethereal and fanciful."[2] In 1905 he claimed he was indifferent rather than antisocialist, but by 1908 he was making positively libelous suggestions that Debs' campaign funds were provided by antiunion capitalists.[3] From these statements, the rejection of socialism and the Socialist Party could scarcely be clearer.

The more positive aspects of "Gompersism"—the attempted integration of labor into American capitalist society—can be interpreted in Gompers' support for the National Civic Federation. As early as 1901 he wrote: "Proper enquiry may lead to the conclusion that despite the clamor which we hear and the conflicts which occasionally occur, there is a constant trend towards agreement between the laborer and capitalists, employed and employer, for the uninterrupted production and distribution of wealth, and too, with ethical consideration for the common interests of all the people."[4] This was the professed belief of the Civic Federation, born at an industrial conference in New York in December 1902 and composed of "some of the largest employers of labor, some of the most conspicuous representatives of organized labor, as well as famous men in public life."[5]

Gompers, of course, had reservations. "It is an error for anyone to believe that the employers who met with representatives of organized labor . . . have suddenly become converts to the cause of unionism," he said. "Or that the representatives of organized labor have changed their attitude upon any essential feature."[6] He had few illusions about giant corporations. The Social Darwinist in him regarded "combinations of capital" as inevitable: "a matter of economy and development and strength."[7] But they interfered with politics and the courts and could be used against the public interest. Though the "logical and inevitable accompaniment and development of the industrial system," the trust was "the voluntary association of the few for their own benefit." The trade union, on the other hand, was "the voluntary association of the many for the benefit of all the community." It was to be found in the "vanguard of public opinion" in attempting to find solutions for the abuses of trusts.[8] Nevertheless, Gompers felt he could work with the representatives of the corporations to achieve industrial harmony.

The National Civic Federation was apparently founded by
Ralph Easley, a Chicago newspaperman, who gave the plan to
the Republican boss, Mark Hanna. Hanna was thus not actually
involved in the foundation, but socialists claimed he gave it real
life, a view shared, interestingly enough, by Terence V. Powderly,
by then in retirement.[9] It has recently been described as the
harbinger of every reform movement from the New Deal to the
"Great Society"—a sincere attempt to deal with social problems
without altering the basic tenets of American capitalism. It is
asserted that the large manufacturers involved—smaller ones remained adamantly opposed to unions—sincerely tried to work
with trade unions for the benefit of all.[10]

Probably all this is true, but motives are usually mixed. One
critic claimed that Easley told Mark Hanna that "the vanity of
the labor leaders could be played upon, and coupled with the
opinions that they sometimes voiced regarding the identity of
interests between the employer and his employee, could be turned
to great advantage, if proper means were utilized."[11] Socialists
naturally stressed the National Civic Federation's negative antisocialism rather than its positive aspects. Hillquit considered it
an insidious poison intended "to rob labor of its independence,
virility and militant enthusiasm."[12] But Gompers didn't see it this
way; one early Civic Federation pamphlet was entitled, *Samuel
Gompers: Socialism's Ablest Foe.*

"Gompersism," therefore, might be described as a rejection of
socialism combined with a search for respectability for labor in its
acceptance by American society as a whole. But to leave it at that
is to attempt to simplify what in fact was very complex. Gompers
probably did feel that his outlook was very simple at times, and
there are innumerable scraps of evidence, plus his memoirs of the
early twenties to confirm this. But at other times he showed himself
to have been very much in two minds: one moment accepting the
theoretical classlessness of American society and the soundness of
its institutions; another moment suspicious of the capitalist system
and its political influence. Most important was his basic mistrust
of politics and determination to rely solely upon economic organization. This policy dominated the outlook of the A.F.ofL. in the
nineties and it survived into the twentieth century. In effect, it
constituted a "syndicalist" side of "Gompersism," which must be
explored.

One thing is clear: Gompers continued to regard the A.F.ofL.

as a class movement, and at times resented any suggestion that it was not. Hugh McGregor, an "old crony" of Gompers', wrote in the *American Federationist:* "Since the time when the workers of this country banded together as workers, and not as citizens, the trade unions have remained a standing manifestation of class-consciousness."[13] This echoes Gompers' statement of a few years earlier, that there was "no other organization of labor in the entire world that is so class conscious as the trade unions."[14] In 1907 he argued that the trade union was "the only successful attempt to give voice to the voiceless masses." "In every trade, in every community where trade unions exist," he argued, "they are recognized as the spokesmen of the workers and in fact of all except the employing and the idle rich classes."[15]

Gompers seems to have retained a theoretical view of class, which seems strangely at variance with his "Americanism." As late as 1902 he seemed anxious to show that trade unionism rather than the Socialist Party was truly Marxist. Of Karl Marx, he said: "There is not a socialist that can find in all his utterances one word for the co-operative commonwealth."[16] "Under the present rules of the game," he wrote in 1916, "the power to control opportunity, whether political, economic or social, is held by those who manipulate the financial agencies of society and thereby control credit. Those who do the real creative work have been dominated by exploiters who usurped the glory and benefits of their achievements. The real power that governs our national life and development is exercised from Wall Street."[17] This statement might have been influenced by the particular events of the time, but even in his memoirs, Gompers writes: "Whoever or whatever controls economic power directs and shapes development for the group or the nation."[18] This seems like a harder line than the Socialist Party's.

A very "Marxist view" of power, of course, does not make a Marxist. Gompers offered no immediate solution to the problem of economic and political power, other than the day-to-day demands of the trade unions. But as he answered Morris Hillquit before the Industrial Relations Commission, these demands could never be satisfied.[19] Considering this statement alongside Gompers' very Marxist concept of power, Hillquit obviously had a point in asserting that Gompers' views were not basically different from the socialists'—even if Gompers chose not to push his arguments to their logical conclusion. The Industrial Relations Commission interview troubled Ralph Easley. "In one place the record has you practically admitting that the unions' goal is to take 'all,' which is about what the socialists propose," he wrote to Gompers. "Hasn't the reporter got that mixed up?"[20]

But Hillquit missed one of Gompers' basic beliefs: his mistrust of politics and the power of the state. Any change in the power structure had to come in the industrial field. Thus at the A.F.ofL. convention in 1900, he denied that the ballot was the only way out, and insisted there was more character built up by the strike than "by a decade of schooling."[21] This "syndicalist" aspect of Gompers' thought contrasts sharply with the views of the Socialist Party, which on the whole seemed to have much greater faith in the efficacy of American institutions. For example, Gompers attacked the American Association for Labor Legislation for efforts to pass health insurance bills as in England and Germany, claiming it was dangerous to give politicians more power. Health insurance schemes, moreover, smacked of more power to employers. When socialist Meyer London brought forward a resolution in Congress for the appointment of a commission to prepare a plan for the establishment of a national insurance fund, Gompers objected. "It has been the constant struggle of the workers through the ages," he maintained, "to get the tentacles of government from the throats of the workers."[22] Besides, measures like social insurance, he felt, took the virility out of trade unions —as in England.[23] Naturally, Gompers was sensitive about suggestions that workers enjoyed better conditions in countries where such legislation existed.

Proposed legislation for shorter hours also found Gompers at odds with socialists. When the issue of an eight-hour law arose at the A.F.ofL. convention in 1916, Gompers remarked, "Do you know where the eight-hour law in California originated? It was started by the Socialist Party of California."[24] That seemed to be a sufficient reply. But the previous year he had made a rather odd statement on the subject in the *Mine Workers Journal*. "The citizens of the United States have regard for the substance of the thing rather than the form," he had argued. "They care more for justice because it is justice than they do for mere enactment of a law." Then Gompers went on: "There is nothing in the history or practice of our country that would lead anyone to think that the citizens of the U. S. hedge laws about in any degree of sanctity, that makes them resent the violation of a law rather than the violation of a principle of justice."[25] From this, the miners were presumably to conclude that, since social legislation was either unnecessary or ineffective, there was no point in having any.

This dispute gave rise to a rather interesting altercation between Gompers and Ed Wallace, the socialist editor of the *Mine Workers Journal*. Wallace had demanded legislation both on general principles and because of the benefits that would accrue to the unorganized, particularly the steel workers. This reference to the unorganized whose plight the socialists constantly had in mind in advocating industrial unionism naturally stung Gompers. In reply, he argued that legislation only weakened the union and would not help the unorganized since the laws were only empty statutes. His conclusion was that only force in the form of the strike was effective. The aim should be organization, which in turn depended upon the spirit being there. The A.F.ofL. had tried with the steel workers—to no avail!

Ed Wallace's reply was unanswerable. The reason for the lack of spirit among the steel workers was precisely the long hours that legislation could overcome. Even the political boss, William S. Barnes, had argued that legislation would only make the workers more restless in their demands. In reply, Gompers took umbrage at having been compared with the boss of New York State.[26]

Of course, it can be argued that "syndicalism" is the wrong expression and that Gompers' mistrust of big government was merely an expression of traditional American "voluntarism." This view is partly justified, for the distinction is somewhat arbitrary in the American context. Saul Yanovsky, the editor of the Ladies Garment Workers journal, once remarked: " 'A Jeffersonian Democrat,' as Gompers expressed himself recently—that is, three-quarters anarchist."[27] But another writer, Juliet Stewart Poyntz, expressed the point better. "We are the native home of social anarchism. The workers get little and hope for little through political action. The capitalist uses his control of politics merely as a convenient additional weapon in the great industrial battle."[28] This seems closer to Gompers' views at the height of his career than the feeble statement in his memoirs to the effect that American institutions were "founded upon the basic principle of equality and American labor had to make plain that it did not request special privilege but equality of opportunity."[29]

Gompers was well aware that the American political tradition was one of equality and consensus. In his view the function of

European socialism was to elevate the working class to a position of full citizenship—a position that Americans had achieved before industrialization. Thus, as John Mitchell expressed it: "The American-bred wage earner does not wish to be the ward of any man or system—classified, numbered, tagged and obliged to carry a card of identification or be subjected to police control or employing class supervision. In fact, the American wage worker who is the product of our general system of education is about the equal of his fellow citizens, and needs only the fair opportunities promised in our republic to work out his own salvation."[30]

But Gompers was also aware of the difficulties of the American position. "Our task was more difficult than that of the British labor movement in dealing with similar issues," he reflected. "England accepted class distinctions and was willing to enact legislation giving wage earners relief without concerning herself closely as to the underlying philosophy that justified the action."[31] In 1912 he summed up the American situation perfectly:

> Nowhere has greater progress been made than here; nowhere have employers of labor been more generally convinced of the justice and practicability and the humanitarian basis of our movement, and it is equally true that nowhere in the civilized world is there such relentless, bitter, brutal war made upon the labor organization and the laboring men as here in the United States. In no country on the face of the globe is corporate wealth, the position of wealth, so powerful as it is here.[32]

Thus, "voluntarism" may be one way of expressing what Gompers stood for, but frustration over the domination of government by capital and the determination to counter this power by economic action makes his "voluntarism" more like European syndicalism. This is borne out by the manner in which Gompers associated his policies with the syndicalist movements then sweeping Europe.

Several articles appeared in the *American Federationist* between 1908 and 1914 showing something of Gompers' thought. The first was a commentary on an accompanying article by William English Walling, the American syndicalist who was to take strong exception to socialist plans for a labor party the following year. Walling, it must be remembered, was an associate of the intellectual socialists at the time, but he was not a party member. To Walling, syndicalism involved two ideas: first, completely freeing the trade union movements from any kind of political influences, such as he believed had been accomplished at the Stuttgart congress; and second, the gradual assumption of power by the labor movement in bringing about a new state of society. In Sorel's words, syndicalism was "the irreconcilable enemy of every despotism, moral or material, individual or collective, including that of the proletariat." Lagardelle, another exponent, explained that although the new movement dropped the old Marxist shibboleths of revolution, it understood "Marx's advice to the working class to go into politics, not as calling for the formation of a political party, but as signifying only that the struggle of labor against capital must eventually become a political struggle in the largest sense of that term, that the working people must some day gain the power of influencing society as a whole."[33]

If Lagardelle as interpreted by Walling was really what European syndicalism was about, then in some ways it was as closely related to the A.F.ofL. as to the I.W.W., with which it is usually associated. As the labor historian Selig Perlman phrased it, syndicalism was merely "a clever working-class strategem to get rid of the intellectuals."[34] This also seems to have been the point of view of Gompers. Of Walling's interpretation he wrote: "The article is especially important, not only as showing the trend of the trade union movement in other countries, but as exemplifying in its philosophy some phases of the situation in this country. We have for many years held that the labor unions must be free and independent of all other class movements and that politically they must consider the interests of the workers as above that of any political party, no matter how aggressive or how friendly the politics of such a party might be."[35]

In 1908 Gompers was most concerned with French syndicalism. By 1910 he drew lessons from the movements in Sweden, Hungary, Italy, Germany, and even Great Britain, all of which caused him to believe that labor organizations in these countries were "coming out of their early crudities."[36] In other words, Gompers was not deceived by the apocalyptic writings of syndicalist intellectuals. In essence the syndicalist movement was the divorce of trade unionism from politics, such as the A.F.ofL. had already achieved. "Nine tenths of their work [was] just the same as that of the A.F.ofL."[37]

European political socialism, in Gompers' scheme of things, aimed primarily at American-style political equalty; social and economic justice, both in Europe and America, could only be obtained through trade unionism. Yet, paradoxically, it was inevitable that even Americans would have to pay some attention to politics. One critic pointed out in 1902 that the platform of the A.F.ofL. and most of the declarations passed at its annual conventions were meaningless without political action,[38] but for the moment Gompers ignored this. What changed his mind was a series of court decisions threatening the entire position of the trade union organization so painfully erected during the preceding generation. Gompers' attention to politics thus was a negative one; it was a purely preventive measure. Nevertheless, it was to become another element in "Gompersism."

Trouble with the courts had been brewing for some time, but for the most part only on a local level. Max S. Hayes had noted in 1902, for instance, that in Michigan a suit could be brought against "unincorporated voluntary associations,"[39] but this apparently received scant attention. Within a few years, however, the writing was on the wall. Two cases, *Lowe v. Lawlor,* usually known as the Danbury Hatters 'Case, and *Buck Stove and Range Co. v. Gompers,* placed the right of boycott in jeopardy. The United Hatters were sued under the Sherman Act in the first case, and individual members would have had their homes foreclosed but for collections made by the A.F.ofL. In the second, Gompers, Morrison, and Mitchell only escaped jail sentences by a technicality for contempt of court, when they refused to obey an injunction restraining publication of their boycott. A third case, *Hitchman Coal and Coke Co. v. Mitchell,* upheld the so-called yellow-dog contract making union organization almost impossible. All three cases were finally disposed of by the Supreme Court and therefore involved several years' litigation, but by 1906 decisions in lower courts showed which way the wind was blowing. The Supreme Court's 1908 decision in the Danbury Hatters' Case, making the Sherman Act applicable to trade unions, was attacked by Gompers as "the most drastic and far-reaching decision it had ever handed down."[40] Even he could scarcely remain complacent, though only one year previously he had justified his nonpolitical stand as the best position for America because, unlike Europe, they had these guarantees of freedom which gave the United States "the opportunity for evolution rather than revolution."[41]

The general effect of the cases was a sense of crisis throughout socialist and labor circles in America, starting in 1906 when home and personal bank accounts of members of the Danbury

Hatters were attached pending the decision of the courts. Perhaps the long years of litigation lessened the drama of the final decisions, but 1906 was a turning point in American labor history—comparable to the Taff Vale decision in Great Britain—but when American labor, for better or for worse, failed to turn.

After the Supreme Court's decision in 1908, the *American Federationist* carried a symposium giving the opinion of labor leaders on what should be done. John B. Lennon, treasurer of the A.F.ofL., thought that unless the Supreme Court reversed its decision there would be a division in the United States on industrial-political lines, as in Germany and England. "If the wage-workers in this country become thoroughly convinced that there is no policy to pursue except that of independent politics," he added, "they will pursue it with a vim and determination and effectiveness that has never been dreamed of by the workers of any country in the world." John Golden, president of the United Textile Workers, considered they were now "passing through the same ordeal that the British trade unionists passed through a few years ago, when it was sought to destroy the power and the effectiveness of the trade unions of Great Britain through and by the aid of the courts. . . . The British trade unionist rose to the occasion. He met the issue squarely, with the result that he sent a fighting force to Parliament, not to knock at the door and plead for his wrongs to be redressed but vested with power and authority to take the floor of the British Parliament and fight for what he considered were his rights and privileges."[42] On the socialist side, Max S. Hayes wrote he was "firmly convinced that the hour [had] struck when calm and cool consideration of the present crises [was] absolutely necessary." Attempting to look at the situation "from the most unbiased standpoint possible, as a socialist and member of a trade union, and with no ill-will towards Samuel Gompers as a man," he wanted to sink their differences and get together in a national conference. Hayes considered this to be the desire of the rank and file everywhere, and he thought that Americans could "proceed along lines of the British socialists and trade unionists."[43]

The demand for a labor party was echoed throughout the succeeding years by many trade unionists at conventions and in the journals. In the A.F.ofL. too, the idea came up at every convention. In 1908 Gompers called a conference in Washington attended by representatives of some of the Railroad Brotherhoods and even some farmers' organizations.[44] For a time, certain members of the executive council took on the title of Labor's Representative Committee, which, even though it did not pursue independent politics, gave the A.F.ofL. a vaguely labor party complexion. One of the more prominent A.F.ofL. organizers tried to call a conference of state federations for the purpose of nominating a presidential candidate. This caused Gompers to write to the presidents of all state federations dissuading them from such a course.[45] With all this feverish activity, it is not surprising that members of the Socialist Party's national executive committee should start laying plans about how to proceed should a labor party be forthcoming.

However, after demands for a labor party over several years, the Committee on Resolutions at the 1913 convention made a statement that seemed significant at the time. Answering a call for "an American Labor Party," and for the Executive Committee to formulate a program and platform, and to approach the leaders of the Socialist Party, Women's Suffrage Leagues, Farmers' National and State Unions, the Railroad Brotherhoods, inviting them to a conference "for the purpose of establishing a working agreement that [would] provide the means of joint action upon the political field," the committee reported that the time was still not right. "While our political developments are encouragingly progressive and should be continued and further developed in the future," it declared, "time has not arrived when, with due regard to the economic movement still young and hopeful in organization, a distinct labor political party should be formed, therefore we are confident that, when our present political activities have suitably matured, a new political party will be the logical result, a party in which will be amalgamated the reform and humanitarian forces, which will represent and stand for protection and supremacy of human rights, giving legislative expression to the sound economic and political position that the producers of wealth are entitled."[46] This is what Lewis Lorwin refers to as a "vague promise."[47] Vague or not, the committee's report got the support of the chief socialist spokesman in the A.F.ofL., Max S. Hayes.

But it was purely talk. Gompers already had entered politics as much as he was going to. What he evolved was what he called his "non-partisan policy"—a policy of "reward your friends, and punish your enemies," irrespective of party. Gompers claimed there was nothing new in his nonpartisan political philosophy, though previously it had not been expressly formulated. In 1908, for the first time, he drew up his "historic bill of labor's grievances," to be presented to both parties, and continued this system at each election afterward. At first he was not too hopeful of the results and stressed instead the educational value of the campaign, but by 1909 he claimed that "at least eighty percent of organized labor's forces voted in accordance with the recommendations of our Federation."[48] Looking back later, he wrote that the reactionaries were definitely in retreat and with the election of Woodrow Wilson "the verdict was clearly interpreted by members of Congress in the short session of the 62nd Congress, and labor measures received unprecedented attention."[49]

All this sounded impressive, but in fact Gompers grossly exaggerated the benefits accruing to labor from his policy. The La Follette Seamen's Act undoubtedly was of great benefit to one sector of American labor, but its passage owed more to the racist appeals of Andrew Furuseth, the seamen's leader, than to the justice of his cause or to the A.F.ofL.'s political tactics. Only Furuseth's claim that bad conditions were driving white men from the seas insured sufficient congressional support for the bill.[50]

The Clayton Anti-Trust Act, "Labor's Magna Carta," as Gompers called it, was claimed as the crowning achievement of his policies. In freeing trade unions from the provisions of anti-trust legislation, he believed it had removed the legal burdens under which labor had suffered since 1906 and which had forced labor into politics in the first place. "The most far-reaching declaration ever made by any government in the history of the world," was his verdict, referring to the phrase, "the labor of a human being is not a commodity or an article of commerce."[51]

Socialists writing in the St. Louis Labor lost no time in contrasting the ecstasy of Gompers over the Clayton Act with the attitude concerning the Supreme Court's annulment of a Kansas act preventing employers dismissing men because they were unionists.[52] But it was not just a question of what the Clayton Act omitted; the Act itself was useless to American Labor. This was not proved until Supreme Court decisions after World War I, but enough voices were raised at the time—and not only among socialists—pointing out the worthlessness of the Act. Gompers, of course, had dismissed such arguments, but perhaps his own fears account for the rather desperate tone of his extravagant praise.[53]

The benefits accruing to labor from Gompers' political policies are therefore questionable, to say the least. One member of the United Mine Workers called it "Reward and get punished" at the hands of the Democrats.[54] But the impact of the nonpartisan policy on American labor amounted to nothing less than the gradual commitment of American labor to the Democratic Party. The possibility of collusion with the Socialist Party became more and more remote.

Some socialists and labor party advocates, like Max S. Hayes, early welcomed the departure from "pure and simple" trade unionism, as bound to lead to the formation of a Labor Party like Great Britain's, or to the "endorsement" of the Socialist Party as the one party that would give unqualified support to labor's demands. But they were bound to disillusionment. A. M. Simons came nearer the mark; he believed that although "the socialist movement was making itself felt," Gompers' policy, taken in conjunction with other statements, looked like a "wide spread plot to side-track socialist sentiment."[55]

Whether deliberate or not, this was perhaps the inevitable result of Gompers' move. He might declare his political action to be genuinely nonpartisan and continue to harp on it, but it really meant selling labor to the higher bidder of the two older parties exclusively. When this became obvious, he justified it in terms of political habits. "Political conditions are such in the United States that the wage earners have been united to one or the other of the two strong political parties and they are bound to these parties by ties of fealty and of tradition," he argued. "It would take years ever to separate any considerable numbers of workers from their fealty to the old party."[56]

Curiously enough, he also claimed to be encouraged in "nonpartisanship" by the British trade unionists. These were the days of the "Lib-labs" when the whole future of the Labour Party as an independent force was in doubt. "The stand of our English brothers was not for socialism, or to form a labor party," Gompers maintained. "They rallied around organizations to fight the decisions of a court, just as we shall have to do now.[57] Gompers got some encouragement from the British themselves. The *Federationist* was full of quotes like that from the English socialist Pete Curran: "If I were in the United States, I should, as a socialist, vote for Bryan." In this way Gompers could insist that American trade unionists still followed the British model, as opposed to the continental socialists' one.[58] By 1910, however, he switched his line. Pointing out that Keir Hardie's prophecies of one hundred labor members had not materialized, he concluded that "the A.F.ofL. [was] on the right political road—at least for America."[59]

The "nonpartisan policy" of relying only on the two old parties did not go unchallenged. Voices within the A.F.ofL. in 1906 warned that "while you stand today, divided between two old parties, looking for your friends in these old camps, you will never succeed in marching one foot forward."[60] In 1908 and in subsequent presidential campaigns, Gompers was bombarded with demands either that the A.F.ofL. remain apolitical or that the Socialist Party be made part of the "nonpartisan" system. These came chiefly from local trade unions and city centrals. The *New Republic,* much to Gompers' annoyance, referred to the A.F.ofL. as going "cap in hand, a self-distrustful supplicant to the ante-rooms and lobbies of the two great parties."[61] Gompers, for his part, claimed that his political movement was not restricted and on occasion did support the Socialist Party on a local level. Nevertheless, he took the trouble to state: "The votes the organized workers give in support of certain radical parties in other localities is less an indication of an acceptance of platform theories than testimony that the immediate practical demands of these parties are in accord with the needs of the wage earners and the communities concerned at the present hour."[62] This was probably true, but his dichotomy between immediate aims and final goals was obviously intended to harm the Socialist Party. Recounting these events in 1917, he claimed that "adopting the socialist political party could not [have been] separated from adopting the socialist theory, socialist utopia, socialist impossibilism, and socialist tactics," most of which was manifestly untrue, whatever he meant by "adopting."[63] But it was not merely a question of "not adopting" the Socialist Party, but of refusing to give credit where it was due, even within his "nonpartisan scheme."

Had the A.F.ofL. and its affiliates maintained an entirely free hand, as Gompers liked to maintain they did, his position might have been unassailable. For instance, two years before embarking on the "nonpartisan" policy, Gompers said it would be "as illogical to commit the labor movement to the Socialist Party, as it would be to commit it to the Republican or Democratic parties."[64] But through the years his policy encouraged what he strove to avoid, in that he got the A.F.ofL. bound up with one of the parties—by "lending the support of organized labor to political machines and cliques."[65]

This was especially so at the level of city centrals and state federations. Since official positions in these labor organizations were unpaid or part-time, local leaders sought political appointments as a means of livelihood. Then once in politics, these men could make themselves popular with the unionists through concessions acquired by political pull. One critic summed it up: "The labor unions are kept quiet and harmless by the stale trick of throwing a few political jobs to a few labor leaders, who in most cases at once forget their zeal for the cause of labor." Once elected, they tended either to sell out or be relegated to obscurity.[66]

All this, of course, did not depend on Gompers' nonpartisan policy. As early as 1900 the Cleveland *Citizen* claimed that city central bodies were an easy prey for the "workingmen's friend" and that "a little influence and beer" could secure endorsement for any office seeker.[67] In other words, the system was widespread long before 1906. But J. H. Maurer, for instance, believed that Gompers' politics led to all sorts of abuses and made large sections of the labor movement easy prey for corrupt politicians.[68] Duncan McDonald of the Mine Workers claimed that he knew of one man who campaigned for the Democratic Party at A.F.ofL. expense. And even worse, McDonald pointed out instances where, because the Democratic Party obtained such influence in the labor movement, the A.F.ofL. was actually supporting Democrats when the Republican candidate himself was a unionist. Naturally, McDonald was one of those aware that the Socialist Party did not seem to come into the so-called nonpartisan movement.[69]

Thus far, we have examined the outlook and policies of the president of the A.F.ofL., but a fuller understanding of "Gompersism" also depends upon appreciating the structure and procedures of the A.F.ofL. Between 1881 and the turn of the century, the oganization had developed gradually; personal, accidental, and environmental circumstances all had a part. But by around 1900 certain groups found themselves in control and the hitherto fluid organization tended to harden. The *status quo* of narrow craft unionism and hostility to socialism had to be preserved. At all levels there were leaders with a vested interest in keeping things exactly as they were.

State federations naturally had a political function and it is therefore not surprising that some were the breeding ground of

third-party politics. Their ability to influence the A.F.ofL., however, was severely limited constitutionally.

City central bodies had once been all-important in the labor
movement and were also historically inclined to adventures. In
1902 the central at Milwaukee made an attempt at a union of
central bodies that caused Gompers some alarm, but it came to
nothing.[70] Still, the A.F.ofL. remained a little afraid of city
organizations and its attitude toward them was highly contra-
dictory. Though an essential part of the trade union movement,
their potentiality as centers of radicalism and independent political
activity caused the federative body to weaken them financially
and constitutionally. Their position in the A.F.ofL. structure was
highly vulnerable, since their charters could be revoked without
much ado.

The basic unit of the A.F.ofL., however, was the national trade
union. In the American experience, production and distribution
on a national scale had to be balanced by union organization on
the same scale. The high degree of labor mobility also required
nationwide control of the labor force in a given trade or industry
if the union was to be effective. Thus the primacy of the national
trade union over other forms of organization is not in dispute.

What we are concerned with here is whether this primacy
excludes the possibility of working class politics. From the
perspective of America since World War II, it has seemed axiomatic that the preponderance of collective bargaining, to the
exclusion of all other activity, is simply the American middle class
psyche in action. In other words, it is held that although union
membership signifies permanent wage-earner status, labor politics
are of no interest to American workers whose aims are irrevocably
middle class. If collective bargaining provides the means of a
middle class style of life, why bother with European-style parties?[71]

If this describes labor attitudes today, it does not do justice to
the situation in the early part of the century. Many of the more
successful unions that did engage in collective bargaining did not
find this incompatible with radical politics. The socialist unionists
did not aim at one form of activity rather than another; they aimed
at both. As we have seen, a radical outlook in politics often contributed to the strength of the union.

On the other hand, some of the most conservative unions
proved surprisingly unsuccessful as collective bargaining agents.
The Amalgamated Assocation of Iron and Steel Workers was
decimated by 1910. Under conservative leadership the Interna-

tional Association of Machinists declined.[72] Considering the aggressiveness of the corporations and their success in the courts in the early twentieth century, the explanation of the victory of exclusive economic activity over radical politics as the deliberate choice of the system that proved most effective makes little sense. In too many cases it simply wasn't effective.

But there is another objection to current theories. Even in those unions which seem to fit the "middle class psyche" explanation, it is not clear that the policies of their leaders adequately represented the wishes of the membership. In many unions a kind of controlling bureaucracy emerged, which owed little to union democracy, yet which managed to take control of their organizations. In the all-important building trades, this class consisted of so-called business agents, who really acted as labor contractors for the numerous subcontractors in the industry. A similar role has been detected in other industries in the form of "autonomous workmen" whose special skills gave them a privileged position between employer and the mass of unskilled workers.[73] Even under normal circumstances these men had little desire to change a system that amply rewarded them, but the opportunities for corruption afforded by their positions made them avidly antiradical.

What makes the position of these "bureaucracies" particularly interesting in the development of American labor institutions is that their outlook was not necessarily shared either by the idealistic founders of the A.F.ofL. or by the rank and file. However, just as the old leadership, chiefly represented by Gompers, accepted these developments with scarcely a murmur, so the rank and file submitted.

This is seen clearly in the carpenters' union, which professional organizers took over and refashioned along conservative lines, completely ousting J. P. McGuire's broad social goals. McGuire had retained massive popular support, which presumably means he represented the rank and file outlook. By means of democratic elections, he had been able to withstand formidable opposition from the "new men," until they were able to overthrow him in 1902 on cooked-up charges of embezzlement. Since McGuire had failed to create a proper democratic hierarchy, he left a vacuum easily filled by the machine of his successor, William Huber. In 1912 the formerly elected executive board was transformed into a staff of administrative officers dependent on the local business agent's machine.[74]

Such groups once in control were in an excellent position to stifle any recalcitrant opinion. In conventions, for instance, all committees were appointed by them, such that resolutions critical of existing union policies could be reported unfavorably, merged with other resolutions, or withdrawn under pressure. As two students of trade union publications have pointed out, "the divergence of opinion within a union is probably not fully reflected in its convention proceedings." It is therefore difficult to gauge rank and file opinion, if such a thing existed. Generally the dominant group also controlled the union periodical, and objectionable editors could be easily dismissed. Letters to the editor "provide almost the only direct indication of the opinion of rank and file union members to be found in the publications," and these are necessarily unsatisfactory sources.[75]

Like some of the larger International Unions, the federative body of the A.F.ofL. itself tended to become "frozen" under the control of an establishment dependent on the *status quo*. The executive board, headed by the president, was re-elected every year at an annual convention just like the convention of an individual union. The annual convention, also through debate on resolutions, decided major policy decisions. The convention consisted of delegates from international unions, local bodies having no international, and central bodies. Delegates from internationals and locals cast one vote for every hundred members they represented, whereas representatives of central bodies cast only one vote each, since members were already represented in their respective internationals. By this means officers were elected annually and resolutions voted upon.

Gompers referred to this system as "the fairest devised by any legislative body in existence."[76] Charles Lane, writing in the *American Labor Year Book* on the 1919 convention, however, pointed out that under the system of representation based upon the average membership of the international and other unions affiliated with the Federation, it was possible for 65 out of the 577 delegates to cast 28,000 out of a possible 34,000 votes.[77] Eva Valesh maintained that "four unions—miners, carpenters, structural iron workers, and maybe railway delegates [could] elect a president."[78]

The means of appointment to an A.F.ofL. convention was therefore crucial. Gompers liked to imagine it was all an example of working democracy, but various writers and contemporaries have referred to the vast political machinery Gompers employed in having "conservative" delegates chosen. One member of the

Typographical Union admitted his union had a huge machine, but added: "You ought to see the machine the A.F.ofL. has! It skins anything they have in this country!"[79] Only once did Gompers lose his election as president during his long reign of forty-odd years. He took care it never happened again. Once the machinery was created it was relatively easy to maintain. John Brophy, speaking of the United Mine Workers—one of the crucial, potentially radical unions—explains how remote the A.F.ofL. was from the average rank and file member. At A.F.ofL. conventions, the union usually had eight delegates, three national officers and five district presidents or national board members. "No rank and file could make it," said Brophy, "because he couldn't get enough votes—wasn't well enough known." He added that the only way to break through was by means of the state federation, which did not make much impression on the A.F.ofL.[80]

Once the A.F.ofL. "establishment" was in control of conventions, it could influence decisions through the president's control of appointment of all committees, particularly the committee on resolutions. Any delegate could get a hearing on the floor of the convention, but in order to become enacted, the measure had to receive the approval of the administrative committee. The refusal of Gompers to allow any socialists, like Hayes or Berger, to sit on important committees, was an effective barrier against propagation of their views. Often delegates from more socialistically inclined unions, given instructions at their own conventions to present resolutions at the A.F.ofL. convention, would find they got nowhere. The procedure for electing officers also caused many socialists to seek new ways of administering the A.F.ofL. Almost every year resolutions were proposed for some system of initiative and referendum for appointment of officers and for passing specific laws that would bring in the rank and file membership—but all to no avail. Writing to his wife from the Atlanta convention in 1911, Max S. Hayes described the situation: "Even the public is disgusted with the dry and listless business that is dragging along. The Socialists are simply up against a blank wall and can't get a thing through no matter what its merit may be. All argument might as well be bottled up. The machine is in absolute control and its creatures feel that they must go along and say 'me too' every time the word is given."[81]

This discussion of the structure and procedures of the A.F.ofL. and its affiliates is not intended to suggest that the whole labor movement in America was somehow a fraud. It simply demonstrates that the A.F.ofL. cannot be viewed in this period as an active democracy. Rather its leadership evolved over the years in a particular way and was passively accepted. Even Max S. Hayes had to admit at one convention that it could not be said that Gompers resorted to unfair methods to infuse his will. "The simple truth [was] that the vast majority of delegates agreed with him, outwardly at least, upon every proposition that he favored.[82]

The general picture of Gompers skillfully directing the A.F.ofL. along conservative lines immediately raises something of an enigma. Had Gompers represented the position of the typical business unionist, his role would be perfectly understandable simply as leader of a self-interested pressure group. But one of the essential features of Gompersism was its view of the A.F.ofL. as a real class movement with broad social aims. These aims were vaguely expressed and sometimes forgotten, but the A.F.ofL. stood for more than the increased bargaining power of particular labor unions. Gompers would blandly assume to represent all wage workers—even those not organized—and no one questioned this assumption. If Gompers attended Civic Federation dinners in evening clothes, in the company of well-known capitalists, it was not without considerable trauma over whether this befitted his position. He remained the typical laboring man at heart, very different from the slick professional union leaders of later years.

Gompers' conception of the labor movement as a socially regenerating force in many respects overlapped that of the revisionist socialists. The puzzle remains, therefore, as to why relations were so bad in the early twentieth century that antisocialism for its own sake sometimes seems the most conspicuous part of "Gompersism."

It might be argued simply that Gompers' personal beliefs are beside the point, and that the pro-capitalist forces hostile to socialism and industrial unionism dominated the A.F.ofL. Gompers often stressed his own powerlessness to initiate alternative policies. He once told the Canadian Club in Ottawa that "the office of presidency of the A.F.ofL. [was] that of an advisor, a counsellor and advocate."[83] He also liked to compare the A.F.ofL.'s constitution with that of the United States, stressing the limited nature of the federal authority. It was so limited according to Gompers that socialists wondered if he confused the U.S. Constitution with the Articles of Confederation.

But the truth is that the A.F.ofL.'s constitution, like its model, was much more flexible than Gompers at times claimed. Philip Taft, though usually stressing the limited power of the federative body, states that Gompers "assumed the role of an active statesman and . . . there was no serious objection to his role," even if there was no provision for it in the constitution.[84] Another biographer has written: "Gompers was an artist at handling men, at building and leading human organizations. Born under other circumstances than those which welded him to the working class, he might have become the head of a great corporation or a great general or the boss of a political machine."[85] Powerlessness, in fact, was often a pose. Eva Valesh, who worked with him for years, claimed that "the autonomous idea was a good shield in cases where he didn't or perhaps didn't think it wise to commit himself." "Theoretically he had little authority," she argues. "But he acquired great influence."[86]

Why then was this influence used against socialists with such telling force, when logic demanded some kind of cooperation with a group that had much to offer the A.F.ofL., especially in the field of organizing ability? One biographer has written: "In Gompers' scheme of things, there had to be a hero and a villain in every piece."[87] If this is true, then by the period of "classic Gompersism" the villain had changed from the employer to the socialist. As Max Hayes put it: "Any and every honest criticism of Gompers or his methods is twisted into 'abuse,' 'vilification,' and so forth, and the manner in which he and his crowd can whine for sympathy would almost shame Uriah Heep. Every time you question Gompers or his politics you attack the labor movement."[88] Gompers' refusal to acknowledge the revisionism of the Socialist Party and his professed belief that they wished to destroy the A.F.ofL. for doctrinaire purposes reveal a stubbornness that can be explained only psychologically. His readiness to write on the subject and the verbose way he attacked socialists belie his frequent assertion that he considered them of no importance. "Gompers could be unrelenting and hard; no man carried grudges further;"[89] he certainly carried them far in dealing with the Socialist Party.

Obviously, a man so intolerant of criticism from socialists would necessarily seek justification in expressing satisfaction in the *status quo*. If the opposition demanded industrial unionism then he would argue that craft unionism was the natural form of organization, even if he fully appreciated its weaknesses. If socialists favored independent politics, then "nonpartisan" politics must prevail, long after their failure was evident. Whatever Gompers' view of the labor movement, by this attitude he obviously played into the hands of the most conservative elements.

But the personal vendetta against socialists constituted a small part of the explanation of "Gompersism." Gompers' policies were too positive to be seen as purely a negative response to the thunder of the left. One thing was clear in his mind and consistently held; whatever American labor was to achieve, it would not be through the corrupting influence of politics. If labor was to contribute to a bettering of society, it would be on its own steam.

Gompers' vision of a better society was never clearly articulated, but it did exist. "Labor's emancipation," his phrase in the nineties, was replaced at the turn of the century by a grandiose vision of evolution toward collective negotiation on a grand scale—the Social Darwinist's dream of fully developed labor and capital meeting as equals. It was the period that launched the national Civic Federation and saw Gompers' specific attacks on socialism as a system. An American solution to the problems of industrialism was taking form.

The idea received a harsh jolt with the collapse of some continent-wide collective bargaining agreements. The aggressiveness of capital intensified rather than diminished. By 1906 its power was felt through the courts and the very legal basis of trade unionism was placed in jeopardy. What made things worse was that the growth of labor organizations stymied at the same time.

Had Gompers underestimated the enemy? Consider the ignominy of letters of condolence from an English socialist as the Supreme Court threatened to incarcerate American leaders. Ben Tillett pointed out that for all British labor's tribulations, they had nothing so archaic as the Supreme Court to back up the "money bugs."[90] Gompers, in a moment of international worker solidarity, wrote Carl Legien, his opposite number in Germany, saying that he "did expect some sort of a letter" in the midst of his trials.[91] American socialists, meanwhile, held their breath as it seemed American labor might follow its British counterpart in the direction of independent politics. But they were disappointed; America would remain different.

Paradoxically, within months, even British labor had second thoughts about political action as the European syndicalist movement spread its influence. European syndicalists might talk of general strikes and revolution, but in practice they represented a good deal of what Gompers had always striven for in America. America had led the way after all.

Throughout these years, it is scarcely surprising that notions of a better society were lost. Only the apparent victory of the Clayton Act could permit such a luxury. By then the European war swelled the American economy and labor relished a new spurt of growth. When Woodrow Wilson launched his crusade for democracy in the world, however, the time had come for renewed discussion of industrial democracy at home.

NOTES

1. A. F. of L., *Proceedings* 1903, 198.
2. A. F. of L., *Proceedings* 1904, 199.
3. *Federationist,* May, 1905, 280-282; September, 1908, 737.
4. *Federationist,* November, 1901, 479.
5. *Federationist,* January, 1902, 23.
6. *Federationist,* February, 1902, 70.
7. *Federationist,* February, 1902, 55-56.
8. *Federationist,* November, 1907, 880.
9. Adolph Germer to T. V. Powderly, May 23, 1911 (Germer Papers, Wisconsin State Historical Society).
10. James Weinstein, "Gompers and the New Liberalism 1900-1909" *Studies on the Left* V (Fall, 1965), 94-105.
11. *International Socialist Review,* March, 1910, 801-810.
12. Morris Hillquit, *The Civic Federation and Labor* (Undated pamphlet).
13. *Federationist,* June, 1905, 354-355.
14. *Federationist,* August, 1897 quoted in *I. S. R.,* December, 1907, 330-345.
15. *Federationist,* November, 1907, 882.
16. A. F. of L., *Proceedings* 1902, 182-183.
17. *Federationist,* November, 1916, 1067.
18. Samuel Gompers, *Seventy Years of Life and Labor,* (New York: E. P. Dutton, 1925), I, 287.
19. U. S. Commission on Industrial Relations: *Final Report and Testimony,* II, 1916, 1474-1475; 1528-1530.
20. Ralph Easley to Gompers, May 26, 1914 (A. F. of L. Papers, (Wisconsin State Historical Society).
21. A. F. of L., *Proceedings* 1900, 134.
22. *Federationist,* May, 1916, 347.
23. *Federationist,* August, 1916, 677.
24. *American Labor Year Book* 1916, 24 ff.
25. *United Mine Workers Journal,* September 30, 1915, 10-11.
26. *Ibid.*
27. *Justice,* (I.L.G.W.U.) September 24, 1920, 4.
28. *Justice,* May 24, 1919, 5-6.
29. Gompers, *Seventy Years* II, 290.
30. *U. M. W. J.,* November 16, 1911, 2.
31. Gompers, *Seventy Years* II, 290.
32. *Federationist,* November, 1912, 921.
33. William English Walling, "The New Unionism in Europe," *Federationist,* June, 1908, 441-446.

34. Selig Perlman, *A Theory of the Labor Movement* (New York: Macmillan, 1932), 288.
35. *Federationist,* June, 1908, 458 ff.
36. *Federationist,* March, 1910, 221.
37. *Federationist,* April, 1914, 301.
38. *Shoe Workers Journal,* July, 1902, 3.
39. *I. S. R.,* March, 1902, 691.
40. *Federationist,* March, 1908, 180.
41. Quoted by Louis S. Reed, *The Labor Philosophy of Samuel Gompers* (New York: Columbia University Press, 1930), 29.
42. *Federationist,* March, 1908, 162, 171.
43. *I. S. R.,* March, 1908, 568.
44. A. F. of L., *Proceedings,* 1908, 28.
45. S. G. to Ex. Council, April 15, 1908. S. G. to Presidents of State Federations, April, 1908 (several letters in A. F. of L. Papers).
46. A. F. of L., *Proceedings,* 1913, 314-315.
47. Lewis Lorwin, *The American Federation of Labor* (Washington D. C.: The Brookings Institution, 1933), 416.
48. A. F. of L., *Proceedings,* 1909, 33.
49. Gompers, *Seventy Years* II, 283.
50. Jerold S. Auerbach, "Progressives at Sea: The La Follette Act of 1915," *Labor History* II (1961), 344-360.
51. *Federationist,* January, 1919, 43.
52. *Federationist,* May, 1915, 356.
53. See Stanley I. Kutler, "Labor, The Clayton Act and the Supreme Court," *Labor History* III (1962), 19-35, and Robert K. Murray, "Public Opinion, Labor and the Clayton Act," *The Historian* XXI (1959), 255-270.
54. *U. M. W. J.,* October 1, 1908, 6.
55. *I. S. R.,* August, 1906, 112.
56. *Federationist,* February, 1917, 111-115.
57. Denver newspaper clipping contained in Max S. Hayes to his wife, November 16, 1908 (Hayes Papers, Ohio State Historical Society).
58. *Federationist,* October, 1908, 875.
59. *Federationist,* March, 1910, 225.
60. A. F. of L., *Proceedings* 1906, 185.
61. *Federationist,* 1918, 286.
62. *Federationist,* December 1910, 1083.
63. *Federationist,* February, 1917, 111-115.
64. *Federationist,* January, 1904, 32-33.
65. Lorwin, *A. F. of L.,* 424.
66. New York *Journal,* January 6, 1904; quoted in *Weekly Bulletin* (United Garment Workers), January 20, 1904, 4.
67. Cleveland *Citizen,* July 28, 1900.
68. J. H. Maurer, *It Can Be Done* (New York: Rand School Press, 1938), 179, 249.
69. United Mine Workers, *Proceedings* 1914, 844.
70. *Federationist,* September, 1902, 507.
71. See, for instance, Lloyd Ulman, *The Rise of the National Trade Union* (Cambridge, Mass.: Harvard University Press, 1955), 578, 604.
72. David Brody, *The Steel Workers: The Non-Union Era* (New York: Harper Torch Books, 1969), Ch. III. Mark Perlman, *The Machinists* (Cambridge, Mass.: Harvard University Press, 1961), 28. Philip Taft, *Organized Labor in American History* (New York: Harper & Row, 1964), esp. 199, chapter 17.

73. Philip S. Foner, *History of the Labor Movement in the United States,* Volume III: *The Policies and Practices of the A. F. of L. 1900-1909* (New York: International Publishers, 1964), 6. Benson Soffer, "A Theory of Trade Union Development: The Role of the Autonomous Workman," *Labor History* I, 2 (Spring, 1960) 141-163, esp. 152, 159.
74. Robert A. Christie, *Empire in Wood* (Ithaca: Cornell University Press, 1956), esp., 66, 78, 104, 151-152, 165.
75. Lloyd G. Reynolds and Charles C. Killingsworth, *Trade Union Publications* (Baltimore: Johns Hopkins University Press, 1944), 8-13.
76. *Federationist*, March, 1904, 222-225.
77. *A. L. Y. B.*, 1919-1920, 149.
78. Columbia University Oral History Project, *Eva Valesh Memoir,* 112.
79. United Mine Workers, *Proceedings* 1914, 842, 855, 859.
80. Columbia University Oral History Project; *Brophy Memoir,* 255.
81. Hayes to his wife, November 23, 1911 (Hayes Papers).
82. *I. S. R.*, December, 1907, 371.
83. Gompers' address quoted in R. H. Harvey, *Samuel Gompers, Champion of the Toiling Masses* (Stanford: Stanford University Press, 1935.), 46.
84. Philip Taft, *A. F. of L. in the Time of Gompers,* (New York: Harper, 1957), XIII.
85. Louis S. Reed, *The Labor Philosophy of Samuel Gompers* (New York: Columbia University Press, 1930), 175.
86. Columbia University Oral History Project, *Valesh Memoir,* 93.
87. Harvey, *Samuel Gompers,* 56.
88. *I. S. R.*, November, 1906, 310-311.
89. Harvey, *Samuel Gompers,* 57.
90. Ben Tillett to S. G., December 26, 1908, (A. F. of L. Papers).
91. S. G. to Carl Legien, January 22, 1909 (A. F. of L. Papers).

6

"War Socialism" and
"Industrial Democracy"

From the turn of the century until World War I, organized labor occupied an ambivalent position in American society, at once critic and participant in the American capitalist system. With the advent of the Wilson Administration, and the apparent political success of the A.F.ofL. crystallized in the Clayton Act, the position seemed to be changing. In 1916 Woodrow Wilson congratulated Gompers on the occasion of the foundation of new A.F.ofL. headquarters, and the following year the President attended the A.F.ofL. convention at Buffalo. By then the nation was at war and it seemed to many that Gompers was the second most important man in the nation. If it were respectability for labor that Gompers craved and the satisfaction of his own vanity, he certainly obtained it during the war years.

Wilson and Gompers bore a striking resemblance to each other. Not at first sight perhaps; the photographs of the two show the one meager, almost parched, the other decidedly obese. But both have the same demanding eyes, and firm, uncompromising lips. Norman Thomas, a novice in the Socialist Party in those years, once said that arguing with Wilson was like arguing with the Holy Ghost.[1] Other socialists said as much of Gompers. Also like Wilson, Gompers had tireless energy in a cause he believed in, and the war provided such a cause. They differed in that Wilson literally killed himself in the effort and in the peace-making attempt afterward, while Gompers seemed to thrive on it. The war, in a sense, provided the kind of psychological stimulus that Gompers needed.

Like the socialists, Gompers had opposed the militaristic tendencies shown in America when war broke out in Europe, knowing only too well they were liable to take an antilabor course. As American participation became more imminent, however, his attitude changed. Undoubtedly, Gompers' patriotism was stirred but his statements during the war period also seem to betray the old need for opposition. Rapidly the "Hun" became the enemy, filling the place formerly occupied by the socialists. Better still, it was the same enemy, for not only was a large proportion of socialists of German origin, but the party opposed the war effort. Gompers was filled with an implacable hatred of anything tinged with pacifism. As one trade unionist pointed out, Gompers went much further than Wilson in this since the President at least distinguished between the German movement and the German people. The President also showed some interest in the socialist peace moves and at least communicated with the Bolsheviks in Russia. Gompers regarded both of these moves with dismay.[2]

But Gompers' war activity has a much greater significance for this study than what it tells us about Gompers personally. The A.F.ofL. leader rapidly saw that war provided opportunities for labor, hitherto denied. It was to be the culmination and vindication of all the policies pursued since the turn of the century. "Now is the time for labor to speak," Gompers announced in a circular to all presidents of national and international unions. "Make sure it has influence in whatever is done for the advance of the nation."[3] To President Wilson, he was almost apocalyptic in his sense of the ripeness of time for a new departure. "We maintain it is a fundamental step in preparedness for the nation to set its house in order," he informed him, "and to establish at home justice in relations between men."[4] One supporter wrote Gompers that "there was never a time in the history of the world when there was such a great opportunity and particularly in our own country to break down class distinction."[5] Gompers already knew. He had written to Newton D. Baker, secretary of war, advocating trade union leaders as officers.[6] Equality and democracy could be furthered by such appointments.

Some of the changes Gompers demanded were not long in coming. Only in 1916 he had complained about the lack of any unionists on congressionally appointed committees, which he claimed were the real government.[7] Within a year, Gompers had a seat on the advisory commission to the council of national defense, which he intended to be more than an honorary post. Using this authority as chairman of the committee on labor, he called a meeting of representatives of labor, management, and the general public just as war broke out, and made himself chairman of the executive committee. The keynote of the committee on labor was cooperation between employers and employees—neither side to take advantage of the war situation to make gains. The suggestion of a no-strike policy caused consternation among some labor leaders as contrary to what the A.F.ofL. had always stood for. Gompers had a hard time explaining that a veto on strikes was not intended, but many still insisted that the policy would give encouragement to employers.[8]

Gompers' initiative and energy in these matters is an interesting indication of the power he exercised in the A.F.ofL. and the extent to which this could annoy even friends. While names as distinguished as John D. Rockefeller, William B. Wilson, and Alton B. Parker gladly accepted positions on the committee on labor, Daniel J. Tobin, president of the teamsters, refused. "I have no confidence in the committee that you are endeavoring to organize," he told Gompers, "because of the fact that things will have to run as you want them to run or they can't run at all." Tobin went on to say that he had recently attended a meeting of leaders of national and international unions, expressly called to advise and counsel members of the executive committee, but only given the opportunity to ratify statements already formulated by Gompers.[9]

These informal arrangements gave way to an agreement with the secretary of war in June 1917—the "Baker-Gompers agreement"—setting up an adjustment committee of three men, one of whom was nominated by Gompers, to cover all construction work involved in the war effort and later repair work as well. The idea of "adjustment" caused some dispute, for the question of whether unions were to be the bargaining agents in war industries soon arose. Both government and employers seemingly wished to avoid this outcome.

As the war progressed, the President created a new agency, the War Labor Policies Board, and appointed Felix Frankfurter head. Frankfurter then appointed a War Labor Conference Board, half of which consisted of representatives of labor. Its task was to work out an overall policy for labor during the remainder of the war. The presidents of the United Mine Workers and the United Brotherhood of Carpenters and Joiners were among the five labor members of the War Labor Conference Board. Though Gompers was not a member, his advice was constantly sought by Frankfurter and the Secretary of Labor, William B. Wilson.

Besides defining principles concerning conditions of work, the

War Labor Conference Board set up a War Labor Board for the express purpose of conciliation and mediation in labor disputes. The great victory of the A.F.ofL.—not to be repeated until the thirties—was that workers were to be represented by "agents of their own choosing," for purposes of negotiation. Thus, although certain voices were raised against some of the policies of the boards, particularly at any attempts made to stabilize wages, the A.F.ofL. had reason to be pleased with its new position of respectability and even of authority. Moreover, there was a new strength felt in the unions' rapidly increasing numbers. While there was no move made in the direction of industrial unionism, the increase of a million and a quarter made an impression even on some socialists.

The improvement in working conditions and rising numbers in trade unions, together with their new-found respectability, must have seemed a complete vindication of the Gompersist policies of the two previous decades. There was, however, one flaw: the wartime success of the A.F.ofL. depended less upon its own efforts than upon the actions of a friendly government. What government gave, it could just as rapidly take away. Meanwhile, the wartime position of labor really depended upon what socialists had long argued for, namely, the political system in friendly hands.

What occurred in America was something common to all belligerents, and best summed up in the phrase, "War Socialism." The Cleveland *Citizen* noted in Germany early in 1918, and prophesied that the old kind of economy would be weakened everywhere.[10] The nationalization of the railroads, the organization of the War Industries and War Labor Boards, and the general supervision of the economy and working conditions, were all manifestations of "war socialism" in the United States. As far as the railroads were concerned, James Maurer considered that "the unions were virtually made partners."[11] The wages in shipyards were fixed at rates higher than the workers had ever known.

But it was not only socialists who observed this tendency. Ralph Easley, for instance, maintained that Great Britain had got in three years what socialists had striven for for fifty. "We have already obtained in this country," he told Gompers in November 1917 "measures of state socialism that seemed as far away as the millenium to our socialists three years ago."[12] W. E. Macey, president of the Civic Federation, was a little more afraid of the term. He denied that measures undertaken by the government as a result of military necessity really constituted socialism, but nevertheless suggested to Gompers that some might be adopted permanently should they prove useful.[13] Macey did not say what he had in mind, but the old "syndicalist" spirit of Gompers revolted against any suggestion of interference by politicians, particularly in schemes for health or social insurance.

Gompers wanted much more than government handouts. After reading a particularly optimistic article by Sidney Webb describing how British labor actually participated in the running of industry, he told Daniel Willard, chairman of the advisory commission, he had the same aims.[14] In the spring of 1918 Gompers was also in correspondence with Robert W. Bruere, another admirer of British labor's accomplishments. Bruere sent Gompers his plans for unified control of war production and manpower under the leadership of organized labor.[15] Gompers, of course, put forward no such demands, but ideas like those of Webb and Bruere seem to have impressed him. Their influence became apparent later.

Though some aspects of socialism made great strides during the war, both among unionists and in the country as a whole, the Socialist Party nevertheless foundered badly. Precisely in what way it failed, however, is open to question. No national convention had met in 1916, but as soon as war was declared in April 1917 an emergency convention met in St. Louis and adopted an antiwar resolution, proposed by a majority of the executive committee.

John Spargo's minority report, stressing socialist ideals and the necessity of maintaining civil liberties but not opposing the war, was defeated in the convention by a small majority. When the decision went against him in referendum, he resigned together with William English Walling, Robert Hunter, J. G. Phelps Stokes, Charles Edward Russell, and others. Spargo admitted that the referendum reflected the opinion of party members, but not necessarily of the socialist vote in the country as a whole. He also argued that the adoption of the minority report could have meant gains for the party.[16] At any rate, as in most countries, the party divided into majority and minority socialists. American socialists were exceptional, however, in that it was the majority that stood against the war. The minority group, forsaking their status as a political party for the moment, constituted themselves as the Social Democratic League of America. Most writers have viewed the party's stand against war as disastrous, since it completely alienated it from the main stream of American life, and made it vulnerable to accusations of disloyalty. Many opinions expressed in trade union journals would support this view. The editor of the United Garment Workers journal reported: "The extent to which prominent socialists are deserting the organized socialist movement in this country is an indication that it has ceased to respond to the demands of members who are imbued with the American idea of democracy and in accord with the spirit that is inspiring the people in its support." Some months later the same journal questioned whether "the attitude of the Socialist Party [was] going to be long tolerated by the patriotic people" of the United States, and referred to the Socialist Party as "the enemy within our gates."[17]

But opinions of this kind were usually expressed in journals already hostile to the socialist movement. The *American Labor Year Book* for 1917, on the other hand, regarded the party's situation among trade unionists as hopeful.[18] The rather hectic activity of Gompers, particularly the time and effort he gave to the prowar American Alliance for Labor and Democracy, suggests he had very real fears. Founded at a convention in Minneapolis, between September 5 and 7, 1917, the main purpose of the Alliance was to counteract the activity of the Socialist People's Council of America for Democracy and Peace, in which many trade unionists showed an interest.

Most of the dissident socialists eagerly supported Gompers in these efforts. J. G. Phelps Stokes became treasurer of the Alliance, while Walling and Simons played prominent roles. Spargo maintained that Gompers' support for it "proved the wisdom of his leadership and the intellectual and moral soundness of the labor movement." Its "Bolshevik" opponents, on the other hand, were untrue to "socialist internationalism, trades unionism and American democracy."[19]

The prominent trade union socialists of the prewar days nevertheless remained with the majority. Max S. Hayes and Victor Berger stood by the party. J. H. Maurer demanded an explanation of why leading trade unionists connected with the Alliance were meeting on the same platform as "some of the leading reactionaries of the country," and felt it was worth while making his feelings known to the press. In a letter widely distributed as a circular, Maurer also wished to know who financed the Alliance and asked what gave Gompers the authority to speak on behalf of the A.F.ofL., which had not taken any action. More to the point, he added that the Pennsylvania State Federation of Labor, of which he was president, had officially taken a stand against the war.[20] Gompers did not reply, but at the next convention of the Pennsylvania State Federation of Labor, business agents of the A.F.ofL. worked against Maurer's re-election. According to Maurer, federal agents also had a warrant for his arrest, only to be used if he lost. He won easily.[21]

One of the A.F.ofL. organizers also reported opposition in Illinois to the war. He felt that if the war were to prove of long duration, the socialists would very likely gain. He recommended a branch of the Alliance in every city with a central body, where members could be "educated to the real facts of the war and the federation's attitude to it."[22]

Milwaukee, as might be expected from Victor Berger's home town, was another stumbling block. The Alliance organizer there regretted that those in charge were not trade unionists, and attributed the lack of support to Berger's control of the *Leader*.[23] Gradually, however, resistance to the war tended to break.

The branch of the Alliance working among the Jewish workers on the east side of New York, where Socialist Party propaganda was strong, was significantly called the Jewish Socialist League. Robert Maisal, the director of the Alliance, made elaborate plans involving "Mothers of Soldiers Clubs" to combat the influence of the Socialist *Forward,* and, as he put it, "to Americanize the East Side," but he could not find speakers. In fact, socialist influence seemed to grow rather than diminish. A special conference of the United Hebrew Trades, called by Gompers to counteract it, was a failure.[24]

An interesting exception among prominent socialist trade unionists was Frank J. Hayes, the president of the United Mine Workers, and later a member of the War Labor Conference Board. According to socialists, Frank J. Hayes was drummed out of the party for supporting local officials of another party, but he claimed he had left before this since it was impossible for a trade union official to comply with the "unfair edicts of the party." He also hinted at an "Impossibilist" takeover. He did not mention the war as a reason for quitting, but took great pleasure in associating himself with antiwar socialists.[25]

But on the whole the effect of the Socialist Party's antiwar resolution was not necessarily adverse among trade unionists. Some historians have recently shown that the same was true of the country as a whole. J. Louis Engdahl considered the elections of 1917 to be "socialism's greatest triumph in America."[26] The economist Paul H. Douglas estimated that if the victories of that year—chiefly in the cities—were projected on a national scale in accordance with the 1912 results, socialist votes would have totaled four million.[27] Thus, far from being yet another manifestation of the Socialist Party's alienation from American life, as has been argued, the antiwar stand was a real political issue that made the meaning of the Socialist Party all the clearer to the public.

Yet the war was nevertheless the party's undoing. The forces in American life that had long regarded the rise of socialism with fear, could now turn on the party under a cloak of patriotism. Their harrassment did not end with the armistice. Antisocialist activity, whether of the strictly legal variety like that stemming from the Espionage and Sedition Acts, or mob violence silently encouraged by officialdom, makes the projection of local votes on to a national scale mere academic speculation. While it is true that party membership did not significantly decline before the Communist secessions in 1919, this disruption is inconceivable without the passions raised within the party in the fact of persecution.

For the duration of the war, the majority socialists were obviously preoccupied with their opposition to it and with their own struggle for survival. This left them little time for any constructive efforts and gave them no opportunity to exploit the social idealism produced by war. In this respect, the prowar minority socialists had much more to contribute.

The behavior of the defectors in some ways is very curious, and it throws considerable light on the relationship between socialists and trade unionism. They felt strongly about the war and were convinced that the Marxist analysis of an imperialist struggle did not quite fit. They were right in disagreeing that it made no difference which side won. After the Russian revolution and Germany's continued invasion of Russia, even the majority socialists felt their original stand at St. Louis should be re-examined. Some of the *Masses* crowd, while facing trial under the Sedition Acts, half changed their minds. But this hardly excuses the way defectors turned on their old comrades, sometimes even calling for their persecution, and providing the government with evidence for conviction. When Spargo spoke at the original meeting of the Alliance for Labor and Democracy, he deplored attacks on free speech and assemblage aimed at the People's Council, but he sat on the same platform as the perpetrators of these attacks.[28]

Most of the minority socialists, it is true, eventually drifted away from the socialist movement. But this was not their original intention. With some justification, they could consider themselves more representative of the international socialist movement than the majority. G. D. Herron, the founder of the Rand School of Social Science, and something of a neutral (he was in Europe during most of the war years), objected to the school's teaching only the point of view of the St. Louis resolution. "The majority of socialists, the world over," he told Hillquit, "favor the military defeat and destruction of German power."[29] W. H. Hyndman, the old leader of the British Social Democratic Federation, now the British Socialist Party and solidly prowar, told Simons that he had high hopes for the dissidents. He believed they would at last have a genuine Social Democratic Party in close touch with the historical development of the United States and "its dominant races."[30] This seems very close to Spargo's point of view.

Like the prowar socialists of the allied countries, the Americans believed that the wartime experience of the nation was about to bring what they had long sought. "Victory for the Allies," Hyndman assured Simons, "means genuine national and international socialism ere long." It was in this spirit that the minority American socialists—the Social Democratic League—sought out the opportunities provided by the war. The immediate opportunity was to work in harmony with the A.F.ofL. through the American Alliance for Labor and Democracy. Considering former relations between Gompers and even the right-wing socialists, they got on remarkably well; there was no saying what this new-found friendship might lead to.

The Minneapolis convention which launched the Alliance, Algie Simons felt, was like one of the first socialist conventions. "All the best brains of the movement are here," he wrote his wife. "There is nothing left in the Socialist Party worth taking."[31] The socialist aspect of the Alliance impressed even Max S. Hayes, who of course had not left the party. Unlike other socialists in the trade union movement, like J. Mahlon Barnes, who attacked the Alliance at the following A.F.ofL. convention, Hayes interpreted its declarations as socialistic, "more advanced by far, than anything that had been advocated by the leaders of the A.F.ofL. in this [A.F.ofL. convention] floor." He congratulated them and hoped they would keep up the good work. "You should have seen the faces of the brothers," he told his wife. "The Reds and others who saw the point waxed enthusiastic, while the conservative brethren grinned or looked rather dazed."[32]

Even Gompers took the minority socialists' advent into the Alliance as a serious move. Describing the movement in a letter to Alexander Kerensky, then head of the provisional government in Russia, he referred to the Minneapolis meeting as a "conference of Labor and Socialists, called to solidify the working class and all the people of the United States."[33] Spargo, too, seemed to be under the impression that the "democracy" in the "Alliance for Labor and Democracy" stood for the Social Democratic League.[34] Socialists, of course, exaggerated the socialist nature of the Alliance and the extent of Gompers' conversion, but their belief in it explains their next moves. Scarcely was the Alliance brought into being than a group of them turned their attention to a new political party.

Perhaps the inspiration for the new party lay in Hyndman's prowar British Socialist Party, for Simons was in correspondence with Hyndman and other members of his group early in 1917. "It is in the interests of socialism generally," one member of Hyndman's group wrote to Simons, "that the United States should do what Europeans are being forced to do—form national parties. You cannot make the U. S. socialist by means of a mob of Europeans who happen to live there."[35] But the Americans had ambitions far in excess of Hyndman's, for they believed that the time was now ripe to bring the labor movement into radical politics. In fact, the British Labour Party itself was their model. Perhaps they could now accomplish what they had failed to do in 1909.

The National Party, as it became called, held its initial conference in Chicago in October 1917, to the consternation of the nonsocialist members of the Alliance. Robert Maisal, the director of the Alliance, suspected that this is what they had been after when they attended its earliest conferences.[36] Chester M. Wright, a member of the executive committee and editor of the Alliance's paper, asked Spargo for a list of names of prominent radicals and a general idea of the character of the gathering, but was told to mind his own business.[37] Maisal thought most delegates had been opposed to forming a new party, and later called the whole thing a fizzle,[38] but Spargo told Gompers a few days later he had been misinformed. There never had been any intention of forming a new *socialist* party, but they did intend forming a new "liberal and radical party . . . by uniting various existing parties and groups." He proudly announced that the new party was now an accomplished fact.[39]

All members of the National Party resented the opposition shown by the labor side of the Alliance. Unless the Alliance was itself a political party, there was no good reason why they should not take whatever political course they thought necessary. They made it clear that they had no intention of being hitched to the Democratic Party because of their new association with labor.[40]

But in spite of all the fuss, the members of the National Party seemed to be under the impression that Gompers was prepared to support them. W.A. Gaylord told the A.F.ofL. president that both he and Simons took the position that "unless the proposed new political organization could be assured of the cooperation directly or indirectly of the organized labor movement of the country," they were not interested. Gaylord maintained, however, that he had been given assurances that the "new party organization would have from the beginning the moral support of the organized labor movement, with the possibility of open and avowed endorsement at a later date."[41] Spargo also remarked to Gompers that he had been assured of his good will. "There were various intimations," he wrote, "that if I would throw over my associates with whom for months I had been working, I should have a chance to work with you in the formation of a new labor party on English lines."[42] D.C. Coates, who became chairman of the National Party after March 1918, actually wrote to Gompers, quoting a statement that he claimed the latter had made. It read that although nonpartisan political activity had brought rewards, Gompers would "not hesitate in the building of a labor party in America" and "be with it body, soul and breeches" were "a more definite political policy . . . pursued along political party lines."[43]

Although statements obviously show their authors' capacity for wishful thinking, their misinterpretations nevertheless reveal something of the sense of a new departure that Gompers exuded at this time. However, the new departure was not to be the National Party. In its search for a wider following, it soon fell under the influence of single taxers and prohibitionists, so that by the time of its national convention in March 1918, most of the minority socialists had lost interest. Spargo proposed that one or two members of the British Labour Party be invited over, "in consideration of the very close accord" of their aims and the National Party's. But he played no other part at the convention.[44] By then, members of the Social Democratic League had had their attention diverted elsewhere.

In January 1918 the British Labour Party, formerly an amalgam of socialist groups combined with the Trade Union Council, reconstituted itself as a proper political party with individual membership. At the same time, the party gave itself a new socialist program based on Sidney Webb's pamphlet, "Labour and the New Social Order." It aimed at "deliberately planned cooperation and distribution for the benefit of all who participate by hand and brain," to be achieved by the "common ownership of the means of production." The new British program had an effect on American liberal and socialist opinion, but its immediate impact was to revitalize the Social Democratic League, by giving it something much more concrete to aim at.

William English Walling played an important part in this development, but he changed the direction of the British scheme. True to this syndicalist leanings as seen in his opposition to the labor party idea in 1909, Walling, though a member of the Social Democratic League, had disapproved of the drift toward the National Party. He believed it was up to the A.F.ofL., the natural product of American conditions, to take the initiative and for the rest to follow. In February 1918 he advised Gompers that the time was ripe for "a program somewhat along the line of the British Labour Party," and that something should be formulated before the June convention of the A.F.ofL. He believed that the general principles laid down by Gompers and the A.F.ofL. since the beginning of the war, together with the platform of the Alliance for Labor and Democracy, would give a sufficient foundation. Other plans which longer wartime experience had enabled the British Labour Party to work out, could then be added.[45]

The interesting part of Walling's scheme, however, is his syndicalist idea of introducing a system of industrial democracy without involving political parties. He was glad the National Party had failed, and it was to forestall some new group from seizing the British Labour Party's ideas, that he felt the A.F.ofL. had to act. "Naturally, I am not suggesting any radical departure in policy," he assured Gompers. "It is chiefly a question of getting the present federation policy into a shape that will appeal more

strongly to the public and also secure support from all the genuine democrats."[45] As he explained to Simons, what he had in
mind was simply "old fashioned Jeffersonian democracy . . . with
the very important amendment that organized labor of the
A.F.ofL. type [would be] taken into partnership with the government."[46]

What Walling meant became clearer with the publication of
the Social Democratic League's "Program of Social Reconstruction," composed by Walling, Simons, and Slobodin.[47] Basically,
they demanded the intensification of the wartime government
control of industry into a gradual process of nationalization,
accompanied by "the direct representation in each industry and
in every economic body and the control of government by industrial labor and the other producing classes." The program was
thus similar to the British one, except that it emphasized much
more clearly the democratization of industry, as opposed to mere
nationalization. The scheme obviously comes closer to G.D.H.
Cole's idea of guild socialism. This is not surprising, for- Cole
acknowledged his debt to prewar syndicalism,[48] which, as we have
seen, also influenced Walling.

Simons, who helped in drafting the Social Democratic League's
plan, was converted by these ideas. Writing to G.D. Herron, he
explained the necessity of labor's gradual participation in the
management of industry which, he believed, would be the next
stage of industrial organization. If this seemed humdrum compared with the big political and social dreams they had formerly
shared, he argued that it was only on such a foundation that
more advanced forms of industrial organization could be built.[49]
During this period, Simons was also in contact with the Belgian
socialist Henri de Man, whose ideas were going through a similar
transformation.[50] De Man's *"planisme,"* as it became called, had
an important influence on Belgian politics.

Walling believed that the ideas expressed in the Social Democratic League's Plan were not far in advance of Gompers', whom
he believed was "contemplating a decided step in advance."[51]
Forwarding the draft Plan to Gompers later, Walling wrote:
"Very possibly you may say there is no socialism about it, but
that it simply carries a little further the ideas of the A.F.ofL."
He added that the members of the League believed that the
entire program would obtain Gompers' enthusiastic approval with
the exception of few references to socialism.[52] At the end of 1918
Simons reported to W.H. Hyndman that Gompers was "steadily

relaxing his hostility to Socialism" and that he had accepted the socialist position on all practical matters and only balked at the name. Simons looked forward to "an entirely new deal in everything."[53]

The members of the Social Democratic League exaggerated Gompers' anticapitalism, for its program said too much about nationalization for Gompers' liking. Moreover, he had a one-track mind, and while the war lasted that track was the defeat of Germany. "Is it not the best course for us to pursue," he asked Spargo, "to secure the greatest possible unity and solidarity of spirit and action, at least for the present, rather than discussing a series of subjects which, after all, can only find free expression after the war has been triumphantly closed?"[54]

Nevertheless, during these months, Gompers reformulated many of his assumptions about the goals of the labor movement and evolved a concept of "industrial democracy" far in advance of the collective bargaining demands of prewar days. Gompers had approved Sidney Webb's ideas about worker participation in the control of industry. He told Spargo that although he dissented from some aspects of the British reconstruction program, he liked its spirit.[55] A few months afterward, the A.F.ofL.'s executive committee reported to the convention its suggestions for a similar program.[56] Besides stressing the opportunity that the war provided for a new departure in industrial relations, this report raised anew the possibility of organizing all workers, skilled and unskilled, in a united working force. The document then suggested that "those contributing to production should have a part in its control"—the phrase that inspired Walling in the belief that Gompers was coming round to the views of the Social Democratic League.[57]

The A.F.ofL.'s "Program of Social Reconstruction," which appeared early in 1919, was something of an anticlimax. Under the section entitled "Democracy in Industry," it stated that the "workers should have a voice in determining the laws within industry and commerce which affect them, equivalent to the voice which they have as citizens in determining the legislative enactments which shall govern them."[58] This could either mean a very advanced form of worker participation or simple collective bargaining; the phrasing is perhaps deliberately ambiguous. But the reconstruction program was not labor's last statement on the subject.

"Industry's Manifest Duty," a manifesto adopted by the

A.F.ofL. convention in 1923, purported to make clear the full implications of trade unionism. Up to World War I only political democracy had been achieved. The war, however, marked a "turning point in human relations" and heralded industrial democracy. Specifically, the document maintained that trade unions had "a deeper meaning than the mere organization of groups for the advancement of group interests."[59] Gompers gave wide publicity to these ideas. In articles in the *Sunday World*, entitled "Samuel Gompers seeks self government for Industry," and "Industrial Democracy must come and surely will come," he embroidered the theme.[60]

Sometimes, Gompers' statements took on a decidedly anticapitalist complexion. After one of his harangues against the "captains of industry and princes of finance" for "their incapacity to rule the industrial destinies of the nation," one old opponent wondered whether the "hazardous winds of spring or some new love" had rejuvenated him.[61] In a private letter at about the same time, Gompers complained of inefficiency and waste on the part of management and its overall social effects. "I grant you that it is not clear to many persons that these are matters which interested the labor movement," he added. "Nevertheless, these are things of the first and foremost interest to the labor movement and this we shall make clear as time and opportunity offers." In the same letter he even contemplated "the elimination of those elements in industry which serve no useful purpose."[62]

It might be thought from these innumerable statements that the war experience had finally brought Gompers back into the socialist camp, at least in spirit. But there remained essential differences. Gompers had abandoned nothing of his suspicion of the state. If socialism had captivated him, it was the "guild socialism" then being propagated by G.D.H. Cole in Britain, but Gompers scrupulously avoided the title.[63] Moreover, all was to be accomplished through natural evolution, not by the state. The first steps in this evolution he detected in the divorce of ownership and management, then being widely discussed.

Many influences were at work on Gompers during this period. The unity and idealism generated by war had their effect. William English Walling and other ex-members of the Socialist Party were in constant touch with him. Perhaps British guild socialist ideas had an appeal. But Gompers' ideas were also a consistent development of that "syndicalism" that had always been an important part of his thought. "The final emancipation of the workers" that Gompers had referred to in the eighteen-nineties was not just an echo from his Marxist past, but a continuing aspiration. Socialist notions of revolution, either peaceful or violent, had no place in America. Through a natural process of evolution, encouraged by the nation's experience in war, industrial democracy was about to be born.

The notion of the natural evolution of social institutions can be a useful concept. But the belief in social evolution can be disastrous if it is simply an excuse for political inaction. It was here that Gompers and Walling were being singularly naive, for they believed that this evolution toward industrial democracy would continue irrespective of politics. What they forgot was that enemies of industrial democracy would be happy to use political, legal, and any other institutions in the forthcoming reaction.

Meanwhile, with the publication of its "Program of Social Reconstruction," the Socialist Democratic League had achieved its main purpose. It continued as a paper organization until 1920, but by the end of 1918 the leadership was already seeking advice about the organization's future. Simons advised a link with the newly emerging Labor Party—the course adopted by some of the majority socialists—but wished himself counted out.[64]

The truth was that some of the leading lights of the Socialist Democratic League had found bigger fish to fry. By the summer of 1918 Simons, Spargo, and Russell had all participated in the American Socialist Pro-War Mission to Europe, with the approval of the government. Spargo, by his own account, went on to become confidante and adviser to President Wilson on Russian matters.[65] Gradually, all drifted away from the socialism. The movement for Social Democracy in postwar America was to lie with their ex-comrades in the Socialist Party.

NOTES

1. Columbia University Oral History Project, *Norman Thomas Memoir*, 17.
2. See discussion in *Advance* (Amalgamated Clothing Workers), April 5, 1918, 8.
3. S. G. to Presidents of National and International Unions, March 2, 1917. (Samuel Gompers Copy Books, Library of Congress).
4. S. G. to Woodrow Wilson, March 6, 1917, (A. F. of L. Papers, Wisconsin State Historical Society).
5. W. P. Bloodgood to S. G. April 1, 1918 (A. F. of L. Papers).

6. S. G. to Newton D. Baker, June 12, 1917 (A. F. of L. Papers).
7. *Federationist,* February, 1916, 105-110.
8. See S. G. to J. W. Kline, April, 1917. G. W. Perkins to S. G., April 10, 1917 and S. G. to Advisory Commission to Council of National Defense, April 17, 1917 (A. F. of L. Papers).
9. Daniel J. Tobin to S. G. March 30, 1917 (A. F. of L. Papers).
10. Cleveland *Citizen,* March 30, 1918.
11. J. H. Maurer *It Can Be Done* (New York: Rand School Press, 1938), 237.
12. Ralph Easley to S. G., November 7, 1917. (A. F. of L. Papers).
13. V. E. Macey to S. G., October 1, 1917 (A. F. of L. Papers).
14. Sidney Webb, "British Labor under War Pressure," *North American Review* (June 1917), 205. Willard to S. G., June 16, 1917. S. G. to Willard, June 17, 1917 (A. F. of L. Papers).
15. R. Bruere, "English Labor and the War," *New Republic,* May 26, 1917. R. Bruere to S. G., March 25, 1918. (A. F. of L. Papers).
16. Columbia University Oral History Project, *John Spargo Memoir,* 211, 239-240.
17. *Garment Worker,* August 10, 1917, 4; May 17, 1918, 4.
1'8. *American Labor Year Book,* 1917, 373.
19. Spargo to S. G., November 20, 1917 (A. F. of L. Papers).
20. J. H. Maurer to S. G., October 4 and 15, 1917 (A. F. of L. Papers).
21. Maurer, *It Can Be Done,* 228-229.
22. Ernest J. Flood to S. G., October 2, 1917 (A. F. of L. Papers).
23. W. B. Rubin to S. G., December 29, 1917. S. G. to James Duncan, January 4, 1918. (A. F. of L. Papers).
24. Maisal to S. G., October 10 and 17, 1917; November 15, 1917; March 8, 1918 (A. F. of L. Papers).
25. Frank J. Hayes to Germer, March 4, 1918 (Germer Papers, Wisconsin State Historical Society).
26. *A. L. Y. B.* 1917, 341.
27. Quoted in James Weinstein, "The Socialist Party: Its Roots and Strength, 1912-1919," *Studies on the Left* I (Winter, 1960) 21.
28. "The Gompers' Circus, September, 1917 (Convention of American Alliance for Labor and Democracy)" Typescript in S. P. Collection, Duke.
29. G. D. Herron to Hillquit, August 7, 1917 (Hillquit Papers, Wisconsin State Historical Society).
30. Hyndman to Simons, July 1, 1917 (Simons Papers, Wisconsin State Historical Society).
31. Simons to May Wood Simons, September 5, 1917 (Simons Papers).
32. Max S. Hayes to his wife, November 10, 1917. (Hayes Papers, Ohio State Historical Society).
33. S. G. to Alexander Kerensky, September 13, 1917 (A. F. of L. Papers).
34. Columbia University Oral History Project, *Spargo Memoir,* 266.
35. F. J. Gould to Simons, January 4, 1917 (Simons Papers).
36. S. G. to Maisal, September 29, 1917 (A. F. of L. Papers).
37. Chester M. Wright to John Spargo, October 2, 1917. Spargo to Wright, October 4, 1917, (A. F. of L. Papers).
38. Maisal to S. G., October 1, 1917; October 5, 1917, (A. F. of L. Papers).
39. Spargo to S. G., October 9, 1917, (A. F. of L. Papers).
40. Chester M. Wright to W. R. Gaylord, October 13, 1917 (A. F. of L. Papers).

41. W. R. Gaylord to S. G., October 5, 1917 (A. F. of L. Papers).
42. Spargo to S. G., October 7, 1917 (A. F. of L. Papers).
43. D. C. Coates to S. G., April 11, 1918 (A. F. of L. Papers).
44. "National Party Report" March 27, 1918 (Printed Copy in A. F. of L. Papers).
45. W. E. Walling to S. G., February 19, 1918 (A. F. of L. Papers).
46. Walling to Simons, April 29, 1918 (Simons Papers).
47. Social Democratic League, "Program of Social Reconstruction (After the War Edition) Revised and Amended," (Simons Papers).
48. G. D. H. Cole, *Guild Socialism Re-Stated* (London: L. Parsons, 1920), 213.
49. Simons to Herron, December 10, 1919 (Simons Papers).
50. De Man to Simons, October 4, 1919 (Simons Papers).
51. Walling to Simons, April 29, 1918 (Simons Papers).
52. Walling to S. G., August 3, 1918 (A. F. of L. Papers).
53. Simons to Hyndman, December 12, 1918 (Simons Papers).
54. S. G. to Spargo, March 22, 1918 (A. F. of L. Papers).
55. S. G. to Spargo, March 22, 1918 (A. F. of L. Papers).
56. A. F. of L., *Proceedings* 1918, 84.
57. Walling to S. G., August 3, 1918 (A. F. of L. Papers).
58. *Federationist,* February, 1919, 129-140.
59. A. F. of L., *Proceedings* 1923, 31.
60. Articles discussed in Harry Lang, "Gompersism," *Justice,* February 1, 1924, 8-9.
61. *Justice,* April 29, 1921, 24.
62. S. G. to W. E. Remington, September 28, 1922 (A. F. of L. Papers).
63. See Louis S. Reed, *The Labor Philosophy of Samuel Gompers* (New York: Columbia University Press, 1930), 50-51.
64. C. E. Russell to Simons, December 6, 1918. Simons to Russell, December 16, 1918. Simons to Slobodin, April 3, 1919 (Simons Papers).
65. Columbia University Oral History Project *John Spargo Memoir,* 340.

7

The Reckoning

Unlike the British Labour Party, the Socialist Party of America in the years immediately following the war was in no position to take advantage of any changes wrought by wartime experience. True, the war brought as many people into its ranks as it lost. At elections, like Morris Hillquit's New York mayoralty campaign in 1917, the party did well. In the presidential campaign of 1920, Debs almost repeated his triumph of 1912 though he was a prisoner under the Espionage Act in Atlanta Penitentiary. But it was a very different party from the prewar days. Gone was the optimism that had looked forward to a steady growth and perhaps even a socialist America in the lifetime of the members. If membership numbers were good compared with the prewar days, their complexion had changed. A majority in early 1919 were non-English speaking. Under other circumstances the party still might have grown, for Debs' popularity, for instance, was untarnished, but the times were not propitious.

Facing a mounting barrage of persecution, as much after the war as during it, the Socialist Party lost its confidence. The conditions of liberty for really healthy growth, according to the Cleveland *Citizen,* were very much on the decline.[1] In some states which in prewar times boasted a sound state machinery—for instance, Oklahoma—the party all but disappeared. Where it remained, as in Wisconsin or Pennsylvania, it tended to be in isolated communities like Milwaukee or Reading. In New York State, where it retained as firm a hold as ever, the party suffered the ignominy of having its five electees in 1920 rejected by the State Assembly.

Attacked from without, the Socialist Party in 1919 also split from within. One section of the left wing quit in June and organized the Communist Party. The remainder of the left, having tried and failed to capture the regular party machinery at the August conference in Chicago, formed the Communist

Labor Party. The Socialist Party of America, so laboriously forged twenty years previously, was falling apart.

Secession had been preceded by expulsion. Lack of discipline was the immediate cause in the case of the Foreign Language Federations—seven immigrant groups directly affiliated with the national party. With large numbers recently arrived from eastern Europe, they were more open to communist influence. The state organization of Michigan, however, was expelled after the state convention resolved to oust those who persisted in advocating legislative reforms. The national party's reaction was probably too quick. Many claimed that even at its worst, the Socialist Labor Party had "never wielded the axe with such ruthlessness."[2]

These secession movements, of course, had been endemic in American socialism all along, as is evident from the divisions in the old Socialist Labor Party in the nineties and the expulsions of 1912. One Ohio socialist told the national secretary, Adolph Germer, that he left in 1919 for the same reason that many were tempted to leave at the 1912 purge.[3] Germer himself noted the similarity between the 1912 group and that in 1919.[4] Thus, it is curious to reflect that a line can be traced from the communist secessionists to the old Socialist Labor Party through Lenin— for the Russian leader apparently claimed to have been influenced by DeLeon. DeLeon, therefore, might be said to have finally wreaked his vengeance on the Socialist Party.[5]

But such statements detract from the catastrophe of 1919 for the American left. For two decades, the Socialist Party of America had provided a consistent alternative to corporate capitalism in the form of democratic socialism. Under its banner the left had united, and, constant wrangles notwithstanding, it had remained united and increasingly influential in American life. Since 1919 the left has comprised a series of warring sects, the most obvious characteristic of which has been futility. American political life has been the poorer for it.

The effect of persecution and division upon trade union support for the Socialist Party is very difficult to gauge. In unions where support had been traditional, as in the needle trades and among the rank and file miners, it probably continued. Several journals attempted sympathetic explanations of the divisions in the Socialist Party.[6] The International Ladies Garment Workers Union journal continued to advocate support, pointing out that as far as New York was concerned no other party voiced the protests of labor.[7] The miners in convention in Cleveland in 1919 came out for nationalization of the mines, thus making their official policy the same as the Western Federation of Miners. All this encouraged Mary Beard, writing in 1919, to believe that the trade unions were finally going to abandon "pure and simple" unionism.[8]

On the other hand, in spite of apparent continued sympathy, one historian estimates a steady decline of union support to a position far below its prewar figure.[9] Probably this can be accounted for less in dramatic changes than in gradual shifts of opinion. Technological changes encouraged the drift. In the Illinois State Federation of Labor, for instance, the influence of the miners waned and was replaced by city unions like the Teamsters.[10] This would undoubtedly mean a lessening of socialist influence as well.

The state of the Socialist Party after the war was therefore not likely to alarm Gompers and the A.F.ofL. leadership. In fact, had the events of the post-war reaction affected only the party, Gompers might have felt supremely confident in his traditional opposition to it. Unfortunately, the super patriots failed to distinguish adequately between labor and socialism, and the corporations took the opportunity to launch an "open shop" drive. The position that Gompers had achieved for labor during the war, even he had to admit, was very speedily lost. Nor was it simply a matter of prestige; numbers declined at an alarming rate. According to James H. Maurer, organized labor was losing eight thousand members a month.[11]

The reaction of 1919 was partly due to the dramatic series of strikes of that year, in particular, the general strike in Seattle, the Boston Police strike, and the steel strike. It has been estimated that one in every five workmen in the United States struck during the year. But although the public associated the strikes with extreme radicalism, both communists and socialists were too much preoccupied with their own affairs to give them much attention.

Seattle's Central Labor Council, which engineered the general strike, did have socialist and radical elements. It constantly advocated industrial unionism and its representatives at A.F.ofL. conventions were on occasion the only delegates to oppose the re-election of Gompers. The West Coast was also a traditional I. W. W. stronghold, and Seattle workers seem to have been particularly class conscious. But William L. Hutcheson of the carpenters union considered I.W.W. successes to be simply the result of A.F.ofL. indifference.[12] The Central Labor Council remained A.F.ofL.-affiliated, while its leader, James A. Duncan, was not even a socialist party member at the time. Seattle's mayor, Ole Hanson might talk of "red revolution," but the strike was essentially a symptom of general unrest and a response to the antiunion drive. I.W.W. presence merely provided employers with an excuse for an attack on all unions.[13]

The Boston Police Strike erupted when some officers were dismissed for forming a union and applying to the A.F.ofL. for a charter; there is no trace of socialism whatsoever. Also during 1919 the miners, a traditional stronghold of socialism, struck in the bituminous fields. But the new United Mine Workers president, John L. Lewis, surprised even the A.F.ofL. by calling off the strike in accordance with a sweeping court injunction.

The steel strike, from the point of view of the issues raised in this study, was probably the most interesting. Quietly dissatisfied since the defeat at Homestead in 1892, the steel workers in the early twentieth century show American labor in microcosm. The principal union, the narrowly craft-based Amalgamated Association of Iron, Steel and Tin Workers, scarcely touched the American-born unskilled, let alone the vast number of immigrant "hunkies" who populated the steel mills of America. The social divisions separating white Americans from immigrants and blacks were fostered by the steel magnates through a system of benefits handed out to the more trusted employees. This mild paternalism, though little affecting the basic capitalist structure or deplorable social conditions—the twelve hour day was standard—was sufficient to sap the moral fiber of unionism. A mild attempt at transforming the Amalgamated into an industrial union after 1909 foundered badly.

Under the benevolent wing of the American government's "war socialism" the situation changed. Steel workers gained a new confidence and unions expanded. By 1918 the men were ready for an all-out organization drive. The steel strike of 1919, which grew out of this drive, gained a notoriety for radicalism. John Fitzpatrick, president of the Chicago Federation of Labor and head of the national committee of all the unions involved in the strike, was a strong labor party advocate. William Z. Foster, the secretary of the committee, was at one time associated with the I.W.W., the author of a pamphlet on syndicalism, and later a well-known communist. The strike also had the support of radical unions like the Amalgamated Clothing Workers. Yet it is surprising how little socialist or really radical activity there was. Fitzpatrick had worked with Foster in organizing the Chicago stockyards, and Foster in 1919 even seems to have been reconciled to craft organization.[14] He probably retained radical ideas but they had little influence on his work.

The stress on the craft principle proved a fatal flaw. It caused dissension among leaders and disrupted finances. It was perhaps also incompatible with the idealism of the rank and file behind the strike. But equally important as a cause of failure was active repression encouraged by a hostile public opinion. The steel strike suffered from the public's fear of radicalism engendered by the earlier strikes, and the strike also intensified that fear. Gompers did his best to defend the strike leaders, particularly Foster, against charges of revolutionism,[15] but in a sense, the A.F.ofL. leaders were partly responsible.

Gompers was in Europe when the Seattle strike occurred, but his deputy on the the *American Federationist,* Mathew Woll, claimed it was "promoted by motives foreign to American trade unionism."[16] It was the kind of attitude Gompers had been expounding himself a little earlier. He had joined in the hue and cry against the Socialist Party as un-American; now the mass hysteria boomeranged against labor and was exploited by the steel companies in their intent to destroy unionism. Letters pouring into Gompers' office from A.F.ofL. organizers about the steel trusts' "brutal and un-American" tactics reveal the bankruptcy of Gompers' appeal to patriotism.[17]

Meyer London, the socialist congressman, speaking before the International Ladies' Garment Workers' Union convention in 1918, had warned of the dangers confronting both socialism and trade unionism. Repudiating the naive notion that socialism was just around the corner, he pointed out that the talk of denationalizing the railroads and building temporary rather than permanent government housing showed that even the achievements of war socialism would be undone.[18] But even London underestimated what was coming. Not only were wartime concessions to labor attacked, but also the gains apparently achieved before the war. In the midst of the hysteria in which civil rights were disregarded, the whole basis of unionism was also placed in jeopardy. James

Maurer claimed antisedition bills introduced into several state legislatures owed their origin to the United States Chamber of Commerce and were aimed at labor.[19] Significantly, the open shop drive was also called the "American Plan."

The antiunion movement to a considerable extent was instigated by the American Anti-Boycott Association, which had earlier won the Danbury Hatters' and the Buck Stove and Range Company cases. It now changed its name to the League for Industrial Rights, and broadened its aims. Besides the open shop drive, the league sought antiunion legislation and encouraged the use of the injunction by the courts.

Probably the sweeping use of injunctions in the years after the war was the most dramatic evidence of labor's loss of power. The final decision of the Supreme Court in the Hitchman Coal and Coke Company case in 1917, upholding an injunction that assumed the legal validity of "yellow dog" contracts, was described as "a five decade retreat from progress."[20] But worse followed. After the Clayton Act—Labor's Magna Carta—Gompers had claimed unions to be free from the provisions of the Sherman Act. But the Supreme Court's 1921 decision in the Duplex Printing Company case undermined the main provisions of the Clayton Act, while in the Coronado decision (the case was not completed until 1925), the United Mine Workers were once again prosecuted under the Sherman Act.

Perhaps some left-wing unionists exaggerated the state of affairs. Ira W. Bird of the Amalgamated Clothing Workers, reflecting on Debs' imprisonment, remarked: "It will be as unsafe to hold May Day parades in America on May 1, as it was in the days of the Czar Nicholas."[21] More to the point, Max S. Hayes at the 1922 convention of the A.F.ofL. claimed that the antiunion drive was so strong that "some organizations [were] even considering the matter of transferring their funds from free America, free republican democratic America, to monarchical Great Britain and its dominions."[22] But even Gompers, the "second most important figure in the nation" only a few months before, and convinced that industrial democracy was about to evolve, now had second thoughts about the success of his policies.

An industrial conference representing labor, management, and the public, called by President Wilson in the midst of the steel strike, ended when Gompers walked out in disgust. Employers had refused even to accept the principle of collective bargaining.[23]

Former friends in government such as Newton D. Baker now joined the drive for an open shop,[24] and in fact the entire United States government seemed to favor it. Gone were the days when Gompers hailed the Clayton Act as the most important legislation ever codified. Now there was present "the greatest conspiracy to destroy democratic government and establish autocratic rule."[25] "When the Clayton law was enacted," Gompers wrote, "it was believed that the day of injunctions in industrial disputes was past. The law provided that no more such injunctions should be issued . . . The Clayton Act told the judge where to stop, but they have manifested as little regard for the law of the land as autocrats certainly manifest."[26] Not only was it the frequency of injunctions, moreover, but their constantly widening scope.

Gompers' tragic failure touched even the socialists. After one harangue delivered at Cooper Union, in which he called for civil disobedience, "friend and enemy alike," according to one reporter, "admit[ted] that the speech was one of the strongest and most effective ever made by him." Significantly, what touched them most was "his expression of bitter disappointment over the results of the war."[27]

But however much Gompers may have expressed his bitterness, when faced with the question of what to do about the onslaught on labor, he gave no answer but to stress the traditional policies of the A.F.ofL. For someone interested in democratic control of industry, for instance, it is a little surprising to find Gompers opposing the Plumb Plan—a scheme to keep the railroads under government control, but with decided moves in the direction of industrial democracy. G. D. H. Cole saw in the Plumb Plan the rudiments of the guild socialist idea,[28] which we have seen seems to have been the direction of Gompers' thought. The railroad brotherhoods favored the scheme; Henry Slobodin, still in the Social Democratic League, maintained that 90 per cent of the fourteen railroad brotherhoods endorsed it.[29] Gompers sought the opinions of many people, including John Spargo and Charles Edward Russell. Russell heartily approved,[30] and though Spargo raised questions about the special privileges railroad workers would enjoy over others, he approved the idea of worker participation.[31] Yet, finally Gompers came down against the plan and objected to the use of his name in connection with it.[32]

At the A.F.ofL. convention in 1920 the issue was clouded by the fact that the proposed resolution called simply for government ownership, as opposed to the Plumb Plan as such. Gompers could then claim he was worried about the right to strike in a nationalized industry, but with the wide use of injunctions and even the provisions of the Esch-Cummins Bill, which returned the railroads to private ownership, this right was far from clear anyway. For once, however, Gompers failed to get his way and the convention endorsed government ownership.[33]

This was a time of rising interest in nationalization. The mine workers made plans, as Brophy explains, to carry out an "educational legislative mandate" on the subject.[34] Nationalization also appealed to the socialist needle trades. The Ohio State Federation of Labor at its convention in 1918 adopted a reconstruction program calling for nationalization of railroads, telegraphs, merchant marine, coal mines, and oil production. Frank Morrison, a vice president of the A.F.ofL., believed that the endorsement of government ownership of railroads was merely carrying out the provisions of the A.F.ofL.'s own reconstruction program.[35]

Considering the diminishing numbers in the labor movement in the postwar period, one might also have expected a greater interest in the old question of industrial unionism. The reconstruction program had made suggestions along this line. But the A.F.ofL. insisted on the steel workers organizing by craft unions, and in spite of the steel strike's disastrous failure, Gompers still lectured his readers two years later that the matter of industrial unionism had been settled at the Scranton and Rochester conventions in 1901 and 1912.[36]

On the political field in particular, Gompers might have questioned the success of traditional policies. Yet in his dealings with the international labor movement, if anything Gompers made a greater display of his antisocialism than before.[37] At home he admitted: "The Congress of the United States has failed to do its duty. It has failed to meet the emergency. It has given encouragement and support to autocratic and reactionary policies. Its dominating thought has been the repression of labor."[38] Yet what was to be done? "Scorned by Congress, ridiculed and misrepresented by many members of both houses," Gompers declared, "the American labor movement finds it necessary to apply vigorously its long and well established nonpartisan political policy."[39]

Gompers' general leadership did not go uncriticized either inside or outside the A.F.ofL. For instance, a number of the so-

called intellectual periodicals—*New Republic, Dial, Survey*—
produced a barrage of criticism of Gompers for his intellectual
bankruptcy and recommended a change of president.[40] What gave
their criticisms a particular potency was the comparison bound
to emerge between American labor and British. As American labor
seemed to meet defeat after defeat, the British Labor Party, newly
reconstituted and equipped with a socialist program, won astound-
ing success at the polls. It was bound to raise questions about
the entire history of American labor.

Gompers started off the argument by dismissing the British
ideas as the work of intellectuals, thinking wholly in political
terms. To the *New Republic,* this attitude only "furthered additional evidence of the deep divergence between European and
American labor—and it is to be feared of a grand failure on the
part of American trade unionists to understand the spirit, motives
and the real nature of the forces animating the new movement
in Europe." It dismissed the A.F.ofL.'s attacks on intellectuals
as "far too narrowly class conscious."[41]

The question of "class consciousness" was always difficult for
Gompers. He used to insist that American labor was "class conscious"—in fact, "the most class conscious movement in the
world." What he meant of course was that it was solely composed
of workers, and not, as he would have termed it, burdened by
professional politicians, theorists, and intellectuals of other classes.
The American labor movement was thus "not the product of
men's imaginations," but a natural growth: it was "truly progressive," and thus truly American. The attacks of socialists and
intellectuals were merely further evidence of "the manner in
which reactionary and radical come together in the effect to
undermine the truly progressive."[42] Gompers embroidered this
same theme two years later when the first Labour government
took office in Great Britain. He offered Ramsay MacDonald
his congratulations, but qualified them by pointing out how many
in America not sympathetic to labor also congratulated him.
"Even conservatives and reactionaries," he noted, "join in pointing with pride to the statesmanship of MacDonald and the
'lamentable differences' not to speak of 'blundering reaction' of
American labor, which insists upon being American in politics
as in all things."[43]

If Gompers considered his brand of "class consciousness" truly
progressive, however, socialists were unconvinced. Commenting

on the *New Republic*'s criticisms, Victor Berger said that the A.F.ofL. leaders were "willing to accept the stigma of inferiority for the masses, so long as they, the great national labor leaders, [were] very considerably better off than the rest of the herd."[44]

But the talk of American labor's class consciousness and its effect was probably embarrassing for Gompers. He must have welcomed Charles Edward Russell's article in the *American Federationist* on "American Labor Wisdom." This article suggested that "labor in a caste country turns [where it can] to political action by its own caste, as its only chance of escape from the terrible and crushing disadvantage the men and women of the lower castes must suffer." On the other hand, "labor in a country without caste [would] never turn to such measures for relief." America, it seemed, had class consciousness represented in the A.F.ofL., but not caste. This was to be the guide to political action.[45]

Within the A.F.ofL., opposition to Gompers and his establishment had always been present, usually with socialists behind it. In the postwar period, as a reflection of Gompers' apparent ineptitude, opposition gathered momentum. In 1918 one member of the old guard, John Lennon, was unseated and replaced by Daniel Tobin. This was not, as the Cleveland *Citizen* pointed out, a socialist victory, but it was certainly regarded as a progressive move.[46] In 1920 there was also talk of a complete reorganization of the A.F.ofL. including even the abolition of the executive council, the stronghold of the old guard.[47]

With the chief opposition centered around the name of John L. Lewis, the matter came to a head at the 1921 convention. What makes this episode odd is that in many eyes Lewis, though later associated with the industrial unionism of the C.I.O., was more conservative than Gompers. For instance, even Gompers' old enemy, the International Ladies' Garment Workers' journal pointed out Lewis' betrayal of his followers in accepting the injunction of 1919 and recommended the re-election of Gompers.[48] John Brophy, who was later to rival Lewis himself as president of the United Mine Workers, claimed Lewis was the "business unionist" par excellence—a lover of power and very much affected by the capitalists he came into contact with. Brophy also argues that Gompers, in contrast with Lewis, saw much more in the unions than just a means of getting more money. In other words, like so many others, Brophy was aware of the social idealism in

Gompers' make-up.[49] On the other hand, Gompers' reluctance to have anything to do with nationalization threw many radicals over to the Lewis side—perhaps more out of desperation than real conviction. But it was all to no effect. The Gompers machine defeated Lewis comfortably; Gompers was to remain at the helm until his death.

The internal opposition to the A.F.ofL. leadership also took another significant form in the postwar era, when many prominent labor figures tried to overthrow the traditional nonpartisan policy and make a fresh attempt at a labor party.

The labor party movement had been alive beneath the surface ever since the origin of the A.F.ofL. and had erupted at various times: the Henry George campaign, the movement in Illinois during the populist period, the labor party in California. It was an idea that appealed to many socialist trade unionists, though not all. What set it off again was the growing success of the Labour Party in Great Britain. As Victor Berger declared: "Since our labor movement has in the past always followed the development of the British labor movement, it is almost certain that socialist ideas will finally get control of the capitalist and reactionary American trade unions."[50] Thus, the British party's meeting with great success naturally appealed to politically minded trade unionists, while at the same time its social program also brought round some socialists traditionally troubled by the idea of fusion. As the *American Labor Year Book* pointed out, "the moving spirits [in the Labor Party in America] were the men and women who have always believed in political action on the part of labor, and some of them had previously supported the Socialist Party in its political campaign."[51] The Cleveland *Citizen* believed that one of the crucial questions was whether there would be real cooperation between the new movement and the Socialist Party. It was optimistic since in both Great Britain and Australia, socialists and laborites had for a long time not agreed, but eventually had come together.[52]

As in the Henry George period, the two main centers of political activity were New York and Illinois. From these two points an attempt was made to form a truly American labor party.

In New York the party was organized in a convention meeting January 11–12, 1919. There were 884 delegates representing the Central Federated Union, the Central Labor Union of Brooklyn, and the Women's Trade Union League, as well as 152 locals,

41 international trade unions, and even the united Board of the
business agents of the building trades. Other groups like the
World War Veterans and the socialists expressed some interest.[53]

The program of the new party was similar in many respects
to the British Labour Party's. Besides demanding a restoration
of free speech, it called for the "democratic control of industry
and commerce, by those who work by hand and brain, and the
elimination of autocratic domination of the forces of production
either by selfish private interests or bureaucratic agents of government, the equitable sharing of the proceeds among all who
participate in any capacity and only among these . . ."[54]

The following year a convention representing organizations in
the state of New York met at Schenectady and adopted a similar
program. According to one adverse report, the party had a
"somewhat radical platform rather like the nonpartisan platform
of the A.F.ofL. and where it differed, leaning toward the Socialist Party."[55]

The movement in Chicago was the stronger of the two. Starting as the Labor Party of Cook County, it soon grew. On
October 6, 1918, the Chicago Federation of Labor voted to
request the president of the Illinois State Federation of Labor
to "call a convention in the immediate future for the purpose of
considering the advisability of forming in Illinois an Independent
Labor Party along the lines of the British Labour Party, but
adapted to American conditions."[56] The president, who at that
time was the socialist mine worker, Duncan MacDonald, re-
sponded favorably, but it meant his resigning from the Socialist
Party. There were grounds for optimism for the new party, for
in municipal elections in 1919, before the convention was due,
some labor tickets did well. John B. Lennon, of all people, "the
veteran treasurer of the A.F.ofL.," got 10,000 votes, only 286
short of election. John Fitzpatrick, president of the Chicago
Federation of Labor, got 55,990 votes in the Chicago mayoralty
race. Though apparently somewhat disappointed by the Chicago
results, Illinois labor decided to go on.

The state convention duly met on April 10, 1919, at Springfield,
Illinois. The preamble to the platform resembled New York's in
making an issue of the fact that it was "the party of the worker
with hand and brain." Significantly too, this convention adopted a
resolution declaring that the Labor Party of Illinois desired "to
place on record a statement of appreciation of the great service

rendered to the cause of labor by the socialist movement by its campaign of education carried on so vigorously and at such noble sacrifice." The statement continued: "We urgently invite all socialists who see larger hopes for the workers through the plans of the Labor Party to come into this party, and become fellow workers with us."[57]

Labor parties appeared elsewhere. In Ohio a convention was called in Cayohoga County (Cleveland) after several postponements. In Pennsylvania and elsewhere similar moves were undertaken by trade union bodies. Support came from all over. The *New Republic* regarded these moves as the most "attractive rallying cry for many decades," and continued to support the Labor Party idea over the following year.[58] The miners' convention in 1919 went on record as favoring the party. Some were tempted to think a majority of rank and file trade unionists favored the move. The Cleveland *Citizen* pointed out that the "much discussed A.F.ofL. policy" had never been approved by A.F.ofL. membership.[59] Even the staunchest supporter of the Gompers' outlook, the United Garment Workers, though doubtful of success, "was not at all sure, but that the present effort may prove successful." The editor of the journal added: "These are exceptional times . . ."[60]

Meanwhile, the state labor parties had catapulted onto a national scale. A meeting was held on December 6, 1919, to form a Labor Party of the United States. Thirty-seven states were represented and fifty-five affiliates of the A.F.ofL. together with the Railroad Brotherhoods. Max S. Hayes, as chairman of the temporary executive committee, tried to bring in dissatisfied groups. J. H. Walker, soon to replace Duncan MacDonald as president of the Illinois State Federation of Labor, was made vice chairman. At the crucial convention in the presidential election year 1920, however, though the Labor Party was joined by the Non-Partisan League and the Committee of Forty-Eight to form the Farmer-Labor Party, the trade unions had a much smaller representation. Only 171 local unions and two central bodies participated. At this convention P. P. Christensen was chosen presidential candidate with Max S. Hayes as his running mate. Hayes meanwhile had had to resign from the Socialist Party.

On the whole, the results of the election were disappointing. Even in Illinois the vote was unfavorable compared with those in 1919, though part is accounted for by the rivalry of the Socialist Party. The Farmer-Labor Party as a national force thus did not survive the 1920 election. As the convention of 1921 witnessed, the Farmer-Labor movement now worked on a state basis. Twenty states had Farmer-Labor parties, and in three—South Dakota, Minnesota, and Washington—they had replaced the Democrats as the second party. But these parties were much more farmer than labor. The Labor Party of Illinois remained in existence, seeking a new national combination. The party in New York disappeared as an independent force.

The idea of a labor party had come and gone once again. It remains to examine, however, the official attitude of the two bodies mainly interested—the federative body of the A.F.ofL. and the Socialist Party.

Mathew Woll, the chief A.F.ofL. spokesman while Gompers was in Europe in 1919, maintained that the dispute between labor party advocates and the old guard was "not one of substance but of procedure." Nevertheless, he felt a Labor Party was inadvisable.[61] Gompers didn't even concede that much. From the start he produced the old arguments dating from the Henry George campaign.[62] A "nonpartisan" policy was the only one for the A.F.ofL., and, as always, that meant it had to choose between the two old parties exclusively. As the Cleveland *Citizen* pointed out, Gompers denounced the two old parties, and then asked American labor to stand by them. He was also guilty of some intellectual dishonesty: the Democrats did not in their platform in 1920 specifically endorse Attorney General Palmer's injunctions, therefore he concluded they condemned them.[63]

But it was basically Gompers' "syndicalist" concepts that seemed to predominate in his public utterances. In spite of his change during the war and the gains he made from it, Gompers' principal reason for avoiding politics was still his mistrust of politicians. Speaking in New York on December 9, 1918, he contrasted the freedom of American labor with that of Europe—in particular, Germany, France, and Great Britain—where the labor movements were all dominated by politicians.[64] When Benjamin Schlesinger demanded to know at the 1919 A.F.ofL. convention whether the organization went on record as being opposed to the new labor parties, Secretary Woll replied: "To render ineffective, or to hamper in any degree, or to lessen the importance and value of trade union economic determinism merely to attain possession of political authority, to place into dominance political parliamentarianism, will not have been a gain but a loss to the advancement of the workers to a fuller, a freer, a better, a nobler life."[65]

The question arose again in the *American Federationist* in

spring 1920. Certain prolabor party members of the A.F.ofL., like
E. N. Nockels, the secretary of the Chicago Federation of Labor,
and William A. Mitch, leader of the Labor Party in Indiana and
secretary-treasurer of the United Miners in the same state, both
advocated action on the British model. Immediately the old
paranoia came out. These men were intentionally trying to hurt
the trade union movement by handing it over to the politicians.
Admittedly, Gompers also maintained that geographical conditions and the lack of homogeneity of the American people made
British conditions inapplicable to America. But his main theme
was the fear of politicians on general grounds. It took Mitch to
point out that any politicians who became merely seekers of power
would simply no longer be supported.[66]

Gompers' opposition to the American Labor Party was largely
for negative reasons. There is little trace in his writings of the
positive argument that Americans were so much better off than
Europeans that a labor party was unnecessary. Nevertheless, this
was argued in other trade union journals, particularly the Shoe
Workers *Journal*. "The reason why a labor party will not succeed
is not because of a weakness of trade unions in number," one
article stated, "but because of the strength of the trade unions as
an economic power which will not allow itself to be dissipated in
the political field."[67] Interestingly, William English Walling, as
syndicalist as ever, later wrote in the same journal on this theme.[68]
But even the Shoe Workers *Journal* echoed Gompers' fears of
politicians, and termed the Labor Party merely "playing toy
politics for the benefit or aggrandizement of the promoters of
such a movement, many of the leaders of which are socialists of
more or less prominence."[69]

In spite of its dislike of the whole idea of a labor party, the
A.F.ofL. leadership at the convention in 1919 had to recognize
the right of affiliated unions, state branches, and central bodies to
do as they wished. This position was repeated at the 1920 convention. But it would be quite wrong to imagine that Gompers and
his cohorts meekly accepted the fact that many affiliated bodies
took an active interest in the movement. On the contrary, they
vehemently opposed it and not merely verbally.

In December, 1918, when the idea was first being propagated,
Gompers called a conference of several A.F.ofL. committees and
as many leaders of labor in and around New York as would come.
Here he made his views plain enough.[70] Almost a year later, when
the American Labor Party was under way, he was ready for more

drastic action. A few days after the launching of the American Labor Party in December, 1919, Gompers called a conference to organize support for the traditional nonpartisan policy. It was to be on a national scale. Represented were eighty-nine national and international unions affiliated with the A.F.ofL., together with the four Railroad Brotherhoods. This conference drew up a new "bill of grievances" called "Labor's Protests, Grievances, and Demands," and chose a special "non-partisan campaign committee" composed of the executive council of the A.F.ofL. and the heads of its departments. One authority has called this "the most extensive political campaign in the history of the A.F.ofL. to defeat the legislative enemies of the workers and elect its friends."[71] Perhaps so, but a principal motive behind it seems to have been to take the wind out of the Labor Party's sails. With justification, the *New Majority,* the publication of the Labor Party, claimed: "The A.F.ofL. is trying to scare everyone to death who dares to rise up and oppose its political ideas."[72]

Gompers also took more direct steps. The Central Federated Union of New York had endorsed the Labor Party by referendum. Gompers induced the Brooklyn Central Labor Union to withdraw support and maneuver the abandonment of the Central Federated Union's radical policies. By a vote of 22 to 18, conservatives carried a motion supporting the nonpartisan policy of the A.F.ofL.,[73] which in this case meant endorsing Tammany Hall.

Before the 1922 elections, the A.F.ofL. dealt a final blow to the Farmer-Labor Party, through the Joint Legislative Board (of the A.F.ofL. and the Railroad Brotherhoods). At a conference in which the Farmer-Labor Party was represented only unofficially, it was announced: "We believe no candidate should be put in the field by the workers themselves except where they have a reasonable assurance of electing such candidates, or where there are no candidates in other tickets that can be depended upon to support labor's program."[74]

Before then, however, the disappointments for the Labor Party in the election of 1920 had made Gompers jubilant. One phrase sums up his attitude: "The Farmer-Labor Party experiment, which was neither farmer nor labor, but merely a combination of foolishness and presumption . . ."[75] "Presumption" is the key word. The Labor Party had presumed to know how to proceed and had been proved wrong. There was unfortunately little to suggest, however, that Gompers' own campaign had been any more successful.

It was also odd for Gompers to argue that a movement had been proved wrong by events, when he himself had done everything in his power to mold these events. The effect of the A.F.ofL. propaganda on the average trade union man and his family is impossible to gauge. Perhaps the Amalgamated Clothing Workers' journal was right in saying that "the average union member would probably [have accepted] a labor party if it [had been] brought to him on a silver platter, made, furnished and completed, and with the blessings of the big labor leaders." The article aptly concluded: "One reason why the movement for independent working class political action is so immobile is the lack of boldness to do the thing that the big rewarders and punishers do not want done."[76]

Of course, it will be argued that a host of other reasons account for the failure of the Labor Party—the frauds, the usual pitfalls of third parties, the normalcy reaction; in fact, the whole American environment. Even if this were all true it is not clear that Gompers had anything to lose by trying. At any rate the A.F.ofL. 1922 convention adopted a rather curious resolution that bears consideration. It called for the support of the nonpartisan policy, but preceded it with this preamble: "Whereas, believing that *while a third party is necessary,* there are too many of our laboring men and women that owe too close an allegiance to the two old parties for inherited national reasons, that they are unwilling to relinquish and renounce . . ."[77] Put in blunt terms, this preamble states that the situation was bleak and a third party necessary, but that labor was powerless because of the deeply ingrained, irrational habits of Americans. Gompers had said as much in the nineties. By the twenties, after the triumphs of the war years, the political helplessness of labor was a bitter pill to swallow. He took refuge in saying his policy was "the American way."

Initially, the Socialist Party's attitude toward the Labor Party movement was equally negative and the national executive committee remained adamant against fusion. In 1919 it issued a special circular addressed to all members of the party, pointing out that the national and all state constitutions of the Socialist Party forbade members joining any other political organizations. The statement seems to have been quite effective in some quarters. Some of the chief opponents of the Labor Party in the Illinois State Federation of Labor, for instance, were socialists who wished the Labor Party to join the Socialist Party. John H. Walker maintained in reply that after twenty-five years' experience with the forces the resolution asked to bring together, he was convinced there would be an explosion the minute they coalesced.[78]

Elsewhere, some long-standing socialists felt obliged to leave the party. The most prominent were Max S. Hayes and Duncan MacDonald, both eminent in the A.F.ofL.[79] Hayes' reasoning was nevertheless peculiar. "The bane of the labor movement in this country has been the so-called intellectuals," he said. "Look at the mess just made of the Socialist Party." He then compared its lack of progress with the strides made by the new Labor Party.[80] The following year, however, Hayes was trying to woo the old socialist party bolters, intellectuals for the most part, into the Labor Party.[81]

The antifusion stand of the Socialist Party was not entirely logical. The 1920 platform, for instance, systematically omitted any Marxist terminology. Though this infuriated Debs, Hillquit considered it a merit.[82] Apparently, he was already thinking seriously about letters he received at this time from Job Harriman, the old labor party advocate still demanding fusion.[83] Under Hillquit's guidance, the Socialist Party eventually took Harriman's advice, but meanwhile the situation was frustrating. James H. Maurer, the president of the Pennsylvania State Federation of Labor, had to decline the Socialist Party's vice presidential nomination, partly because of the embarrassment its acceptance would cause in opposing candidates on the Labor Party ticket.[84]

Socialist opposition to the Labor Party made an interesting break with British precedent, noted by friends and enemies alike. The now conservative Shoe Workers *Journal,* for instance, got a fine opportunity to point out the anomalous situation when Arthur Henderson was invited by the American Labor Party to visit the United States. "Doesn't Henderson know," they asked, "that the American Labor Party of greater New York is taboo with good comrades, and has been officially disavowed and otherwise frowned upon by the party and its members denied permission to affiliate? What does Henderson mean by coming to America to organize workers away from the Socialist Party? Why doesn't somebody tip him off before he gets across the Atlantic and gets tangled up in the various left and right wings of the Socialist Party? One of the little groups of serious thinkers will have to denounce him, and what will the comrades think then?"[85]

Many socialist trade unionists, attracted by the idea of the Labor Party, were bewildered by the party's intransigence. The Amalgamated Clothing Workers, whom Gompers surprisingly accused of being behind the Labor Party,[86] complained of a lack of clearness in the party's attitude in 1919: "One would be justified in expecting more clearness of mind, and consistency of action of the Socialist movement than of that as yet vague formation that is generally known as the labor movement. The labor organizations and individuals who have supported the Socialist movement in the political field have a right to look to it for advice and guidance at this important juncture." A year later, however, the same journal decided that the party should stay out. "The Labor Party surely realizes," it argued, "that it will not elect its candidate . . . The Labor Party can be no more than a protest in the coming campaign. Why then not make the protest as ringing and challenging as possible."[87] The means was to vote for Debs.

The International Ladies' Garment Workers' Union, on the other hand, adopted the opposite view. In 1919 one article in the journal expressed the hope that "the socialists, being the most intelligent and conscious element of the labor world will in America, as they did in England, become the leaders of the party, and so gradually convert the workers to socialism."[88] A year later, in reply to a correspondent who feared the dangers of fusion, the editor replied he was for socialism, but not necessarily for the Socialist Party. "If the Socialist Party proves itself to be faulty and ineffective to achieve the desired end," he said, "a more effective and sharper instrument must be devised."[89]

It must have been a relief to socialist trade unionists when the 1922 Socialist Party convention amended the constitution and permitted state parties to cooperate with "organizations of labor and working farmers within their state, in independent political action." The party still wished to make sure, however, that its separate identity would be maintained.[90]

Exciting developments had been taking place on the political scene that made this departure from traditional socialist policy seem advisable. Both the farmers and certain parts of American labor, particularly the Railroad Brotherhoods, were again politically restless. Perhaps more than the A.F.ofL., the Brotherhoods sensed the gulf between their wartime position under government control and the postwar situation. There was certainly a far drop from the harmony of the Federal Railroad Administration, which the Plumb Plan had sought to preserve, to the Daugherty injunction against the striking Railroad Shopmen in 1922.

With the talk of new political activity in the air, the Detroit convention of the Socialist Party in 1921 had passed a resolution, proposed by Hillquit, instructing the national executive committee to explore the possibility of cooperation with other progressive groups. With this mandate, the party answered an invitation sent out by the Railroad Brotherhoods to attend a conference of progressive groups in Chicago in February, 1922. A permanent organization called the Conference for Progressive Political Action was then founded. The decision of the 1922 Socialist Party convention to permit cooperation on a state level was therefore a logical step.

It could be argued, of course, that the socialists' agreement to work with the diverse elements that constituted the C.P.P.A. is evidence of desperation rather than of conviction. Certainly it is a little difficult to understand otherwise the sudden willingness to work in harmony with the Farmer-Labor Party of Illinois, a group of former "Bull Moose" progressives called the Committee of Forty Eight, and the Railroad Brotherhoods, who in spite of their early association with Debs were never too friendly toward socialism. Obviously the changed conditions of the twenties had caused the Socialist Party to have second thoughts about the possibilities of American socialism. Hillquit, in fact, felt the entire role of the Socialist Party had changed. "It has no interests of its own," he told one critic. "Its sole aim in politics is to educate the workers to the necessity of organizing their own political power." Rather astonishingly, he added that the Socialist Party had never cared for "votes as votes or office as office."[91]

But equally important in making this new departure was the continuing success of the British Labour Party, now rapidly abandoning its "third party status." When Bertrand Russell argued in New York that the first British Labour government in 1924 was not really socialist, Hillquit for one would have none of it.[92] Two years before he had suggested some communication with the British party in order to acquire information about its practical methods and propaganda.[93] He also pointed out that the British Labour Party had only 365,000 members twenty years before, but by 1923 it had close to five million. With the British example to guide them, Hillquit believed Americans could accomplish the same in five years. An interesting piece of evidence for the influence of the British example is provided by the chronological charts that the socialists brought out at this time, comparing events in Great Britain and the U.S.A. over the previous decades.[94]

Once involved, the socialists' immediate aim in all their dealings with the C.P.P.A. was the creation as soon as possible of a new party. At the first convention in February, 1922, Hillquit was appointed to the committee that was drawing up a statement of purpose, and he felt he made an important impact by drawing the conference back to the labor party idea. He remained disappointed at the two C.P.P.A. meetings in February and December 1922, however, since no new party emerged. At this point the Illinois Farmer-Labor Party withdrew and attempted to organize a new national labor party on its own. At its 1923 meeting, however, it was taken over by the Communist Workers Party, headed by Earl Browder and William Z. Foster, now thoroughly involved in the Communist movement. The Illinois State Federation of Labor at its convention in Decatur, therefore, with Fitzpatrick and Walker in the lead, decided to abandon the party. They never forgot the experience. Walker led the opposition to the labor party motion at the 1923 A.F.ofL. convention; when the labor party issue was raised again in the thirties, Fitzpatrick opposed. A few enthusiasts in the Illinois labor movement tried to keep the state party in operation, but the motion was easily defeated.

The socialists, meanwhile, determined to stay with the C.P.P.A. and to use whatever influence they had to create third parties at state level. In greater New York where their party was strong, they immediately tried to put this policy into operation. Socialists participated in a convention in July 1922 called by the "Joint Committee for Independent Labor Political Action." It was made up of three groups: the Socialist Party, the Farmer-Labor Party of New York, and the trade unions, most of whose representatives were from the needle trades of New York City. The convention formed the Independent Labor Party, which subsequently changed its title to "the American Labor Party of New York." Having drawn up a platform and chosen candidates, it called upon the Central Trades and Labor Council of New York to "scrutinize carefully the records of its nominees and platform, in accordance with the resolution of the Central Trades and Labor Council itself, and also of the Chicago conference of the C.P.P.A."[96] The executive committee then proceeded to elect a campaign committee to fight the elections of 1922.

The second convention of the American Labor Party of New York in February 1923, following the December 1922 meeting of the national C.P.P.A., seems to have been more concerned with thwarting the Communists, who were also creating difficulties. By the time of the third convention in September 1923, however, a crisis had occurred in New York that almost brought Socialist Party participation in the national C.P.P.A. to an end. This crisis was caused by a self-styled C.P.P.A. conference at Albany, New York, during the summer of 1923.

The American Labor Party of New York considered itself the state C.P.P.A. affiliate. But since it was really concentrated in greater New York City and most, though not all of its trade union and Farmer-Labor representatives were socialist or socialist sympathizers, it is not altogether surprising that the Railroad Brotherhoods in New York chose to ignore it and call a new state C.P.P.A. convention at Albany. What is surprising is that, although socialists were duly invited to attend, the Brotherhoods used Albany to stage a violent attack on the Socialist Party on the grounds that it had run candidates opposed to labor candidates at the recent elections. When the matter was reported to the third convention of the American Labor Party of New York in September 1923, Hillquit explained the attack as the action of some Tammanyites trying to force the C.P.P.A. in New York to follow the A.F.ofL. "nonpartisan" policy.[97]

Meanwhile, a special emergency meeting of the executive committee of the American Labor Party of New York had decided not to break away from the C.P.P.A., but instead to persevere. A letter was sent off to William H. Johnston, president of the International Association of Machinists and chairman of the national C.P.P.A., explaining the situation. It claimed that the Albany conference was not a *bona fide* state organization, but a group of men who deliberately prevented the formation of such an organization. It was called irregularly and conducted undemocratically and in complete disregard of the C.P.P.A. rules. The letter took care to point out, however, that all of the Railroad Brotherhoods' members were not guilty.[98] Fortunately, by the time of the calling of the third national C.P.P.A. meeting at St. Louis in February 1924, the matter had blown over.

At St. Louis, though socialist hopes of a new party were again dashed, at least a half victory was gained in the decision to call a convention in July for the selection of candidates, separate from the two old parties, in the forthcoming presidential election. It soon became apparent that the choice for presidential candidate would be Robert M. La Follette. Socialists possibly hoped for James H. Maurer as his running mate. As a long-time trade unionist with experience in Pennsylvania politics, Maurer might have been suitable, but he himself felt it was more important to gain the confidence of the more conservative labor unions, and advised against nominations from the floor on his behalf. The vice-presidential nomination instead went to the former Democratic senator, Burton K. Wheeler of Montana, who it was felt could carry the Far West. Nevertheless, if the American Labor Party's reports are to be believed, when Hillquit took the rostrum at the C.P.P.A. convention he was given an overwhelming reception— a great tribute to the position traditionally held by both the Socialist Party and the progressive labor organizations he represented.[99]

The Socialist Party convention of 1924 met in Cleveland immediately after the C.P.P.A. nominations. It then endorsed them and threw itself into the fight. The contribution of the party in winning almost five million votes—the highest ever gained by any group outside the two main parties except for the "Bull Moose"— is hard to assess. Senator-elect Magnus Johnson of Minnesota told the American Labor Party of New York in convention in 1923 that even Hillquit would not get too good a reception in his state, but he thought the farmers were changing.[100] Nevertheless, in areas like Cleveland and Rochester the socialists did earn the respect of the voters. Moreover, as the historian of the 1924 campaign has pointed out, both socialist experience and local organization, neither of which the hastily formed C.P.P.A. possessed, proved invaluable.[101] The enthusiasm that the Socialists gave to the movement, too, must have been inspiring. As the socialist campaign manager J. M. Barnes told the party workers: "In joining the C.P.P.A., the Socialist Party puts all into the balance. . . . We offered the supreme sacrifice even to the life of our party for unity in the political field."[102]

Meanwhile, as workers for La Follette and Wheeler, the Socialist Party had been joined by the A.F.ofL. As Hillquit proudly announced to Fred Adler of the Labor and Socialist International: "For the first time in the political history of our country, all forces of the organized labor movement are united in support of an independent candidate for the President of the United States."[103] Gompers' last campaign was to follow a course he had scrupulously avoided since the Henry George mayoralty race—the support of a candidate from other than the two major parties. But his support was a sad, half-hearted affair.

A "nonpartisan" political campaign committee had appeared

early in the year and duly submitted labor's demands to the
Republican and Democratic conventions. It was rebuffed by both
—"by the Republican convention in an arrogant manner," as the
committee reported to the Atlantic City A.F.ofL. convention, and
by the Democratic convention "by that evasiveness which is the
customary mark of insincerity."[104] Gompers, by now old and sick,
had flown into a rage in his Atlantic City hotel when he heard
the news. His secretary, afraid for his health, saw fit to draw up a
memorandum. It explains how Gompers said he felt like the
Irishman who put five dollars instead of a penny into the church
collection: "It's for the church so to hell with it!" Thus Gompers
risked physical collapse: "It is for the cause, the cause which is
eating me up; to hell with it!"[105]

The A.F.ofL. had thus turned to La Follette and Wheeler.
Nevertheless, the committee took the trouble to declare: "Cooperation hereby urged is not a pledge of identification with an
independent third party nor can it be construed as support for such
a party, group or movement, except as such action accords with
our non-partisan political action."[106] There was therefore no
endorsing a third party as is sometimes stated. A third party, in
fact, did not exist (though there were plans to form one after the
election). Instead, the A.F.ofL. stressed the personal candidacy
of La Follette and Wheeler. In an odd way the fact that La Follette
was an "independent Republican" and Wheeler an "independent
Democrat," both "running as such" seemed to lend them
respectability.

In addition, the federative body made only too clear that it in
no way associated itself with any third party involved with the
C.P.P.A., by which it meant the Socialist Party in particular. At
times, Gompers became explicitly nasty about this: "The candidates have the support of minority groups in themselves of no
great importance, with whose doctrines we not only do not agree
but with which we are and have been in the sharpest kind of
disagreement. We shall continue to oppose these doctrines at all
times." All this, too, in an article entitled, "We are in to win."[107]

At other times Gompers deplored La Follette's economic views,
especially his attitude toward the trusts. The *American Federationist* also insisted that for all La Follette's recommending
government ownership of railroads, and semipublic corporations,
he was no socialist. This contrasts with the editorial attitude of
the I.L.G.W.U. journal, which maintained that many of

La Follette's schemes, such as the full return for labor, were feasible only under socialism.[108] In general the A.F.ofL. seemed so reluctant in support that Gompers was eventually forced to make a public display of personal friendship with La Follette in an endeavor to arouse labor's interest.

Some constituent unions of the A.F.ofL., of course, did not need any initiative from the A.F.ofL. In the needle trades particularly, unions followed the Socialist Party's lead. The United Mine Workers also made a large contribution. Outside the A.F.ofL., the Amalgamated Clothing Workers were equally enthusiastic. A labor survey committee of the C.P.P.A. in January 1924 also reported interest in independent politics from the United Cloth Hat and Cap Makers, the International Molders' Union, the Upholsterers Union, the International Ladies' Garment Workers Union, and the International Fur Workers Union. The last convention of the Amalgamated Association of Iron Steel and Tin Workers adopted a resolution to be presented to the A.F.ofL. in favor of a labor party.[109] Among other unions, however, the lead given by the A.F.ofL. was uninspiring, to say the least.

The only admission the A.F.ofL. leadership ever seems to have made to a departure from traditional policy was the statement at the 1924 convention that further changes were possible: "There is noticeable throughout the world the manifestations of a change of political groupings, representing on the one hand the desire to conserve the domination of material forces, and wealth, property and property rights, and, on the other, the hope and ambition to substitute the human aspirations and personal well-being of all our people as the controlling influence in our governmental affairs."[110] It was a mild hint that the A.F.ofL. might have gone on had a new party materialized.

The A.F.ofL. in one sense, therefore, never abandoned its "nonpartisan" policy. And yet in another sense it did. "Nonpartisanship," as the chapter on "Gompersism" explains, really meant a commitment to the two-party system, even if it were supposed to entail a free choice between them. The year 1924 brought a significant change. But in breaking with tradition, Gompers did not make a new start; it was rather a confession of failure. "To use political parties and be used by none," was the motto of the "nonpartisan" policy. It had not worked. With the legal and economic disasters and rapidly diminishing numbers, labor needed politics. But both major parties could ignore the

A.F.ofL., even to the point of not bothering to pay lip service to its demands. The only alternative was the C.P.P.A.

The road had come full circle since the Henry George campaign when Gompers had last plunged into "partisan" politics. Again, the overall result, almost five million in the popular vote, was not unimpressive. But apart from a few major cities like Cleveland, the vote was largely agricultural. Laboring men had not followed the rather hesitant advice of their leaders.

Explanations of La Follette's defeat in 1924 are varied. Prosperity in some areas—even agriculture had a temporary recovery that summer—made "Keeping Cool with Coolidge" reasonably attractive. There is probably less truth in the assertion that the natural antipathy of farmer and laborer defeated La Follette. True, the antipathy was there. Even in 1923 James G. Livingstone, a Montana socialist, was overwhelmed by the manner in which exploited farmers—even members of the "Non-Partisan" League —joined in breaking a railroad strike.[111] But on the other hand, the Socialist Party in its heyday had enjoyed a large degree of farmer support and the remains of this undoubtedly went to La Follette in 1924.

Whatever is said about city workers opposing country "hicks," the fact remains that a very large number of actively interested farm voters backed a man who explicitly supported labor's cause, and whom the Socialist Party faithfully bolstered. City workers, members of the constituent unions of the A.F.ofL. did not. It would probably have been surprising if they had. The experience of the past is after all cumulative. It took a generation of hard work by labor leaders and a world upheaval to get British laboring men to cast a vote in what was obviously their own interest. During the same period, Gompers and his associates had joined the corporations in condemning the Socialist Party together with all independent labor politics as somehow un-American and undesirable. It would have been surprising indeed if at the drop of a hat the American worker had suddenly changed.

With La Follette's defeat, labor's leaders turned yet again to "traditional" policies, which by their own admission had failed. Gompers died soon afterward. His last words were: "God bless our American institutions. May they grow better day by day."[112] His statements over the previous few years suggest there was indeed room for improvement. The projected conference of the C.P.P.A., which might have launched the new labor party, ended dismally. The Socialist Party, having staked all on the C.P.P.A., almost lost all. Debs, just about to follow Gompers to the grave, thought the 1925 convention of the party demonstrated as clearly as anything could that the Socialist Party was "as near a corpse as a thing can be and still show signs of life."[113]

NOTES

1. Cleveland *Citizen,* January 31, 1920.
2. Michigan Party Bulletin, 1919 (Tamiment Institute).
3. J. F. Denison to Germer, August 17, 1919 (Germer Papers, Wisconsin State Historical Society).
4. Statement by Germer to National Office, June 20, 1919, headed "Socialist or Factionalist" (Germer Papers).
5. Though the influence of DeLeon on Lenin has been questioned. See Don K. McKee, "Daniel DeLeon: A Reappraisal," *Labor History* I (Fall, 1960), 264.
6. E.g. *Justice* (I.L.G.W.U.), May 3, 10, 17, 1919.
7. *Justice,* September 6, 1919, 1 and Oct. 14, 1921, 1.
8. Mary Beard, *A Short History of the American Labor Movement* (New York: Harcourt, Brace & Howe, 1920), 168.
9. David J. Saposs, *Left Wing Unionism* (New York: International Publishers, 1926), 40.
10. Eugene Staley, *A History of the Illinois State Federation of Labor* (Chicago: University of Chicago Press, 1930), 314.
11. J. H. Maurer, *It Can Be Done* (New York: Rand School Press, 1938), 237.
12. William L. Hutcheson to S. G., December 4, 1919 (A. F. of L. Papers).
13. J. Perkins to S. G., December 5, 1919 (A. F. of L. Papers).
14. David Brody, *Labor in Crisis* (New York: J. B. Lippincott Co., 1965), 64, 142.
15. Brody, *Labor in Crisis,* 142.
16. *Federationist,* March 1919, 242-244.
17. E.g. Henry W. Raisse, Secretary of Organizing Committee to S. G., October 10, 1919 (A. F. of L. Papers).
18. I.L.G.W.U., *Proceedings* 1918, 288-292.
19. Maurer, *It Can Be Done,* 203.
20. *Federationist,* March, 1918, 216-220.
21. *Advance,* (Amalgamated Clothing Workers) April 30, 1920, 6.
22. A. F. of L., *Proceedings* 1922, 394.
23. S. G. to William G. Willcox, October 25, 1919 (A. F. of L. Papers).
24. *Justice,* December 29, 1922, 7.
25. Gompers quoted in *Justice,* February 6, 1920, 4.
26. *Federationist,* December, 1921, 1011-1012.
27. *Justice,* May 27, 1921, 4.
28. G. D. H. Cole, *Guild Socialism Re-Stated* (London: L. Parsons, 1920), 215.
29. H. Slobodin to Ex. Comm. of S. D. L., March 18, 1919 (Simons Papers).
30. C. E. Russell to S. G., September 28, 1919 (A. F. of L. Papers).
31. Spargo to S. G.. September 23, 1919 (A. F. of L. Papers).
32. S. G. to Ralph Easley, June 28, 1920 (A. F. of L. Papers).

33. A. F. of L., *Proceedings* 1920, 399-420.
34. Columbia University Oral History Project, *Brophy Memoir*, 336, 357, 365.
35. Cleveland *Citizen*, October 21, 1918.
36. *Federationist*, May 22, 1922, 341.
37. *Advance*, August 5, 1921, 4.
38. *Federationist*, March 1920, 233-235.
39. A. F. of L., *Proceedings* 1920, 76.
40. See *Federationist*, June 1919, 513-517.
41. *New Republic*, July 13, 1918, 307.
42. *Federationist*, January, 1922, 53-57.
43. *Federationist*, April, 1924, 324-327.
44. Milwaukee *Leader*, March 24, 1918.
45. *Federationist*, February, 1924, 132-133.
46. Cleveland *Citizen*, May 18, 1918.
47. Cleveland *Citizen*, May 22, 1920.
48. *Justice*, June 17, 1921, 4.
49. Columbia University Oral History Project, *Brophy Memoir*, 600, 611, 616, 636.
50. Milwaukee *Leader*, June 15, 1918.
51. *American Labor Year Book*, 1919-1920, 199.
52. Cleveland *Citizen*, December 28, 1918.
53. New York *Herald Tribune*, June 12, 1919.
54. *A. L. Y. B.* 1919-1920, 202.
55. *Garment Worker*, June 4, 1920. 4.
56. Staley. *History of Illinois State Federation of Labor*, 361.
57. *A. L. Y. B.*, 1919-1920, 200.
58. *New Republic*, January 18, 1919, 324.
59. Cleveland *Citizen*, May 1, 1920.
60. *Garment Worker*, July 16, 1920, 4.
61. *Federationist*, February, 1919, 149-151.
62. *Federationist*, January, 1919, 38.
63. Cleveland *Citizen*, May 1, 1920; July 24, 1920.
64. A. F. of L., *Proceedings* 1919, 102-108.
65. A. F. of L., *Proceedings* 1919, 373-374.
66. *Federationist*, March, 1920, 257; April, 1920, 332-335; May, 1920, 436-442.
67. *Shoe Workers Journal*, January 1919. 15-16.
68. *Shoe Workers Journal*, October, 1924, 1-2.
69. *Shoe Workers Journal*, March, 1920, 13-15.
70. *Federationist*, January, 1919, 37-45.
71. Staley, *History of Illinois State Federation of Labor*, 371.
72. Quoted in Staley, *History of Illinois State Federation of Labor*, 373.
73. *Garment Worker*, May 28, 1920, 4.
74. Staley, *History of Illinois State Federation of Labor*, 382.
75. *Federationist*, December, 1920, 1081-1082.
76. *Advance*, August 24, 1923, 4.
77. A. F. of L., *Proceedings* 1922, 476 (Italics added).
78. Staley, *History of Illinois State Federation of Labor*, 376.
79. Cleveland *Citizen*, August 23, 1919, 3.
80. Report of National Conference of the Labor Party of Illinois, August 18, 1919, in Hayes Papers, Ohio State Historical Society.
81. Hayes to his wife, June 19, 1920 (Hayes Papers).
82. Hillquit to Debs, June 30, 1920 (Hillquit Papers).
83. Harriman to Hillquit, June 14, 1920 (Hillquit Papers).

84. Maurer to Hillquit, April 16, 1920 (Hillquit Papers).
85. *Shoe Workers Journal,* November, 1919, 822-823.
86. *Federationist,* June, 1919, 516.
87. *Advance,* February 14, 1919, 4; July 16, 1920, 4.
88. *Justice,* April 26, 1919.
89. *Justice,* August 6, 1920, 4.
90. *A. L. Y. B.* 1923-1924, 131.
91. Hillquit to Thomas E. Ryan, October 1, 1923 (Hillquit Papers).
92. Bertrand Russell-Hillquit Debate in New York, May 5, 1924 (Report in S. P. Collection, Duke).
93. Hillquit to Fred C. Howe, April 6, 1922 (Hillquit Papers).
94. *Minutes of Third Convention of A. L. P. of N. Y.,* September 30, 1923 (Tamiment Institute).
95. Hillquit to his wife, February 20, 1922 (Hillquit Papers).
96. *Proceedings of Conference of A.L.P. of N.Y.,* 17. *Minutes of Ex. Comm.* August 7, 1922. (Tamiment Institute).
97. A. L. P. of N. Y., *Proceedings,* September 1923, 58.
98. Letter of Wm. H. Johnston, August 8, 1923 follows minutes of Ex. Comm. meeting, August 3, 1923.
99. Organizer's Report to General Council of A. L. P., July 30, 1924.
100. Address of Magnus Johnson, Third Convention of A. L. P. of N. Y. 1923 (Tamiment Institute).
101. Kenneth C. McKay, *The Progressive Movement of 1924* (New York: Columbia University Press, 1947), 179-199.
102. Letter from J. M. Barnes, Socialist Campaign Manager, August 15, 1924 (S. P. Collection, Duke).
103. Hillquit to Fred Adler, September 13, 1924 (Hillquit Papers).
104. *Federationist,* September, 1924, 705-711.
105. Memorandum by Lee Guard, August 7, 1924. (A. F. of L. Papers).
106. *Federationist,* September, 1924, 710.
107. *Federationist,* September, 1924, 741-743.
108. *Federationist,* September, 1924, 745; November, 1924, 889. *Justice,* September 26, 1924, 6-7.
109. Labor Survey Committee Report, January 1924, in James O'Neal to Hillquit, February 4, 1924 (Hillquit Papers).
110. A. F. of L., *Proceedings* 1924, 271.
111. James G. Livingstone to Otto Branstetter, March 14, 1923. (S. P. Collection, Duke).
112. Bernard Mandel, *Samuel Gompers: A Biography* (Yellow Springs: Antioch Press, 1963), 529.
113. Debs to Bertha Hale White, June 3, 1925. (Hillquit Papers).

Conclusion

It has become a cliche in labor history that the American trade union movement is a reflection of the dominant middle class psyche of the nation. "The individualistic and business like temper of the wider community," as Lloyd Ulman phrased it, "ultimately fashioned a labor movement in its own image."[1] Louis Hartz's "irrational Lockean Liberalism"[2] affected even American workers. Their institutions accordingly are mere "pressure groups" within the capitalist system; the socialism of other countries had no place.

Nothing could better describe the labor movement of today. The preceding pages, however, have been concerned with whether these ideas characterize labor in the era of Samuel Gompers. Undoubtedly, business agents of one kind or another created a "business union" mentality in some unions. The A.F.ofL.'s stress on craft autonomy also encouraged a "pressure group" outlook. Nevertheless, the image presented by labor's best known leaders and carried over by individual union organizers is surely pertinent. As reflected in public statements by the president of the A.F.ofL., and generally throughout the trade union press, organized labor constituted a class movement with broad social aims, very different from the "pressure group" unionism of today. In Gompers' words, the trade union was "the only successful attempt to give voice to the voiceless masses."[3] It urged them "to unite for mutual protection to secure both material welfare and intellectual advancement."[4]

And yet Gompers spent a great deal of energy opposing even the revisionist socialists whose aims certainly overlapped his own. It is this opposition that has given a certain credibility to the argument that the A.F.ofL. was already business unionist in the modern sense. But this is a wrong deduction.

Gompers had a surprisingly sophisticated conception of the place of democratic socialism in western countries. As far as he was concerned, its accomplishments would be political, not social. Socialism would raise the working class to full citizenship. It was

183

part of the process of what recent historians have called "nation building."[5] In short, socialism was procuring what Americans had already achieved through the Revolution. Gompers maintained that if he had lived in Germany he would have been a socialist.

Gompers was under no illusion that political equality had anything to do with social or economic equality, or that it provided for the full development of the potential of each individual. But socialist parties in his view provided no solution. The working class could achieve its full share of the good things of life only through trade unionism. For this reason he welcomed European syndicalism not as the revolutionary movement it sometimes posed as, but as a frank recognition of the inefficacy of political action to achieve social and economic equality. It was largely what the A.F.ofL. had always stood for.

Gompers' conception of European revisionist socialism showed considerable perspicacity. But he missed the other side of it. Full citizenship was obviously one aim, and part of its function has been to extend political democracy. But socialist parties have also stood for much besides. They have provided the possibility of public ownership and control in place of the domination of corporate enterprise, and have created a positive role for the state as the agent of public welfare. The extent and success of their programs has obviously varied from country to country, but unquestionably their presence is an essential factor in the political life of the Western democracies.

Leaders of American labor wished no such role on the part of the state. All labor expected was the guarantee of the right to pursue its aims independently. But these aims encompassed vast changes in the structure of American economic and social life. This is what Gompers meant by voluntarism—a different meaning from the exclusively "business union" connotations of the term today. But if American labor made no claim on the state, the corporations were less self-denying. When their influence was felt through the courts, revisionist socialists expected a change in policy, for the same issues had forced a realignment in British politics and given British socialism a mass base. In America labor entered politics but on a "nonpartisan" basis. The political changes anticipated by socialists and labor party advocates were not forthcoming.

This work has argued that decisions taken by labor leaders on certain critical occasions determined this outcome. Whether they

were wise decisions must depend on rather obvious value judg-
ments. Whether alternative decisions could have changed labor's
development is not answerable. But they were decisions taken in
the face of viable alternatives.

Most historians, however, have explained American developments not by the actions of the leadership, but by immutable
factors which precluded changes along the lines of other industrialized countries. In particular, attention has been given to the
fact that even if solidly united, the American working class constituted a permanent minority in the American community.
Political parties must be nondoctrinaire, flexible enough to cover
different social groups spread over a wide area. In a community
dominated by middle class values, parties that questioned the
sanctity of private property or seemed to cater to only one social
group could not succeed. Besides, according to determinists,
there are other difficulties. The two major parties are flexible
enough to absorb third parties, which serve merely as pressure
groups. The presidential system dominates political life as to
preclude gradual growth at a local level. The difficulties are so
numerous, in fact, that one wonders why Americans ever even
contemplated a third party.

But the fact remains that the Republican Party was once a
"third party" that breached the system. It did so because the two
existing parties were unresponsive to the problems of the time.
The transformation of the American economy in the late nineteenth century that brought the corporations to their dominant
position touched every American. To say that only a minority
was affected is nonsense. For two generations after 1880 Americans seemed about to storm the bastions of privilege symbolized
by Wall Street; but they failed. Conservatism triumphed.

The consensus historians explain this as further evidence of
the peculiar power of Lockean liberalism. Americans complained,
but really wished to change little. The populist and progressive
upheavals were antimonopoly crusades, or at most aimed at corporate regulation. But in any case, American reformers remained
firmly attached to the principle of private property and individual effort.

Such syntheses are distorting and give a unity to the reform
movements that didn't exist. The Populists made a stand clearly
overlapping that of social democrats, and for this reason many
socialists of the day supported them.[6] Many of those who created

the ferment of Progressivism—not all by any means members of the Socialist Party—analyzed the problems of industrial America as identical with those of Great Britain, and formulated a constructive role for the state along social democratic lines. Undoubtedly the traditional culture and the political system presented a problem. Left-wing progressives were aware of American confusion over private property and its relationship to the private corporation, or the place of true individualism in a world of corporate enterprise. Lacking a mass base of support, it seemed safer to think in terms of infiltrating the Democratic Party rather than building a third party. Analysis was not a guide to action.[7]

In this welter of confusion, the factor of leadership was all important. As the outstanding spokesman for American labor for more than forty years, Samuel Gompers was the pivotal figure. Gompers' grasp of economic realities meant he was never beguiled by antimonopolism. His clear conceptions of class and power in the capitalist systems must have robbed any notion of the state-regulated private corporation of the appeal it had for others. Yet in place of providing some clear substitute political goal, his energies were spent destroying any other group within the A.F.ofL. that did. Under his leadership the mass base which the labor movement lent democratic socialism in other countries proved impossible.

Max S. Hayes, Gompers' opponent in the A.F.ofL. over many years, asked if he provided any leadership at all. "The British trade union leaders, the officials, were real leaders," he said. "They did not wait to see how the rank and file was going to march and then run round the corner and get at the head of the procession. That is not leadership; that is pure, unadulterated cowardice."[8]

Cowardice was part of it. Gompers quickly retreated from his own belief in the organization of blacks and the unskilled at the first sign of opposition. A corrupt bureaucracy emerged in some unions unchecked by the A.F.ofL. But a greater error was miscalculation. Disappointment with politics after 1886, a general mistrust of politicians, and experience with DeLeon's opposition to the A.F.ofL. colored Gompers' future attitude toward socialists and labor party advocates. His professed solution to America's grave social problems was the growth of the labor movement to an unassailable position from which it could shape new forms of economic organization with industrial democracy. What exactly this meant varied from collective bargaining for all workers to something more akin to guild socialism. In any case he believed American institutions to be flexible enough to permit its evolution.

Socialist warnings and his own experience notwithstanding, Gompers staked all on this belief, and lost. The trade unions, sadly in decline, were rescued by the New Deal and the war economy that followed, and so they have remained. The "betterment of humanity" that Gompers promised even while he lambasted the socialists is conspicuously absent from their program.

NOTES

1. Lloyd Ulman, *The Rise of the National Trade Union* (Cambridge, Mass.: Harvard University Press, 1955), 603.
2. Louis Hartz, *The Liberal Tradition in America* (New York: Harcourt, Brace & World, 1955).
3. *Federationist*, November 1907, 882.
4. *Federationist*, June 1908, 459.
5. See Val R. Lorwin, "Historians and other Social Scientists: the comparative analysis of Nation-building in western societies," in *Comparative Research across Cultures and Nations* (Paris, 1968), 102-114.
6. Norman Pollack, *The Populist Response to Industrial America* (New York: W. W. Norton & Co., 1966).
7. See Kenneth McNaught, "American Progressives and the Great Society," Journal of American History LIII 3 (December, 1966), 504-520.
8. A. F. of L., *Proceedings* 1922, 393.

Bibliography

PRIMARY SOURCES

MANUSCRIPT COLLECTIONS, ETC.

American Federation of Labor Archives, Washington, D.C. Samuel Gompers Copy Books, 1881-1924 (Now in Library of Congress).

Duke University, North Carolina. Socialist Party Collection, especially, Correspondence and Press Releases, National Office File, State Files, Labor File.

Milwaukee County Historical Society. Papers of Victor L. Berger, including editorials from Milwaukee *Leader*.

Labadie Collection, University of Michigan, Ann Arbor, includes a file of *John Swinton's Paper,* 1884-1887.

Ohio State Historical Society, Papers of Max S. Hayes, Charles E. Rothenberg.

New York Public Library, Henry George Scrap Books, 1886-1888. Tamiment Institute, New York. American Labor Party of New York, Papers, including Minutes of Executive Committee Meetings, and Proceedings of three party conventions, 1922-1924. Debs Clipping Books. Pamphlets and papers of DeLeon.

Wisconsin State Historical Society, Madison, Wisconsin. A. F. of L. Papers, Series 11, Files of the Office of President. Socialist Labor Party Papers, including Daniel DeLeon Papers. Papers of Adolph Germer, Morris Hillquit, Algie M. Simons, William English Walling.

TRADE UNION PUBLICATIONS

American Federation of Labor. *Reports of Proceedings of Conventions,* 1881-1924.

Boot and Shoe Workers Union. *Proceedings,* 1894-1924. *The Union Boot and Shoe Worker,* 1900-June 1902. *The Shoe Workers Journal,* July, 1902-1924.

Cigar Makers International Union of America. Proceedings, c. 1880-1924. *Cigar Makers Official Journal,* 1875-1924.

Carpenters and Joiners of America, United Brotherhood of. *Proceedings,* 1881-1924. *The Carpenter,* 1906-1924.

Clothing Workers of America, Amalgamated. *Proceedings,* 1914-1924. *Advance,* 1917-1924.

Garment Workers of America, United. *Proceedings,* 1892-1924. *The Garment Worker,* April, 1893-August, 1903. *The Weekly Bulletin,* February 18, 1903 to October 18, 1912. *The Garment Worker,* October 25, 1912-1924.

Garment Workers Union, International Ladies. *Proceedings,* c. 1900-1924. *The Ladies Garment Worker,* 1910-1918. *Justice,* 1919-1924.

Knights of Labor. *Proceedings,* c. 1878 to c. 1900 (irregular) *Journal of United Labor,* 1880-1889. *Journal of Knights of Labor,* 1889-c. 1900.

Machinists, International Association of. *Proceedings,* 1893-1924 (irregular). *Journal,* 1889-1891. *Monthly Journal,* 1891-1902 (irregular). *Machinists' Monthly Journal,* 1903-1924.

Mine Workers of America, United, *Proceedings,* 1890-1924. *The United Mine Workers' Journal,* 1891-1924.

Textile Workers of America, United, *Proceedings,* 1902-1924 (irregular). *The Textile Worker,* 1912-1924.

OTHER PRINTED SOURCES

Commission of Inquiry, The Interchurch World Movement. *Report on the Steel Strike of 1919.* New York, 1920. *Public Opinion and the Steel Strike.* New York, 1921.

Socialist Party. *Proceedings of National Conventions:* May 1-6, 1904; May 10-17, 1908; May 12-18, 1912. Chicago, 1904, 1908, 1912.

Socialist Party. *Proceedings of the National Congress of the Socialist Party,* May 15-21, 1910. Chicago, 1910.

Socialist Party. *Weekly Bulletin.* 1903 on. Microfilm labelled. Socialist Party, U.S., Labor and Socialist Press News. 3 reels.

Socialist Party. *Monthly Bulletin* (originally *Official Bulletin*), Chicago: September 1904 to April, 1913 (microfilm).

Socialist Labor Party. *Proceedings.* New York 1877 to 1932 (microfilm).

United States Commission on Industrial Relations. *Industrial Relations: Final Report and Testimony.* Washington, D.C., 1916, 11 vols. Especially Volume 2.

NEWSPAPERS, PERIODICALS, ANNUALS

American Labor Year Book. New York: Rand School of Social Science, 1916-1924.

Citizen, Cleveland, 1891-1924.

International Socialist Review. Chicago, July 1900 to February 1918.

Masses. New York, 1911-1917.

New Republic. New York, 1914-1924.

People. New York, April, 1891 to August, 1900.

People. New York, July 1899 to April 1901. Later changed to *Worker,* April, 1901 to April, 1908. *New York Socialist,* April, 1908 to December, 1908. *New York Call,* May 30, 1908 to September 30, 1923.

MEMOIRS, LETTERS, SPEECHES, ETC.

Ameringer, Oscar. *If You Don't Weaken.* New York: H. Holt & Co., 1940.

Bisno, Abraham. Abraham Bisno, *Union Pioneer.* Madison, University of Wisconsin Press, 1967.

Bloor, Ella Reeve. *We Are Many.* New York, International Publishers, 1940.

Brophy, John. *A Miner's Life,* edited and supplemented by John O. P. Hall. Madison, University of Wisconsin Press, 1964.

Chaplin, Ralph. *Wobbly,* Chicago, *The Rough and Tumble Story of an American Radical,* University of Chicago Press, 1948.

Debs, Eugene Victor. *Debs, His Life, Writings and Speeches, with a biography by S. M. Reynolds.* Chicago: Charles H. Kerr & Co., 1908.

Debs, Eugene Victor. *Walls and Bars.* Chicago, Socialist Party, 1927.

——. *Speeches of Eugene V. Debs,* introduction by Alexander Trachtenberg. New York: International Publishers, 1928.

——. *Writings and Speeches of Eugene V. Debs,* introduction by A. M. Schlesinger, Jr. New York, 1948.

——. *Debs: His Life, Writings and Speeches,* with a department of Appreciations. Girard, Kansas: The Appeal to Reason, 1908.

DeLeon, Daniel. *Speeches and Editorials,* 2 vols. New York, 1918.

Eastman, Max. *Enjoyment of Living.* New York: Harper, 1948.

Goldman, Emma. *Living My Life.* New York: Knopf, 1934.

Gompers, Samuel. *Seventy Years of Life and Labor.* New York: E. P. Dutton, 1925.

Haywood, William D. *Bill Haywood's Book.* New York: International Publishers, 1929.

Hillquit, Morris. *Loose Leaves from a Busy Life.* New York, Macmillan, 1934.

Luhan, Mabel Dodge. *Movers and Shakers,* New York, 1936. Vol. III of *Intimate Memories.* New York: Harcourt, Brace & Co., 1933-1937.

Marx, Karl, and Frederick Engels. *Letters to Americans, 1848-1895. A Selection,* ed. by Alexander Trachtenberg. New York: International Publishers, 1953.

Maurer, James Hudson. *It Can Be Done.* New York, Rand School Press, 1938.

Powderly, Terence Vincent. *Thirty Years of Labor, 1859-1889.* Columbus, Ohio: Excelsior Publishing House, 1889.

Powderly, Terence Vincent. *The Path I Trod: The Autobiography of Terence Victor Powderly,* edited by Harry J. Carman, Henry David, and Paul N. Guthrie. New York: Columbia University Press, 1940.

Russell, Charles Edward. *Bare Hands and Stone Walls: Some Recollections of a Side-Line Reformer.* New York, C. Scribner & Sons, 1933.

Wayland, Julius Augustus. *Leaves of Life: a story of twenty years of socialist agitation.* Girard, Kansas: Appeal to Reason, 1912.

Columbia University Oral History Project. Memoirs of: John Brophy, Albert J. Hayes, Benjamin McLaurin, H. L. Mitchell, John O'Hare, William Pollock, Upton Sinclair, John Spargo, Norman Mattoon Thomas, Eva McDonald Valesh, Mary Heaton Vorse.

CONTEMPORARY BOOKS, ARTICLES, PAMPHLETS

Brower, Charles. *Why Socialism has failed in the U.S.,* Washington, D.C.: Rossi-Bryn Co., 1924.

Cole, G. D. H. *Child Socialism Re-Stated.* London: L. Parsons, 1920.

Debs, E. V. *The American Movement.* Chicago: C. H. Kerr & Co., e. 1904.

———. *Unionism and Socialism.* Terre Haute, Ind.: Standard Publishing Co., 1904.

DeLeon, Daniel. *The Burning Question of Trade Unionism.* New York; New York Labor News Co., 1921.

———. *Reform or Revolution.* New York; New York Labor News Co., 1929.

DeLeon, Daniel. *The Socialist Trade and Labor Alliance versus the 'pure and simple' Trade Union.* New York Labor News: New York, 1900.

———. *Unity.* New York: New York Labor News, 1914.

Ely, Richard T. *The Labor Movement in America.* New York: T. Y. Crowell & Co., 1886.

———. *Recent American Socialism.* Baltimore: Johns Hopkins University, 1885.

Engdahl, J. L. *Trade Unions and the Present Social Crisis.* Chicago: Socialist Party, 1914.

Ghent, W. J. *Mass and Class: A Survey of Social Divisions.* New York: Macmillan, 1904.

———. *Socialism and Organized Labor.* Girard, Kansas, 1916.

Gompers, Samuel. *Labor and the Employer,* edited by Hayes Robbins. New York: E. P. Dutton & Co., 1920.

———. *American Labor and the War.* New York: George H. Doran Co., 1919.

———. *Labor in Europe and America.* New York: Harper, 1910.

Hagerty, Thomas J., "The Function of Industrial Unionism," *Voice of Labor,* III (March, 1905), 5.

Hanna, Mark, "Senator Hanna on Labor Unions and Socialism," *The Literary Digest,* XXVIII (January 30, 1904).

Haywood, William D., "Industrial Unionism," *Voice of Labor,* III (June, 1905), 2.

———. and Frank Bohn. *Industrial Socialism.* Chicago: C. H. Kerr & Co., 1911.

Hillquit, Morris, Samuel Gompers and Max S. Hayes, "The Double Edge of Labor's Sword." Discussion, testimony and cross-examination before the U. S. Committee on Industrial Relations. Chicago, 1914.

Hillquit, Morris. *Socialism in Theory and Practice*. New York: Macmillan, 1912.

——. *Socialism Summed Up*. H. K. Fly Co., New York, 1913.

Hoehn, Gustavus. *Labor and Capital and the Object of the Labor Movement*. St. Louis, 1893.

Hunter, Robert. *Labor in Politics*. Chicago: The Socialist Party, 1915.

——. *Violence and the Labor Movement*. New York: Macmillan, 1919.

International Ladies' Garment Workers Union. A Letter to Delegates of the 17th biennial convention of the I. L. G. W. U. from the executive board. Boston, 1924.

Korngold, Ralph. *Are there classes in America*. Chicago: The Socialist Party, 1914.

Lynch, Daniel. *Socialism and Trade Unionism*. Chicago, 1900.

McNeill, George E. *The Labor Movement: The Problem of Today*. Boston: M. W. Hazen Co., 1887.

O'Neal, James. *Sabotage: or Socialism vs. Syndicalism*. St. Louis, Mo.; National Rip-saw Publishing Co., 1913.

——. *The Workers in American History*. 4th ed. New York: Rand School of Social Science, 1921.

Russell, Charles E. *Why I am A Socialist*. New York: Hodder & Stoughton, George H. Doran Co: 1910.

Schlesinger, Alexander. *Gomperism and Socialism*.

Socialist Labor Party. *Daniel DeLeon, The Man and His Work, A Symposium*. New York, 1920.

Spargo, John. *Americanism and Social Democracy*. New York: Harper, 1918.

——. *Syndicalism, Industrial Unionism and Socialism*. New York: B. W. Huebsch, 1913.

——. *Applied Socialism*. New York: B. W. Huebsch, 1912.

——. *The Common Sense of Socialism*. Chicago, C. H. Kerr & Co., 1908.

——. *Socialism: A Summary and Interpretation of Socialist Principles*. New York, Macmillan, 1909.

——. *The Substance of Socialism*. New York, B. W. Huebsch, 1909.

Stone, N. I. *The Attitude of the Socialist towards the Trade Unions*. New York, 1900.

Sullivan, J. W. *Socialism as an Incubus on the American Labor Movement*. New York, B. H. Tyrrel, 1918.

Tannenbaum, Frank. *The Labor Movement: Its Conservative Functions and Social Consequences*. New York; G. P. Putnam's Sons, 1921.

Untermann, Ernest, "The Trade Union Resolution and the Working Programme," *American Labor Union Journal*. May 19, 1904.

Wood-Simons, May. *Socialism and the Organized Labor Movement*. Chicago, 1904.

Walling, William English. *Labor-Union Socialism and Socialist Labor-Unionism*. Chicago, 1912.

———. *Socialism As It Is: A Survey of the World-Wide Revolutionary Movement*. New York, Macmillan Co., 1915.

SECONDARY SOURCES

MONOGRAPHS

Adamic, Louis. *Dynamite, the Story of Class Violence in America*. New York, Viking Press, 1934.

Barker, Charles A. *Henry George*. New York, Oxford University Press, 1955.

Baratz, Morton S. *The Union and the Coal Industry*. New Haven: Yale University Press, 1955.

Beard, Mary. *A Short History of the American Labor Movement*. New York: Harcourt Brace & Howe, 1920.

Bedford, Henry F. *Socialism and the Workers in Massachusetts, 1886-1912*. Amherst: University of Massachusetts Press, 1966.

Bell, Daniel. *The End of Ideology: on the exhaustion of political ideas in the fifties*. New York, Collier Books, 1961.

Bernstein, Samuel. *The First International in America*. New York: A. M. Kelley, 1965.

Berthoff, Rowland Tappan. *British Immigrants in Industrial America*. New York, Russell & Russell, 1953.

Bonnett, Clarence E. *History of Employers Associations in the United States*. New York: Vantage Press, 1956.

Brissenden, Paul Frederick. *The I. W. W. A Study of American Syndicalism*. New York: Columbia University Press, 1920.

Brody, David. *The Butcher Workmen, A Study of Unionization.* Cambridge, Mass.: Harvard University Press, 1964.

———. *Labor in Crisis: The Steel Strike of 1919.* New York; J. B. Lippincott Co., 1965.

———. *Steelworkers in America: The Nonunion Era.* New York: Harper, 1969.

Budish, J. M. and George Soule. *The New Unionism in the Clothing Industry.* Harcourt, Brace & Howe: New York, 1920.

Carnes, Cecil. *John L. Lewis, Leader of Labor.* New York: Robert Speller Publishing Corp., 1936.

Carrol, Mollie Ray. *Labor and Politics.* New York: Houghton Mifflin Co., 1923.

Christie, Robert A. *Empire in Wood: A History of the Carpenters' Union.* Ithaca, N. Y., Cornell University Press, 1956.

Clegg, H. A., Alan Fox and A. F. Thompson. *A History of British Trade Unions since 1889, Vol. 1, 1889-1910.* Oxford: Clarendon Press, 1964.

Cole, G. D. H. *The Second International 1889-1914; A History of Socialist Thought.* London, Macmillan, 1960-62.

Coleman, McAlister. *Eugene V. Debs, A man unafraid.* New York: Greenberg, 1930.

Commons, J. R. and Associates. *History of Labor in the United States. 4 vols.* New York, Macmillan, 1918-1935.

David, Henry. *The History of the Haymarket Affair.* New York: Russell & Russell, 1936.

Destler, Chester M. *American Radicalism, 1865-1901.* New London, Conn.: Connecticut College, 1946.

Draper, Theodore. *The Roots of American Communism.* New York: Viking Press, 1957.

Dubofsky, Melvyn. *When Workers Organize: New York City in the Progressive Era.* Amherst, Mass.: University of Massachusetts Press, 1968.

Dubofsky, Melvyn. *We Shall Be All; A History of the I.W.W.* Quadrangle Books, Chicago: 1969.

Dulles, Foster Rhea. *Labor in America: A History.* 2nd Edition. Thomas Y. Crowell Co., New York.

Egbert, D. D. and Stow Persons. *Socialism and American Life.* 2 vols. Princeton: Princeton University Press, 1952.

Evans, Chris. *The History of the United Mine Workers of America.* Indianapolis, 1918-1920.

Fay, C. N. *Labor in Politics*. Cambridge, Mass.: Priv. Print. at University Press, 1920.

Fine, Nathan. *Labor and Farmer Parties in the United States, 1828-1928*. New York: Rand School of Social Science, 1928.

Foner, Philip S. *History of the Labor Movement in the United States*. New York: International Publishers: 4 vols. to date, 1947-1965.

Friedheim, Robert L. *The Seattle General Strike*. Seattle: University of Washington Press, 1964.

Galenson, Walter, ed. *Comparative Labor Movements*. New York: Russell & Russell, 1952.

Gavett, Thomas W. *Development of the Labor Movement in Milwaukee*. Madison: University of Wisconsin Press, 1965.

Gay, Peter. *The Dilemma of Democratic Socialism: Edward Bernstein's Challenge to Marx*. New York: Columbia University Press, 1952.

Ginger, Ray. *Eugene V. Debs: A Biography*. New York; Collier Books, 1962.

Ginzberg, Eli and Hyman Berman, eds. *The American Worker in the Twentieth Century: A History through Autobiographies*. New York: Free Press of Glencoe, 1963.

Glocker, Theodore W. *Government of American Trade Unions*. Johns Hopkins Press: Baltimore: 1913.

Gluck, E. *John Mitchell, Miner*. New York, 1929.

Green, Marguerite. *The National Civic Federation and the American Labor Movement*. Washington, D. C.: Catholic University of America Press, 1956.

Gregory, C. O. *Labor and the Law*. W. W. Norton & Co.: New York: 1946.

Grob, Gerald N. *Workers and Utopia: A Study of Ideological Conflict in the American Labor Movement, 1865-1900*. Evanston: Northwestern University Press, 1961.

Hardman, J. B. S., ed. *American Labor Dynamics in the Light of Post-War Development*. New York: Harcourt, Brace & Co., 1928.

Harvey, Rowland Hill. *Samuel Gompers, Champion of the Toiling Masses*. Stanford: Stanford University Press, 1935.

Hillquit, Morris. *History of Socialism in the United States*. New York: Funk & Wagnalls, 1903.

Hinrichs, Albert Ford. *The United Mine Workers of America and the non-union coal fields.* New York, 1923.

Hoxie, Robert Franklin. *Trade Unionism in the United States.* New York: D. Appleton & Co., 1917.

International Ladies Garment Workers Union. *I. L. G. W. U. news-history, 1900-1950.* ed. Max D. Danish, Leon Stein. New York, 1950.

Jensen, Vernon H. *Heritage of Conflict; labor relations in the non ferrous metals industry up to 1930.* Ithaca: Cornell University Press, 1950.

Josephson, Mathew. *Sidney Hillman, statesman of American labor.* Garden City, N.Y.: Doubleday, 1952.

Karson, Marc. *American Labor Unions and Politics, 1900-1918.* Boston: Beacon Press, 1965.

Kipnis, Ira. *The American Socialist Movement, 1897-1912.* New York: Columbia University Press, 1952.

Laslett, John H. M., *Labor and the Left.* Basic Books Inc.: New York, 1970.

Lieberman, Elias. *Unions before the Bar.* New York: Oxford Book Co., 1960.

Lorwin, Lewis L. *The Women's Garment Workers.* New York, B. W. Huebsch, Inc., 1924.

———. *The American Federation of Labor; History, policies and prospects.* Washington, D.C.: The Brookings Institution, 1933.

Lorwin, Val Rogin. *The French Labor Movement.* Cambridge, Mass.: Harvard University Press, 1954.

Madison, Charles A. *Critics and Crusaders.* New York: Frederick Ungar Publishing Co., 1959.

Mandel, Bernard. *Samuel Gompers, A Biography.* Yellow Springs, Ohio: Antioch Press, 1963.

McDonald, David J. and Edward A. Lynch, *Coal and Unionism: a history of the American coal miners' unions.* Indianapolis: Cornelius Printing Co., 1939.

MacKay, Kenneth Campbell. *The Progressive Movement of 1924.* New York: Columbia University Press, 1947.

Morris, James O. *Conflict within the A. F. of L.; a study of craft versus industrial unionism, 1901-1938.* Ithaca, N.Y.: Cornell University Press, 1958.

Murray, Robert K. *Red Scare; a study in national hysteria.* Minneapolis, University of Minnesota Press, 1955.

Oneal, James. *A History of Local 10, I.L.G.W.U.* New York: Ashland Press, 1927.

Painter, Floy Ruth. *That Man Debs, and His Life and Work.* Bloomington, Indiana: Indiana University Graduate Council, 1929.

Pelling, Henry. *America and the British Left; from Bright to Bevan.* New York: New York University Press, 1957.

———. *American Labor.* Chicago: University of Chicago Press, 1960.

Perlman, Mark. *Labor Union Theories in America, background and development.* Evanston, Ill.: Row, Peterson, 1958.

———. *The Machinists: A new study in American trade unionism.* Cambridge, Mass.: Harvard University Press, 1961.

Perlman, Selig. *A History of Trade Unionism in the United States.* New York: Macmillan, 1922.

———. *A Theory of the Labor Movement.* New York, Macmillan, 1928.

Perry, Louis B., and Richard S. *A History of the Los Angeles Labor Movement, 1911-1941.* Berkeley: University of California Press, 1963.

Petersen, Arnold. *Daniel DeLeon: Social Architect.* New York: New York Labor News Co., 1941.

Pollack, Norman. *The Populist Response to Industrial America.* New York: W. W. Norton & Co.: 1966.

Quint, Howard J. *The Forging of American Socialism.* Bobbs-Merrill Co.; 1953.

Rayback, Joseph G. *A History of American Labor.* Free Press, New York, 1966.

Reed, Louis S. *The Labor Philosophy of Samuel Gompers.* New York: Columbia University Press, 1930.

Rogoff, Hillel. *An East Side Epic: the life and work of Meyer London.* New York: Vanguard Press, 1930.

Saposs, David J. *Left Wing Unionism: a study of radical policies and tactics.* New York: International Publishers, 1926.

Savage, Marion D. *Industrial Unionism in America.* New York: The Ronald Press Co.

Seidman, Joel. *The Needle Trades.* New York: Farrar & Rinehart, Inc., 1942.

Shannon, David A. *The Socialist Party of America: A History.* New York: Macmillan, 1955.

Sombart, Werner. *Warum gibt es in den Vereinigten Staaten Keinen Sozialismus?* Tubingen: J. C. B. Mohr, 1906.

Soule, George Henry. *Sidney Hillman, labor statesman.* New York: Macmillan, 1939.

Staley, Eugene. *A History of the Illinois State Federation of Labor.* Chicago: University of Chicago Press, 1930.

Starr, Mark. *Labor Politics in the U.S.A.* London, Fabian Publications, 1949.

Stetler, H. G. *The Socialist Movement in Reading, Pennsylvania, 1896-1936.* Storrs, Conn., 1943.

Stolberg, Benjamin. *Tailors' Progress: the story of a famous Union and the men who made it.* Garden City, N.Y.: Doubleday, Doran & Co., 1944.

Symes, Lillian and Clement Travers. *Rebel America; the story of social revolt in the U.S.* New York: Harper, 1934.

Taft, Philip. *The A. F. of L. in the Time of Gompers.* New York: Harper, 1957.

——. *Organized Labor in American History.* New York, Harper & Row, 1964.

Thorne, Florence Clavert. *Samuel Gompers, American statesman.* New York: Philosophical Library, 1957.

Tracy, George A. *A History of the Typographical Union.* Indianapolis: International typographical union, 1913.

Ulman, Lloyd. *The Rise of the National Trade Union.* Cambridge, Mass., Harvard University Press, 1955.

Ware, N. J. *The Industrial Workers, 1840-1860.* Houghton Mifflin Co., Boston: 1924.

——. *The Labor Movement in the United States, 1860-1895.* D. Appleton & Co., New York, 1929.

——. *Labor in Modern Industrial Society.* Boston: D. C. Heath & Company, 1935.

Watkins, Gordon S. *Labor Problems and Labor Administration in the United States during the World War.* Urbana: University of Illinois Press, 1920.

Webb, Sidney and Beatrice. *The History of Trade Unionism 1666-1894.* London: Longman's & Co., 1894.

Wechsler, James A. *Labor Baron. A portrait of John L. Lewis.* New York: W. Morrow & Co., 1944.

Weinstein, James. *The Decline of Socialism in America, 1912-1925.* New York: Vintage Books, 1967.

———. *The Corporate Ideal in the Liberal State, 1900-1918.* Boston: Beacon Press, 1968.

Wolman, Leo. *Ebb and Flow of Trade Unionism.* New York: National Bureau of economic research, 1936.

———. *The Growth of American Trade Unions, 1880-1923.* New Yirk: National bureau of economic research, 1924.

Yearly, Clifton K. *Britons in American Labor.* Johns Hopkins University Studies in History and Political Science. (Series 75, No. 1). Balitimore, Johns Hopkins Press, 1957.

Yellen, Samuel, *American Labor Struggles.* New York: Harcourt Brace & Company, 1936.

Yellowitz, Irwin. *Labor and the Progressive Movement in New York State, 1897-1916.* Ithaca, Cornell University Press, 1965.

Zaretz, Charles E. *Amalgamated Clothing Workers of America; A study in progressive trades-unionism.* Ancon Publishing Co., 1934.

ARTICLES

Auerbach, Jerold S. "Progressives at Sea: The LaFollette Act of 1915," *Labor History* II, 1961.

Berthoff, Rowland. "The Working Class," *The Reconstruction of American History,* ed. John Higham. London, 1962.

Barnett, George E. "Growth of Labor Organization in the United States, 1897-1914," *Quarterly Journal of Economics,* August, 1916.

Bell, Daniel. "The Background and Development of Marxian Socialism in the United States," *Socialism and American Life,* ed. D. D. Egbert and Stow Persons. Chapter VI, Princeton, 1952.

Brooks, George W. "Reflections on the Changing Character of American Labor Unions," *Proceedings of the 9th Annual Meeting of Industrial Relations Research Association,* December 29, 1956.

Commons, John R. "Karl Marx and Samuel Gompers," *Political Science Quarterly,* Vol. 41, 1926.

Cummins, E. E. "Political and Social Philosophy of the Carpenters' Union," *Political Science Quarterly,* Vol. 42, 1927.

Derber, Milton. "The Idea of Industrial Democracy in America, 1898-1915," and "The Idea of Industrial Democracy in

America, 1915-1935," *Labor History,* VII, 3 (Fall, 1966);
VIII, 1 (Winter, 1967).

Douglas, Paul H. "The Socialist Vote in the 1917 Municipal
Elections," *National Municipal Review,* March, 1918.

Dubofsky, Melvyn. "The Origins of Western Working Class
Radicalism, 1880-1905," *Labor History,* VII, 2 (Spring,
1966).

——. "Success and Failure of Socialism in New York City,
1900-1918: A Case Study," *Labor History,* IX, 3 (Fall,
1968).

Flower, B. O. "Socialism in Europe and America," *The Arena,*
XXVI (October, 1901).

Fraina, Louis. "DeLeon," *New Review,* 11 (July, 1914).

Frank, Henry. "The Meaning of the Invasion of European Socialism," *The Arena,* XXXVIII (September, 1907).

Gitelman, H. M. "Adolph Strasser and the Origins of Pure and
Simple Unionism," *Labor History,* VI, 1 (Winter, 1965).

Greenbaum. "The Social Ideas of Samuel Gompers," *Labor History,* VII, 1 (Winter, 1966).

Grob, Gerald N. "Knights of Labor, Politics and Populism,"
Mid America, V. 40, ns. V. 29 (January, 1958).

——. "Organized Labor and the Negro Worker, 1865-1900,"
Labor History, 1, 2 (Spring, 1960).

——. "Terence V. Powderly and the Knights of Labor," *Mid
America,* V. 39 n.s. Vol. 28 (January, 1957).

Grubbs, Frank L., Jr. "Council and Alliance Labor Propaganda,"
Labor History, VII, 2 (Spring, 1966).

Gulick, Charles A. and Melvin Bers. "Insight and Illusion in
Perlman's Theory of the Labor Movement," *Industrial and
Labor Relations Review,* VI (July, 1953).

Kennedy, John Curtis. "Socialistic Tendencies in American Trade
Unions," *The Journal of Political Economy,* XV (October,
1907).

Knoles, Harmon George. "Populism and Socialism, with special
reference to the Election of 1892," *Pacific Historical Review,*
XII, 3 (September, 1943).

Kutler, Stanley I. "Labor, the Clayton Act, and the Supreme
Court," *Labor History,* III, 1962.

Laslett, John. "Reflections on the Failure of Socialism in the
American Federation of Labor," *Mississippi Valley Historical Review,* 2, 4 (March, 1964).

Levine, Louis. "Development of Syndicalism in America," *Political Science Quarterly,* XXVIII (September, 1913).

Lorwin, Val. "Recent Research on Western European Labor Movements," *Industrial Relations Research Association, Proceedings of Seventh Annual General Meeting.*

——. "Reflections on the History of the French and American Labor Movements," *Journal of Economic History,* XVII, 1 (1957).

——. "Syndicats et action politique aux Etats-Unis," *Socialisme* (Brussels), No. 56 (March, 1963).

Mandel, Bernard. "Gompers and Business Unionism, 1873-1890," *Business History Review,* XXVIII (September, 1954).

——. "Samuel Gompers and the Negro Worker," *Journal of Negro History,* XL (January, 1958).

McKee, Don K. "Daniel DeLeon: A Reappraisal," *Labor History,* 1, 3 (Fall, 1960).

McNaught, Kenneth. "American Progressives and the Great Society," *Journal of American History,* LIII, 3 (December, 1966).

Murray, Robert K. "Public Opinion, Labor, and the Clayton Act," *Historian,* XXI, 1959.

Soffer, Benson. "A Theory of Trade Union Development: The Role of the 'autonomous' Workman," *Labor History,* 1, 2 (Spring, 1960).

Sturmthal, Adolph. "National Patterns of Union Behaviour," *Journal of Political Economy,* LVI (1948).

Taft, Philip. "On the Origins of Business Unionism," *Industrial and Labor Relations Review,* Vol. 17, No. 1 (October, 1963).

Urofsky, Melvin I. "A Note on the Expulsion of the Five Socialists," *New York History,* (January, 1966).

Wakstien, Allen M. "The Origins of the Open Shop Movement, 1919-1920," *Journal of American History,* LI, 1964.

Weinstein, James. "Anti-War Sentiment and the Socialist Party, 1917-1918," *Political Science Quarterly,* (June, 1959).

——. "Gompers and the New Liberalism, 1900-1909," *Studies on the Left,* V, (Fall, 1965).

——. "The Socialist Party, Its Roots and Strength, 1912-1919," *Studies on the Left,* 1, 2 (Winter, 1960).

Wolman, Leo. "The Extent of Labor Organization in the United
    States in 1910," *Quarterly Journal of Economics* (May,
    1916).
——. "The Extent of Trade Unionism," *Annals of the American
    Academy of Political and Social Science,* (January, 1917).

Index

5